1981

A Reader's Guide to
Fifty American Poets

Reader's Guide Series

General Editor: Andrew Mylett

A Reader's Guide to
Fifty American Poets

by Peter Jones

Heinemann – London
Barnes & Noble – Totowa, New Jersey

Heinemann Educational Books Ltd

LONDON EDINBURGH MELBOURNE AUCKLAND HONG KONG
SINGAPORE KUALA LUMPUR NEW DELHI IBADAN NAIROBI
JOHANNESBURG KINGSTON PORT OF SPAIN

First published 1980 by Pan Books as
An Introduction to Fifty American Poets
in the Pan Literature Guides Series
First published in this casebound edition 1980

British Library CIP Data
Jones, Peter
  A reader's guide to fifty American poets. –
  (Reader's guide series).
  1. American poetry – 19th century – History
  and criticism
  2. American poetry – 20th century – History
  and criticism
  I. Title   II. Series
  811'.009   PS316

ISBN 0–435–18491–1

ISBN (USA) 0–389–20140–5

Published in Great Britain by
Heinemann Educational Books Ltd
22 Bedford Square, London WC1B 3HH
Published in the U.S.A. 1980 by
Barnes & Noble Books

Printed and bound in Great Britain by
Richard Clay (The Chaucer Press) Ltd,
Bungay, Suffolk

Contents

Foreword

The composer Lukas Foss in a BBC interview pointed out that it was irrelevant to say that he was born in Berlin. He was an *American* composer. He was thus stating his own deep conviction, and that of other American artists: namely, that he acknowledged and believed in an American tradition; that he was working within that tradition; and that the older traditions should acknowledge it and not condescend to it. He has, while living in America, developed from a 'conservative' composer into a powerful exponent and composer of the *avant-garde*. Yet he remains American in both his early and his later work. The American tradition is such that Foss – German by birth and upbringing – can be a part of it. His commitment highlights the difference between an artist who professes to be a 'nationalist', and one who works within a national tradition. The former profession can and often does lead to jingoism with little purpose beyond immediate excitement; while the latter bears witness to the past, accepting its lessons, and accepting, too, the possibility of full expression that can only come from working within a developed tradition, either by consolidating it or reacting against it. There is richness in the consolidation and purpose in the reaction.

A nation's artistic maturity is reached when such opposing movements evolve naturally from the cultural tradition, extending it. Although American poets had not yet found a distinctive American voice at the beginning of the nineteenth century, they attained a voice and a maturity well before the century closed. I hope the chapters of this book describing the figures of that period provide the necessary evidence. The prime movers were Emerson and Poe, both in the principles they argued and in their attacks on one another – often contradictory but always pointing the paradoxes which others have explored.

Emerson clarified the American poet's choices, emphasizing the power of intuition and instinct as opposed to intellect, yet reminding us – in his essay on Shakespeare, for instance – that 'the greatest genius is the most indebted man'. And Poe, working precisely on the art of poetry, was able to clarify and define its functions. Both men stressed the high calling of the poetic art – a point frequently overlooked in the wide-spread contemporary misunderstanding of Emerson's praise of instinct and the misinterpretation of Poe's advocacy of originality. The literary pioneer work of Emerson and Poe meant that Whitman was able passionately to compose free verse in a crowded world, and Emily Dickinson in her seclusion could express herself with burning sincerity and develop in her concise poems a poetic power that was unprecedented in English. The American tradition contains them both.

There was a sense of literary pride in being American, and the 'leading-strings of our British Grandmamma', to use Poe's expression, were 'snapped asunder'. But the foundation of a national tradition was not without its hazards. A startling statement of Melville's indicates that facile nationalism was not far away. 'Let America, then,' he wrote in 'Hawthorne and his Mosses', 'prize and cherish her writers; yea let her glorify them ... let America first praise mediocrity even, in her children, before she praises (for everywhere merit demands acknowledgement from everyone) the best excellence in the

children of any other land.' Poe was sensitive to this
danger. In his 'Exordium' of 1842 he underlined the
folly of 'finding ourselves daily in the paradoxical di-
lemma of liking, or pretending to like, a stupid book the
better because (sure enough) its stupidity was of our
growth, and discussed our own affairs.'

The power of the greatest American poets – the pion-
eers and the consolidators – Emerson, Poe, Whitman,
Dickinson, Frost, Stevens, Crowe Ransom, Carlos
Williams, Pound and Eliot – has kept that danger at bay.
Movements and trends have developed naturally, multi-
plying the possibilities of the rich tradition. Imagists,
Projectivists, Objectivists, the New Criticism, the Beat
poets and others are all part of it. Only in recent years
are the larger figures obscure. Time has yet to make its
choice and one wonders, for example, how the work of
Ginsberg – already recognized for its individual rhetoric
and dubious influence – will be regarded in fifty years'
time.

The social and political insecurity of recent decades has
infected mature poets with an equivalent doubt that has,
in some cases – as with the poets of the so-called 'Tragic
Generation' – led to suicide (Plath, Jarrell and Berryman), to a form of literary withdrawal (Laura Riding), or
an almost desperate search for adequate styles that has produced several incidences of stylistic *volte-face* in mid career
(Merwin, Rich, Ashbery). Robert Lowell survived the
period with conviction, though even he fumbled for a
secure voice in *Notebook* and the subsequent collections
that developed from it, except perhaps in his posthumous
volume *Day by Day*, where a firmer control is evident.
Current anthologies such as *The New American Poetry*
edited by Donald M. Allen or *A Controversy of Poets*
edited by Paris Leary and Robert Kelly help to emphasize the polarities and obscure the common ground.
James Atlas's *Ten American Poets* reveals in a new generation of writers that the mis-named 'academic' poetry of

the school of Lowell, Bishop and Fitzgerald is thriving, and the anthology includes figures worth following.

Of the poets described in this book, none I feel could have been omitted if a clear picture of the diverse maturity of American poetry were to emerge. Those whom I have not included – particularly among recent writers – seem to me either to be working along lines similar to those of other poets, in a movement, and are mentioned in the context of another poet; or to have completed as yet an insufficient body of significant work to require an essay. I regret that I was unable to include Trumbull Stickney (1847–1904), mentioned in the essay on Conrad Aiken who acknowledged his debt to that 'forgotten figure'. Stickney, writing in a period of transition, was able to combine a metrical style and a robust, and at times highly poetic, tone, with a colloquial diction – a curious fusion that produced some memorable poems:

Leave him now, quiet by the way
To rest apart.
I know what draws him to the dust alway
And churns him in the builder's lime:
He has the fright of time.

Stickney died at the age of thirty. He was, however, one of the first American 'moderns'.

It is not my intention here to distinguish and assess the Englishness of English verse or the American-ness of American. The reader will be able to do that by supplementing the brief quotations given in the text and referring to the bibliography for further reading. He may sympathize with Matthew Arnold, who, on seeing an advertisement for a *Primer of American Literature*, declared that 'we are all contributors to one great literature – English Literature'. But he is more likely to agree with W. H. Auden in his introduction to the *Faber Book of Modern American Verse*, that 'from Bryant on there is scarcely one American poet whose work, if unsigned, could be mistaken for that of an Englishman.'

I hope the majority of the poets in this volume may remind us that the poetic vocation is not one of narrow self-esteem but that, in Emerson's words, the poet 'stands among partial men for the complete man, and apprises us not of his wealth but of the commonwealth'.

Manchester 1975, 1979

Anne Bradstreet 1612?-1672

Eternal substance do I see,
With which inriched I would be;
Mine eye doth pierce the heavens, and see
What is invisible to thee.

– 'The Flesh and the Spirit'

It is difficult to understand what made Anne Bradstreet
write verse – particularly the verse of charm and wit for
which she is still read, traditional and derivative yet
identifiably her own. She was a teenager when she arrived
in America, a wife in a wilderness surrounded by natural
and human hostility – forest, untillable soil and fractious
Indians. She was called upon to build and plant and bury.
She bore eight children and suffered chronic illness for
much of her life. Yet she was the first American poet, at
a time when it was thought unbecoming – even a sign of
madness – for a woman to write.

As a girl she read books in the library of the Earl of
Lincoln at the Castle of Sempringham, and she never
forgot her favourite authors: Edmund Spenser, Joshua
Sylvester's translation of du Bartas, and most of all
Francis Quarles, Sir Philip Sidney, Michael Drayton and
Sir Thomas Browne. Her reading included Sir Walter
Raleigh's *History of the World*, Robert Burton's *The
Anatomy of Melancholy*, and of course the Bible. Her

own poems, written in the new world, were in part a nostalgic exercise, and she composed elegies on Queen Elizabeth and Sidney. But there was a deeper motive: a struggle to establish continuities, to maintain a sense of home and family in an absolutely different milieu.

One of her most engaging qualities is her strength of spirit. She expressed annoyance at being condescended to as a woman:

I am obnoxious to each carping tongue
Who says my hand a needle better fits,
A poet's pen all scorn I should thus wrong,
For such despite they cast on Female wits:
If that I do prove well, it won't advance,
They'l say it's stoln, or else it was by chance.

– 'Prologue'

The tone is characteristic. Her strength of will is hardly surprising. Born in England, near Northampton around 1612, she emigrated with her parents and her young husband, Simon, a graduate of Cambridge, when she was eighteen. They sailed on the *Arbella* with eleven other families. On landing, they met the original colony of pilgrims who had arrived ten years earlier. According to Anne's father, they were, 'in a sad and unexpected condition, above eight of them being dead the Winter before; and many of those alive, weak and sick ...' During their own first winter, he reports he had 'no table, nor other room to write in than by the fireside upon my knee'.

The family settled first in Ipswich and later in North Andover, Massachusetts. During the deprivations and trials, Anne Bradstreet's faith was tested and clarified. Single-mindedly she pursued the common Puritan goals: to lead a Christian life strictly by the light of the Scriptures in the harsh, depriving interpretation placed on them by the Puritan fathers; to help found the Kingdom of God. Her occasional doubts and final acceptance resulted in some of her best poetry, in particular the *Contemplations*.

By 1646 she had written a number of long works, including *The Foure Elements*, a conventional debate on the relative virtues of one element over another. It is a tedious and characterless work, imitating Sylvester's pentameter couplets. Other imitations of Sylvester's translation of du Bartas were based on the same principle of 'fours': *Of the Foure Humours in Man's Constitution*, *The Foure Ages of Man*, *The Foure Seasons of the Yeare*, and – based on Raleigh's *History* – *The Four Monarchies*. 'Youth' in *The Foure Ages of Man* is not without its power:

Whole nights with Ruffins, Roarers, Fidlers spend.
To all obscenity mine ears I lend:
All counsell hate, which tends to make me wise,
And dearest friends count for mine enemies.

But this is dull stuff to come from a life rich in incident and beset by *new* trials and sufferings. She confesses ingenuously at the end of *The Foure Seasons*, 'My subjects bare, my brains are bad,/Or better lines you should have had.'

Her friends thought otherwise. A brother-in-law, the Reverend John Woodbridge, returned to England in 1647 and, unbeknown to the author, took with him a manuscript of her poems. It was published in England in 1650 as *The Tenth Muse Lately Sprung Up In America*. Anne Bradstreet, when the news reached her, worried and delighted, immediately set about revising the book, adding new poems and a proem called 'The Author to her Book':

Thou ill-form'd offspring of my feeble brain,
Who after birth didst by my side remain
Till snatcht from thence by friends less wise than true
Who thee abroad expos'd to publick view

Made thee in raggs, halting to th' press to trudge
Where errors were not lessened (all may judge) ...
I washt thy face, but more defects I saw,
And rubbing off a spot, still made a flaw.
I stretcht thy joints to make thee even feet,
Yet still thou run'st more hobbling than is meet.

The child, the book, was published in Boston in 1678, six years after her death.

Despite revisions, the long poems remain tedious. It is on the shorter poems that her individual achievement is founded. A few passages are of a quality on a par with the better work of her English contemporaries. She was not ambitious to discover a new style. In 'To my Dear and Loving Husband' she writes,

If ever two were one, then surely we.
If ever man were lov'd by wife, then thee.
If ever wife was happy in a man,
Compare with me, ye women, if you can.
I prize my love more than whole Mines of gold,
Or all the riches that the East doth hold ...

Conventional conceits – yet with unquestionable sincerity and directness. Another poem refers to her children:

I had eight birds hatcht in one nest,
Four Cocks there were, and Hens the rest,
I nurst them up with pain and care,
Nor cost nor labour did I spare,
Till at the last they felt their wing,
Mounted the Trees, and learn'd to sing.
Chief of the brood then took his flight,
To regions far, and left me quite;
My mournful chirps I after send,
Till he return, or I do end ...

The shift of emphasis from the homely to the universal reveals the best of her art. The shorter poems were written out of necessity, with almost confessional authority. They are not literary exercises. Despite the flatness of rhythm, the direct simplicity is authentic.

There were many trials of faith, among the most acute a fire in 1666 which destroyed the Bradstreet house and library of eight hundred volumes. 'Many times,' she wrote in a prose book for her children, 'hath Satan troubled me concerning the verity of the Scriptures.' She attempted to pacify her doubts after the fire:

I, starting up, the light did spye,
And to my God my Heart did cry
To strengthen me in my Distresse
And not to leave me succorlesse.
Then coming out beheld apace
The flame consume my dwelling place.

And, when I could no longer look,
I blest his Name that gave and took,
That layd my goods now in the dust:
Yea so it was, and so 'twas just.
It was his own: it was not mine;
Far be it that I should repine.

In the lines that follow, with intense regret she dwells on the perished pleasures too intently for an undoubting Puritan.

Here stood that Trunk, and there that chest;
There lay that store I counted best:
My pleasant things in ashes lye,
And them behold no more shall I.
Under my roof no guest shall sitt,
Nor at thy Table eat a bitt.

When in the last line, renouncing the loss, she declares, 'My hope and Treasure lyes above,' the controlled anguish of the poem gainsays the declaration. The poem expresses a positive trial of will which later produced her

Religious Meditations. Their titles indicate the personal themes that compelled her to write: 'For Deliverance from a Fever', 'From Another Sore Fitt', 'For the Restoration of my Husband from a Burning Ague, June 1666', and so on. These were vital matters for her.

Some of the poems are slight, but within their formal bounds a sincere fire burns, even through the traditional hymn form:

II

I sought him whom my soul did love,
With tears I sought him earnestly;
He bow'd his ear down from Above,
In vain I did not seek or cry.

III

My hungry soul he fill'd with Good,
He in his Bottle putt my teares,
My smarting wounds washt in his blood
And banisht thence my Doubts and feares.

It is a sincerity of determination and will rather than of easy belief, and the poem is the stronger for it.

Her doubts were finally resolved in the *Contemplations*, the technical and emotional climax of her work. A walk in New England provides the starting point for a long contemplative poem in which the processes of nature and the ephemerality of human life are made analogous, provoking her meditations on the purpose of life:

When I behold the heavens as in their prime,
And then the earth (though old) stil clad in green,
The stones and trees, insensible to time,
Nor age nor wrinkle on their front are seen;
If winter come, and greeness then do fade,
A Spring returns, and they more youthfull made;
But Man grows old, lies down, remains where once he's laid.

Her last poem bids farewell to the burning sun, the

storms, the hungry wolves and other dangers of this world and offers up a passionate prayer for rest in the next.

Oh how I long to be at rest
   And soare on high among the blest.
  This body shall in silence sleep,
Mine eyes no more shall ever weep ...

Lord make me ready for that day:
   Then Come deare bridegrome Come away.

She died in 1672 at the age of sixty. Her son recalls the event. 'Her death was occasioned by a consumption being wasted to skin and bone & she had an issue made in her arm bec' she was much troubled with rheum, & one of the women that tended herr dressing her arm, s'd shee never saw such an arm in her Life. Aye, s'd my most dear Mother, but that arm shall bee a Glorious Arm.'

Edward Taylor 1642?–1729

Lord, blow the Coal: Thy Love Enflame in mee.
– 'Meditation One'

There is a curious paradox in Edward Taylor's work.
His fully sensuous verse flowed from the pen of a Puritan
preacher. But the paradox runs deeper, for though he
attempted to make certain that the poems would not be
published after his death, none the less he bound them up
carefully and left them in good hands – those of his
grandson, Ezra Stiles, President of Yale College. Stiles
handed the manuscripts on to the poet's great grandson,
who deposited them in the Yale library. There they were
discovered in 1937. Despite Taylor's direction that his
heirs should never publish the poems, in 1939 a number
appeared in print, and most of the remainder in 1960.
Thus the outstanding Colonial poet was discovered two
centuries after his death.

There is a roughness in his writing. It flashes with un-
formed brilliance, startles even at its most contemplative.
Yet the poems reconcile the puritan conscience and the
sensuous imagination in an original manner. If Taylor is
a Metaphysical poet two generations after the English
Metaphysicals, he has virtues other than technical
originality.

The 'plain stile' was reserved for the pulpit. In the
twelve Puritan commentaries on the Bible in Taylor's

library, we find an interpretation of the Scriptures relying on an allegorical and symbolic approach. The poetry built from these, starting with sensuous detail – an insect, a passage from 'The Song of Solomon' – and bringing to the interpretation a brilliant coherence, discovering through contemplation the implicit significance, the presence of the divine pattern:

My shattred Phancy stole away from mee,
(Wits run a Wooling over Edens Parke)
And in Gods Garden saw a golden Tree.
  Whose Heart was All Divine, and gold its barke.
  Whose glorious limbs and fruitful branches strong
  With Saints, and Angells bright are richly hung.

– 'Meditation 29. John, XX,17'

Edward Taylor was born in Leicestershire and emigrated to Massachusetts at the age of twenty-six, having been evicted as a schoolmaster, prevented from studying at either Oxford or Cambridge, and threatened with imprisonment if he were to preach or attend a nonconformist service. The Restoration of King Charles and the Act of Uniformity of 1662 made it impossible for him in conscience to remain in England.

As a schoolmaster he had a good foundation in Greek, Latin and Hebrew. No doubt he had used George Herbert's poetry as a model of poetic composition in class. His own poems often echo Herbert's in form and in phrase. He felt a strong attraction, too, for others of the Metaphysicals, particularly Henry Vaughan, Thomas Traherne and Richard Crashaw. With Anne Bradstreet he shared an enthusiasm for Sylvester's translation of du Bartas and for Francis Quarles.

He left England for Bay Colony in 1668. He attended Harvard as an advanced student with Samuel Sewall, who later became Chief Justice of Massachusetts and from whose *Diary* we learn much of the period and the people.

Taylor planned to stay at Harvard after graduation but changed his mind and took up ministry in the small frontier town of Westfield, where he settled as pastor for the rest of his life.

The township was a hundred miles west of Boston and Taylor wrote in a letter of 'these remotest swamps where little save Rusticity is'. He became the town physician as well as pastor. He married twice and fathered a large family, none of whom survived him.

Taylor was a confirmed Calvinist. He believed in an all-powerful God who had selected certain souls for salvation. Salvation could be achieved by *faith*, total and unwavering, and not by works. Hell was a vivid reality waiting for those not chosen. Sewall records a visit Taylor made to Boston to deliver a sermon which 'might have been preached at Paul's Cross'. Taylor believed without wavering, and he was exemplary in his conscientiousness. He knew the doctrine and the history of his church, composed *A Metrical History of Christianity*, fourteen sermons on the Incarnation, and the *Poetical Works*.

He wrote meditations in verse at intervals of roughly six weeks as part of his private spiritual preparation. These comprise the bulk of his poetry – some 217 poems written in six-line stanzas under the heading, *Preparatory Meditations Before My Approach to the Lord's Supper. Chiefly upon the Doctrine Preached upon the Day of Administration*. Some of the poems deal with homely topics; for example: 'Upon a Spider Catching a Fly', 'Upon a Wasp Child [Chilled] with Cold', and 'Upon Wedlock, and the Death of Children'. The poems invariably point a moral. There is a group specifically addressed to prominent New Englanders, and there is a long poem, with a fine preface, called *God's Determinations Touching His Elect*, resolutely bearing its Calvinist message.

The poet's greatest skill is his ability to surprise the reader into a sudden vision of the divine pattern, a vision of attainable unity with God through the created world. Although the roughness of the verses might at times trouble the ear, it is the same quality of roughness we find in the work of Emily Dickinson. It is felt particularly when Taylor uses ordinary images to approach the mystery, as in 'Upon a Wasp Child with Cold':

Her petty toes, and fingers ends
Nipt with his breath, she out extends
Unto the Sun, in greate desire
To warm her digits at the fire.
Doth hold her Temples in this state
Where pulse doth beate, and head doth ake.
Doth turn, and stretch her body small,
Doth Comb her velvet Capitall ...

Taylor was a meticulous observer of nature, and his use – like Emily Dickinson's – of the unexpected word surprises us with its aptness. The wasp moves her 'digits' over her temples as if 'her little brain pan were/A Volume of Choice precepts cleare', and 'As if her velvet helmet high/Did *turret* rationality' (my italics). The poem culminates with the arresting couplet, 'Where all my pipes inspir'de upraise/An Heavenly musick furrd with praise.'

Sometimes the surprise is inherent in the verse form skilfully developed, as in 'Upon a Spider Catching a Fly':

Whereas the silly Fly,
  Caught by its leg,
Thou by the throate took'st hastily
  And 'hinde the head
    Bite Dead.

The last line is mimetic, as quick and final as the action. The drama is redolent of Herbert. Sometimes the surprise is in the dramatic use of line ending and the careful development of the syntax. Taylor writes in 'The Joy of Church Fellowship Rightly Attended', 'In Heaven soaring up, I dropt an Eare/On Earth ...' In 'Address to the Soul Occasioned by Rain' he asks,

Shall I be made
  A sparkling Wildfire Shop,
Where my dull Spirits at the Fireball trade
  Do frisk and hop?
    And while the Hammer doth the Anvill pay,
    The fire ball matter sparkles ev'ry way.

In the *Preparatory Meditations* both the individual power and the limitations of Taylor's art are revealed. These periodic exercises in meditation are sometimes so intense as to be obscure, sometimes so cerebral as to provide grotesquely over-extended metaphors and analogies. The full sensuousness of Taylor's imagination is displayed in them – the decorated altars, the spices, jewels, perfumes, elements with overtones of Roman Catholic ritual. But in Taylor they are the properties of Heaven, not of earth. They are the rewards.

Would God I in that Golden City were,
  With Jaspers Walld, all garnisht, and made swash,
With Pretious Stones, whose Gates are Pearles most cleare
    And Street Pure Gold, like to transparent Glass
    That my dull Soule, might be inflamde to see
    How Saints and Angells ravisht are in Glee.

Excessive, perhaps, but not too far removed from Bunyan. Or, another example:

When that this Bird of Paradise put in
  This Wicker Cage (my Corps) to tweedle praise
Had peckt the Fruite forbad: and so did fling
    Away its Food, lost its golden dayes,
    It fell into Celestiall Famine sore:
    And never could attan a morsell more.

Alas! alas! Poor Birde, what wilt thou do?

The images, despite their richness, are drawn in part

from a plain life, in part from the Bible. The diction is generally homely. It is the unexpected words and images – 'fling', 'Celestiall Famine', 'golden dayes' – that elevate the poetry. Again, the homely metaphor is raised up:

Yet were thy silver skies my Beer bowle fine,
    I find my Lord would fill it to the brim.

When Taylor is not looking round about him for images, he uses the diction and the common trappings of Protestant tradition, evoking the mystical marriage of Christ and his elect in terms of the biblical Song of Solomon, with characteristic passion:

Shall I not smell thy sweet, oh! Sharons Rose?
    Shall not mine Eye salute thy Beauty? Why?
Shall thy sweet leaves their Beautious sweets upclose?
    As half ashamde my sight should on them ly?
    Woe's me! For this my sighs shall be in grain,
    Offer'd on Sorrow's Altar for the same.

For Edward Taylor, with his Bible, his Herbert and Crashaw, his commentaries on the Scriptures, such was his everyday vision and idiom. There is finally no difficulty in reconciling the sensuous vision with the Puritan priest pursuing his duties in the felt presence of his God. Even the most incongruous metaphors have a charming rightness in Taylor's derivative yet unmistakable poetry. In the 'Preface' to *God's Determinations Touching His Elect*, he exclaims:

Who Spread its Canopy? Or Curtains Spun?
Who in this Bowling Alley bowld the Sun?

William Cullen Bryant
1794–1878

These are the gardens of the Desert, these
The unshorn fields, boundless and beautiful,
For which the speech of England has no name –
The Prairies. I behold them for the first,
And my heart swells ...

– 'The Prairies'

William Cullen Bryant, American by birth, was the first programmatically American poet. In his essays and lectures he explored the possibility of a specifically American literature. He pleaded that writers deal honestly with American landscape and character and thus deserve well of their countrymen. In the *North American Review* he protested, 'We do not praise a thing until we see the seal of transatlantic approbation on it!' His own life and writings mark the transition between the Puritan tradition, firmly grounded in European models, and the native romantic transcendentalism that followed.

He was born of Pilgrim stock in 1794 in Cummington, Massachusetts, and lived – one of seven children – with his parents at the home of his formidable grandfather, Ebenezer Snell, an extreme Calvinist and Federalist. Harsh justice was Ebenezer's governing principle. In the home he compelled thrift and industry.

Cullen was a sickly baby with an alarmingly large head.

It is said that his father, a physician, used to plunge him into an icy spring every morning to reduce the size of the offending member. The weakling survived, however, into his eighty-fourth year. He was taught to work hard in the fields, and his father insisted that he take long walks in the woods to strengthen his constitution. These walks contributed to the development of his individual response to nature. He wrote later that he was 'a delighted observer of external nature – the splendors of a winter daybreak over the wild wastes of snow seen from our windows, the glories of the autumnal woods, the gloomy approaches of the thunderstorm ... the return of spring, with the flowers, and the first snowfall of winter.' The pleasure of escaping from Ebenezer's house for hours at a time was intensified by the pleasure of close observation.

The poetic vocation was early in evidence. At the age of ten he composed a poem printed in the *Hampshire Gazette*, versifying the first chapter of Job. Cullen's father wrote verses too, and had in his library the poems of the eighteenth-century poets. His son was able to study Samuel Johnson, Joseph Addison, and most ardently 'Pope's celestial fire'. At the age of thirteen he composed a satire against Jefferson:

When shall this land, some courteous angel say,
Throw off a weak, and erring ruler's sway?
Rise, injur'd people, vindicate your cause!
And prove your love of liberty and laws ...

Such poems were concealed from Ebenezer, left in a drawer and published years later by his father.

None of the early poets he read instilled in the boy a positive poetic regard for nature. It took an extreme experience to stimulate his vision. Ebenezer's predisposition to thrift prevented the boy's ambition to go to Harvard. Instead he was sent to a more orthodox and cheaper college – Williams. Cullen objected to the intellectual poverty of Williamstown and left. Ebenezer then forestalled his going to Yale. Melancholy, Cullen turned to wandering in the countryside near his home, meditating on death and his unhealthy childhood. He composed a poem which proved to be among his best. At seventeen he completed the first draft. Strongly influenced by Robert Southey, William Cowper, and Milton, 'Thanatopsis' – a meditation on death – evokes Cullen's own vision of nature and life. This poem Cullen assiduously concealed from Ebenezer: the theme is that man may face death with serenity through his *own particular faith*. The resemblance, both in diction and in poetic disposition, to Wordsworth, is the more remarkable when we realize that at this time Cullen had not read Wordsworth.

Cullen's father discovered the poem and took it to the editors of the *North American Review*. It appeared in 1817. When R. H. Dana, a founder of the magazine, read it, he exclaimed to his editor, 'Ah, you have been imposed upon. No one on this side of the Atlantic is capable of writing such verses!'

In an expanded form, the poem was included in a collection called *Poems* in 1821. The style is detached and cool. The poem opens with the lines,

To him who in the love of Nature holds
Communion with her visible forms, she speaks
A various language; for his gayer hours
She has a voice of gladness, and a smile
And eloquence of beauty, and she glides
Into his darker musings, with a mild
And healing sympathy, that seals away
Their sharpness, ere he is aware. When thoughts
Of the last bitter hour come like a blight
Over thy spirit, and sad images
Of the stern agony, and shroud, and pall.
And breathless darkness, and the narrow house,
Make thee to shudder, and grow sick at heart –
Go forth, under the open sky, and list

To Nature's teachings, while from all around –
Earth and her waters, and the depths of air –
Comes a still voice ...

Nature is a teacher whose lesson becomes clear in the closing lines of the poem:

So live, that when thy summons comes to join
The innumerable caravan, which moves
To that mysterious realm where each shall take
His chamber in the silent halls of death,
Thou go not, like the quarry-slave at night,
Scourged to his dungeon, but, sustained and soothed
By an unfaltering trust, approach thy grave,
Like one who wraps the drapery of his couch
About him, and lies down to pleasant dreams.

The maturity of the verse is evident in the controlled and varied rhythm, the development of the syntax, the quality of the thought, and the use of simple language with a dignity in the unforced archaisms. Many critics see 'Thanatopsis' as Bryant's poetic masterpiece.

Matthew Arnold, on the other hand, preferred 'To a Waterfowl', which he considered one of the best short poems in the language. The style, quite distinct from that in 'Thanatopsis', again admirably suits the content. The poem marks a change in Bryant's philosophy, towards a religious liberalism in which Nature and deity are fused. Seeing a waterfowl, he asks,

Seek'st thou the plashy brink
Of weedy lake, or marge of river wide,
Or where the rocking billows rise and sink
On the chafed ocean-side?

In the bird's flight he discerns a purpose. Nature guides it. And 'on my heart/Deeply has sunk the lesson thou hast given ...' Bryant resolves to trust in the same natural purpose and guide:

He, who, from zone to zone,
Guides through the boundless sky thy certain flight,
In the long way that I must tread alone,
    Will lead my steps aright.

The words 'certain', 'alone', and 'aright' confirm that
Bryant has come to terms with God through Nature, as
the early Puritans had come to terms with Nature
through their vision of God.

The poem was suggested by an actual observation:
Bryant saw such a bird in flight. He wrote in a letter to
his brother, chastising him for his derivative, literary and
un-American approach to poetry: 'I saw some lines by
you to the skylark. Did you ever see such a bird? Let me
counsel you to draw your own images, in describing
Nature, from what you observe around you ... The skylark is an English bird, and an American who has never
visited Europe has no right to be in raptures about it.'

Actual observations of nature often spark off Bryant's
poems. In 'A Scene on the Banks of the Hudson' he
describes,

Cool shades and dews are round my way,
And silence of the early day;
Mid the dark rocks that watch his bed,
Glitters the mighty Hudson, spread,
Unrippled, save by drops that fall
From shrubs that fringe his mountain wall.

Though the diction is literary in the manner of Pope's
'Windsor Forest', the landscape is not aestheticized. And
when Bryant relinquishes the heroic couplet, his rhetoric
becomes more natural and resonant, as in 'The Prairies':

    Lo! they stretch,
In airy undulations, far away,
As if the Ocean, in his gentlest swell,
Stood still, with all his rounded billows fixed

And motionless forever. Motionless? –
No – they are all unchained again.

When Bryant was prevented from attending Yale, he studied law and was admitted to the bar at the age of twenty-one. He disliked it. After his marriage five years later, he was ready to leap at an invitation to contribute to a new magazine, *The United States Literary Gazette*. This period proved the most prolific of his literary career, and some of his best poems, mainly on nature themes, were written and published. 'A Walk at Sunset' and 'Autumn Woods' are among the best. 'Thanatopsis' had been influenced by the so-called 'Graveyard School' of English poets – Edward Young and Thomas Gray. But now Bryant had assimilated the Romantics.

In New England the Lake Poets were disliked. The Puritan ethic was still strong, and Bryant felt constrained by the unwelcoming atmosphere.

When breezes are soft and skies are fair,
I steal an hour from study and care,
And hie me away to the woodland scene,
Where wanders the stream with waters of green ...

He complained:

Though forced to drudge for the dregs of men,
And scrawl strange words with the barbarous pen,
And mingle among the jostling crowd,
Where the sons of strife are subtle and loud ...

Paradoxically it was the 'jostling crowd' that Bryant joined in New York. He moved there at the age of thirty to edit a magazine, and then to the New York *Evening Post* in 1826, where he became editor and eventually part-owner. His fame as a champion of liberal causes spread. He came to be known as one of New York's most distinguished citizens. When Dickens visited America his first words on disembarking are reported to have been,

'Where's Bryant?' Bryant was instrumental in establishing Central Park and the Metropolitan Museum of Art. He accepted the Unitarian faith and the humane vision that went with it. His editorials were provocative. He opposed slavery, supported Free Trade and in 1856 stoutly defended a group of tailors who had formed a union and thereupon been fined for conspiracy. 'If this is not SLAVERY,' he cried, 'we have forgotten its definition.' He spoke out for the rebel John Brown and backed Lincoln's emancipation programme. He continued to publish verse, in a new *Poems* (1832), *The Fountain* (1842), *A Forest Hymn* (1860), and *The Flood of Years* (1877), but the poetry had, predictably, suffered. It came to have less of the directness and passion that characterize the early work. As he grew older, he became something of a martinet – imposing and unapproachable. James Russell Lowell wrote,

There is Bryant, as quiet, as cool, and as dignified,
As a smooth, silent iceberg that never is ignified . . .
He may rank (Griswold says so) first bard of our nation,
There's no doubt he stands in supreme ice-olation . . .

Yet his achievements were hardly in doubt. Poe wrote in 1837, 'Mr Bryant's poetical reputation, both at home and abroad, is greater, we presume, than that of any other American. British critics have frequently awarded him high praise; and here, the public press have been unanimous in approbation.'

If he is less than a great poet, there is considerable dignity in much that he wrote, and his persistent introduction of *things* American – even if the idiom was not wholly native – showed the way for some of his successors. His critical writings about poetry show him to be the first self-consciously American critic of stature. His essay 'On the Use of Trisyllabic Feet in Iambic Verse' was in its way radical at a time predisposed to strict Augustanism. So too was his review of Solyman Brown's *An Essay on American Poetry*. He condemned American Augustans for their 'balanced and wearisome regularity'. His own experiments were among the first in his period to break with the heroic couplet.

His lectures, too, are fascinating, not least for the light they cast on his own composition. 'On the Nature of Poetry', 'On the Value and Uses of Poetry', 'On Poetry and its Relation to our Age and Country' and 'On Originality and Imitation' partake of an aphoristic style. Each sentence relates to Bryant's basic themes: 'emotion is the great spring of poetry'; 'poetry which does not find the way to the heart is scarcely deserving of the name'; 'the most beautiful poetry is that which takes the strongest hold on the feelings'. Yet Bryant did not discard the strict calm metres of the classical and Augustan tradition. After the death of his wife, when he was seventy-six, he began translating both the *Iliad* and the *Odyssey*.

His eventual fame was such that the Russian Academy elected him, together with Longfellow, as an honorary member in 1873. Tennyson was the only other contemporary English language poet to be thus honoured. He died in 1878 at the age of eighty-four, from concussion of the brain on falling in Central Park after delivering an address at the unveiling of a statue to Mazzini. The day was hot and Bryant was bare-headed.

Ralph Waldo Emerson
1803–1882

... it is not metres, but a metre-making argument, that makes a poem, – a thought so passionate and alive. that like the spirit of a plant or an animal, it has architecture of its own, and adorns nature with a new thing. The thought and the form are equal in the order of time, but in the order of genesis the thought is prior to the form. The poet has a new thought: he has a whole new experience to unfold; he will tell us how it was with him, and all men will be the richer in his fortune. For the experience of each new age requires a new confession, and the world seems always waiting for its poet.

– Emerson's essay on 'The Poet'

Any reader of American literature must come to terms with Emerson if he is to understand the intellectual traditions of America in the nineteenth century, and the source of many of the ideas that have informed writers of the twentieth century. One would like to use the image of this tall, blond figure, dressed in black, striding across nineteenth-century American literature, but it would be inappropriate. He was essentially a static, almost a passive character in spite of the flurries of protest his speaking and writing occasioned early in his career. And he was always a man of paradoxes. He described books as being merely 'for the scholar's idle times', recommending *experience* as the way to self-knowledge and fulfilment.

Yet his *Journals* – which fill ten printed volumes, include passages such as (October 1842): 'Thou shalt read Homer, Aeschylus, Sophocles, Euripides, Aristophanes, Plato, Proclus, Plotinus, Jamblicheus, Porphyry, Aristotle, Virgil, Plutarch, Apuleius, Chaucer, Dante, Rabelais, Montaigne, Cervantes, Shakespeare, Jonson, Ford, Chapman, Beaumont and Fletcher, Bacon, Marvell, Moore, Milton, Molière, Swedenborg, Goethe.' There is a paradox too in his opposition to slavery. He spoke out against it, but took no action apart from writing an 'Ode' to a critic who chastised his passivity. Yet his was an 'active passivity' – he practised what he preached, basically an ethic of 'to thine own self be true'. It is his emphatic honesty in this that commands our respect. It is also due to this that he is an undisciplined philosopher and writer.

Though his biography is hardly rich in incident, the personal struggle towards his mature serenity was considerable. 'So much of our time is preparation, so much is routine, and so much retrospect, that the pith of each man's genius contracts itself to a very few hours,' he wrote in *Experience*. His own 'few hours' of literary genius lasted forty years, from the publication of 'Nature' – a prose essay – in 1836 when he was thirty-three, to his *Letters and Social Aims* in 1876.

Born in Boston in 1803, one of four sons, he was descended from generations of New England ministers. His father, a Unitarian minister, died when Waldo was eight. An upbringing in genteel poverty followed. At times, it is said, there was only one coat between the four brothers.

Waldo was fortunate in his sympathetic aunt, Mary Moody Emerson. Many letters passed between them in which the beginnings of his self-examination are evident. His aunt guided him to books – to Shakespeare, Bacon, Milton and Burke. Despite her fervent Calvinism, he found her sympathetic and she contributed to his plain commonsense and perhaps to his aphoristic directness in prose and verse.

In spite of poverty, his mother's initiative made it possible for all four sons to attend Harvard, Waldo at the age of fourteen. He helped to pay his way, working in the kitchens and waiting on table. Though not a brilliant scholar, he read widely. Already he recognized solitude and independence as prime requisites for his imagination. 'A room alone was the best thing in my college course.'

After college he became a teacher, helping his brother William to run a Boston finishing school from 1821 to 1825. He then decided to become a Unitarian minister. In 1826 he was approbated to preach and declared, 'I deliberately dedicate my life, time and talent and hopes to the church.' He became Pastor of the Old Second Church of Boston. In 1829 he married a young consumptive, Ellen Tucker. This was a crisis period for Emerson. He became ill and had to travel to Florida for his health. On his return he found his brother Edward on the verge of madness. His wife died after less than two years of marriage.

The doubts about his religion intensified. He found that he could no longer in conscience administer the sacrament. In his final sermon, he said, 'It is my desire in the office of a Christian Minister to do nothing which I cannot do with my whole heart. Having said this, I have said all. I have no hostility to this institution; I am only stating my want of sympathy with it.' His retirement from the ministry epitomizes both his integrity and his faith in his individual instinct. 'Nothing is at last sacred but the integrity of your own mind.'

In 1832 he travelled to Europe. In Italy he met Walter Savage Landor. In Paris, a visit to the Jardin des Plantes confirmed in him a sense of the dark affinity between the human and animal worlds, the transcendental unity of man and nature, and the essential unity of all things. This formed the basis of much of his philosophy: 'Compound it how she will, star, sand, fire, water, tree, man, it is still one stuff, and betrays the same properties,' he wrote two years later in 'Nature'.

He travelled to England and met Coleridge, whose writings had helped him to distinguish between the logical and the intuitive roads to truth. He met Wordsworth and Carlyle as well, forming a fruitful friendship with the latter. They shared much in common as prophets rebuking the materialism of their time and cautioning against the tyranny of democracy, yet they were unlike in temperament, for Emerson was quiet and basically an optimist.

In 1833 he returned to New England and began the work that would, with that of Thoreau, Hawthorne, Melville and Whitman, establish a firmly American tradition and shake off the provincial stigma attached to American literature. Implicit in his programme was a challenge to religious authority and to rationalism, the ascertion of the doctrine of human individuality. American literature would be ambitious, explore the 'nature of the universe, the origin of evil'. In effect, the programme was intended to set American literature on an independent footing, worthy to stand beside other world literatures.

Emerson settled in Concord, Massachusetts, and in 1835 married a second time. He spent the remainder of his life writing and lecturing. The last forty-seven years of his life were settled and, on the surface, hardly eventful.

His first major essay, 'Nature' (1835), was published anonymously the next year. It expresses clearly his 'transcendentalist philosophy'. An historical approach, he says, involves a second-hand relationship with nature and God. It is the direct relationship that it essential to true understanding, the trusting and intuitive approach. 'We are escorted on every hand through life by spiritual agents, and a beneficent purpose lies in wait for us ... if, instead of identifying ourselves with the work, we feel that the soul of the workman streams through us, we shall find the peace of the morning dwelling first in our hearts ...'

'Every moment instructs, and every object: for wisdom is infused into every form.' 'A man does not tie his shoe without recognizing laws which bind the farthest regions of nature ...' The essay does not depend on a logical framework; rather it trusts an intuitive, spiritual approach, an acknowledgement of man's oneness with things around him and with things higher than himself, and yet a knowledge which still cherishes the uniqueness of the self. The idea that nature provides man with symbols has been adapted from Swedenborg. Emerson goes further than Bryant. For him, 'the whole of nature is a metaphor of the mind.'

This published lecture attracted little support or animosity. The book it appeared in hardly sold. But strong reaction came in 1837 when he was invited to give the address at the public announcement of the new members of Phi Beta Kappa at Harvard. The distinguished assembly recoiled from his views that nature and instinct, not learning and books, were man's best guide: 'This is my music; this myself ... The world is nothing, the man is all; in yourself is the law of all nature ... in yourself slumbers the whole of Reason; it is for you to know all; it is for you to dare all.'

This address, 'The American Scholar', was called by Oliver Wendell Holmes, 'Our Intellectual Declaration of Independence'. It was followed in 1838 by the 'Divinity School Address', which seemed to draw the wrath of Boston down upon Emerson. Orthodoxy was challenged powerfully. Transcendentalism had become a living force to be reckoned with.

In brief, the basic assumptions were these. Everyman might commune with God if he so willed. God is the Over-Soul, and there can be unobstructed communication between Him and the soul of everyman: 'I am born into the great, the universal mind,' declares the soul in the essay on 'The Over-Soul'. 'I am part and parcel of God.' Deity has lost its definite article; formal religion is rejected for intuitional experience. An element of eternity exists in everyman; in him are the seeds of all knowledge. Nature is 'the gigantic shadow of God cast on our senses' and each law and pattern in nature has a counterpart in the intellect: 'Whenever you enumerate a physical law, I hear in it a moral rule.' The structure of the universe duplicates the structure of the individual self. Self-knowledge therefore will find all knowledge, and happiness will depend on self-realization. 'The reliance on authority measures the decline of religion, the withdrawal of the soul.' In Emerson's new faith there was scope not only for a revolt against Unitarianism, but also against the continuing cultural dependence of America on Europe.

Though much of the content of Transcendentalism has its source in Coleridge, Cousins and Carlyle, Emerson's essay on 'The Over-Soul' reveals the individuality and originality of the new programme. 'The simplest person, who in his integrity worships God, becomes God ...' The action of an individual with self-knowledge is prompted by his own nature. No vocation is inherently ignoble.

The five great Transcendentalists interpreted the doctrine in their own ways. Emerson, Thoreau and Whitman saw it as a decree of optimism. For Hawthorne and Melville it represented an unattainable ideal – hence the pervasive sense of resigned pessimism in their writings. Emerson's optimism provoked a telling charge against his work: Yeats's statement that it lacked 'a sense of evil'. There is some justification in the charge.

Although there was no manifesto, a group formed around Emerson in Concord. This 'Transcendental Club' included Thoreau, Bronson Alcott, W. H. Channing, George Ripley and Margaret Fuller. Emerson's house was referred to as 'a cure of souls'. But – true to their beliefs – they did not work as a group, preferring to regard each person as his own law. They attracted criticism. Poe's is particularly telling. 'Put in something about the Supernal

Oneness,' he wrote. 'Don't say a syllable about the Infernal Twoness. Above all, study innuendo. Hint everything – assert nothing.'

Their writings were published in *The Dial*, which Emerson himself edited from 1842 to 1844. It was about this time that he began reading the *Vegas, Bhagavad-Gita* and *Vishna Purana*, which influenced his thought considerably. In 1841 the first volume of his 'Essays' – including 'The Over-Soul' and 'Self-Reliance' – was published. In 1844 a second volume followed, and his poems appeared in 1847. *Representative Men* – a volume of essays on Plato, Swedenborg, Montaigne, Shakespeare, Napoleon and Goethe – was published in 1850. In 1856 came *English Traits, The Conduct of Life* in 1860, *May-Day and other Pieces* in 1867 and *Society and Solitude* in 1870. *Letters and Social Aims* (1876) was his last notable work. He died in 1882 and was buried in Sleepy Hollow Cemetery in Concord.

His prose style often reaches the intensity of poetry, but frequently there is a failure of progression within a paragraph, a wilfulness of organization. His mind proceeds intuitively, asserting unity, progressing elliptically. 'Society is a wave. The wave moves onward, but the water of which it is composed does not. The same article does not rise from the valley to the ridge. Its unity is only phenomenal. The persons who make up a nation today, next year die, and their experience dies with them.' It is a tone of public address, a lecture formed from notes in his *Journal*. It lacks at times the rhythm of speech and the rhythm of thought.

A lack of convincing rhythm in his poetry, too, has put off many readers. The poetry must be approached, however, not through its sound but through its sense. It is his philosophy in concentrated form, and when the intrinsic importance of the content is accepted his originality as a poet can be appreciated. In 'Merlin' he writes:

Great is the art,
Great be the manners, of the bard.
He shall not his brain encumber
With the coil of rhythm and number;
But, leaving rule and pale forethought,
He shall aye climb
For his rhyme.
'Pass in, pass in,' the angels say,
'In to the upper doors,
Nor count compartments of the floors,
But mount to paradise
By the stairway of surprise.'

Much of the quality of the poetry is epitomized in that 'stairway of surprise'. The surprises are normally not in the language or imagery but in the odd unities the poems seem to discover, between normally unrelated areas of experience and perception.

Emerson began composing poetry early when at college, and was invited in 1834 to contribute the customary Phi Beta Kappa poem for the anniversary at Harvard. Poems were printed in the *Western Messenger* and later in *The Dial*. After the small 1847 collection, twenty years passed before a second book – made up largely of poems from *Atlantic Monthly* – was published. It was a small body of work, but an influential one. The oracular tone of the poems earned a number of parodies, but Emerson's style is uncannily original in the sense that it is inimitable. 'Poetry,' he says, 'was all written before time was ... The men of more delicate ear write down these cadences ...' Though Emerson's own ear was not very delicate, he heard the transcendental music. The poet's role was that of a bard making himself passive so that the cadences can flow through him.

There is, of course, more to the process than that. Many of the poems rise out of suggestions in the *Journal*. In May 1847 he wrote, 'The days come and go like muffled and veiled figures sent from a distant friendly party, but they say nothing, and if we do not use the gifts they bring, they carry them as silently away.' In 'Days' the conceit was developed further:

Daughters of Time, the hypocrite Days,
Muffled and dumb like barefoot dervishes,
And marching single in an endless file,
Bring diadems and fagots in their hands.
To each they offer gifts after his will,
Bread, kingdoms, stars, and sky that holds them all.
I, in my pleached garden, watched the pomp,
Forgot my morning wishes, hastily
Took a few herbs and apples, and the Day
Turned and departed silent, I, too late,
Under her solemn fillet saw the scorn.

There is little sense that the poem is being spoken *through* Emerson. There is a definite purpose of action here, a particular meaning to be conveyed. The poet might see himself as an Aeolian harp, 'trembling to the cosmic breath', but the message, if not the music, is his own. There is a deep stylistic difference between the two poems quoted. Each rises out of an idea, not directly out of an experience. Though the idea may initially be as spontaneous as one of Whitman's, the expression is calculated, gauged. Only the oracular tone is common to both poems.

'Merlin' illustrates Emerson's use of the irregular line, the intrusion of the sudden short line, the immediate and unexpected rhyme, all point to the freedom of movement he preached – and yet how well-gauged the freedom is, how contrived. He developed a theory that phrase and line rhythms and lengths should be determined by breathing – a theory later developed by Charles Olson. This in part accounts for the irregularity of the lines, distributing stress and emphasis with some dramatic effect. The 'Ode: Inscribed to W. H. Channing' includes some of his best lines in this manner:

The God who made New Hampshire
Taunted the lofty land
With little men; –
Small blat and wren
House in the oak: –
If earth-fire cleave
The upheaved land, and bury the folk,
The southern crocodile would grieve.
Virtue palters: Right is hence;
Freedom praised, but hid;
Funeral eloquence
Rattles the coffin-lid.

The poem develops Emerson's passive commitment to the anti-slavery cause.

Emerson was at his best, as the 'Ode' shows, when using a striking visual image. He was an acute observer of nature and men as his *Journals* reveal. A number of the poems were suggested by his walks in all weathers in the countryside near Concord. 'The Snow Storm' mingles his rhetorical and his precise style effectively:

Announced by all the trumpets of the sky,
Arrives the snow, and, driving o'er the fields,
Seems nowhere to alight: the whited air
Hides hills and woods, the river, and the heaven,
And veils the farmhouse at the garden's end.
The sled and traveller stopped, the courier's feet
Delayed, all friends shut out, the housemates sit
Around the radiant fireplace, enclosed
In a tumultuous privacy of storm.

Come see the north wind's masonry.

The best of Emerson's poems open strongly, unexpectedly, with some of the haunting dignity we associate with Emily Dickinson. And the linking together of unusual words – a noun and an unexpected adjective, as in 'tumultuous privacy' – contributes to the verse's controlled authority. 'A swan-like form invests the hidden thorn,' he writes. A world of analogies, in which the concrete and the abstract are fused, is created.

And when his hours are numbered, and the world
Is all his own, retiring, as he were not,
Leaves, when the sun appears, astonished Art
To mimic in slow structures, stone by stone,
   Built in an age, the mad wind's night-work,
   The frolic architecture of the snow.

Many of the poems have no rhyme scheme as such, but a number rely on short-line rhyming couplets, at first glance a strange choice, since he handles unrhymed verse deftly while many of his rhymes are forced. But the opening of the second section of 'Merlin' offers a partial explanation. His obsession with the oneness of nature, god, art and man, with the manner in which structures in nature seem to be echoed in man, dictates the choice of a rhyming or echoing. In 'Merlin' he describes the correspondence between nature and poetry:

The rhyme of the poet
Modulates the king's affairs:
Balance-loving Nature
Made all things in pairs.
To every foot its antipode;
Each color with its counter glowed;
To every tone beat answering tones,
Higher or graver;

Emerson's rhyming couplets and quatrains echo 'balance-loving Nature', with its duplication in echo, reflection and shadow, by reflecting the principle in sound. The irregular line at the end of the passage must be one of those that non-plussed his admirers and amused his critics. But as Emerson points out in the first part of 'Merlin',

Thy trivial harp will never please
Or fill my craving ear;
Its chords should ring as blows the breeze,
Free, peremptory, clear.
No jingling serenader's art,
Nor tinkle of piano strings,
Can make the wild blood start
In its mystic springs.
The kingly bard
Must smite the chords rudely and hard
As with hammer or with mace;

The didactic, self-conscious poem about poetry tells us in mimetic terms how poetry should not be. The 'jingling' here is almost certainly Poe's, since Emerson referred to him as 'the jingle man', and Poe's approach to poetry was anathema to Emerson, who saw his role as that of prophet and seer, interpreting the emanations of Nature and the promptings of the 'still small voice' within. In the *Journal* he writes, 'I believe I am more of a Quaker than anything else. I believe in the still small voice, and that voice is Christ within us.' And Nature itself symbolizes all:

Over me soared the eternal sky,
Full of light and of deity;
Again I saw, again I heard,
The rolling river, the morning bird; –
I yielded myself to the perfect whole.

This poem, 'Each and All', presents us again with 'deity', stripped of the definite article and even, in this case, of the capital letter. The idea of the complete interrelation between things, the identity of the forms underlying the substance, and circularity of all processes, each in time encompassing its opposite, is best expressed in 'Uriel'. The poem was written in response to the critics of his 'latest form of infidelity', the 'Divinity School Address' delivered at Harvard Divinity School in 1838.

'Line in nature is not found:
Unit and universe are round;
In vain produced, all rays return;
Evil will bless, and ice will burn.'
As Uriel spoke with piercing eye,
A shudder ran around the sky ...

The poems 'Brahma', 'Saadi' and 'Hamatreya' show the influence of Emerson's Eastern studies and confirm his sensitivity to the larger themes. There are numerous analogies between his Transcendental vision and the vision of the Eastern philosophies. The wide range of formal variations, too, indicates that his poetry attempted to develop organically, miming the development of his philosophy. Each subject demands its own idiom, each part of the poem is related naturally to the other parts. In the later poems, he concentrated more and more on the symbol. In his essay on 'The Poet' he wrote, 'I find that the fascination resides in the symbol'.

But it was his free verse style, his idea of the 'organic', that helped show the way for Whitman, and Emerson was among the first to give enthusiastic encouragement to the author of *Leaves of Grass*. Some critics contend that Emerson's eloquent fusion of oriental mysticism and individual detachment has contributed to recent trends in 'spontaneous art' and extempore performance. The strength of his personality remains, and his intellectual influence is still felt with much of its original urgency and novelty in the work of many contemporary writers.

Henry Wadsworth Longfellow
1807–1882

Longfellow is the sort of counteractant most needed for our materialistic, self-assertive, money-worshipping Anglo-Saxon race, and especially for the present age in America – an age tyrannically regulated with reference to the manufacturer, the merchant, the financier, the politician ... I should have to think long if I were asked to name a man who had done more, and in more valuable directions, for America.

– Walt Whitman

Longfellow was a rare phenomenon in the world of poetry: a best-selling author. Ten thousand copies of *The Courtship of Miles Standish* were reported sold in London in a single day, and *The Song of Hiawatha* was translated into most modern languages and into Latin, too – the Latin version by Cardinal Newman's brother. It is easy to dismiss the poet as a sentimental moralist singing parlour songs or versifying romantic tales. It is easy, too, to overcomplicate him. Some recent critics have tried to assess him in Freudian terms, discovering a mind replete with depressing symptoms, suggesting that his verse was a positive antidote, expressing a desire for a traditional world of legend and 'beauty'. Each explanation is incomplete. The poet was emotionally, if not intellectually, clear about his objectives from the beginning. The first poem in his first collection, *Voices of the Night,* ends:

Look then into thine heart, and write!
  Yes, into Life's deep stream!
All forms of sorrow and delight,
All solemn Voices of the Night,
That can soothe thee or afright, –
  Be these henceforth thy theme.

Longfellow was born in 1807 in Portland, Maine, a sea-port. He was the second child in a family of eight. His mother, a strong character, was of Pilgrim stock. Although his father, a prominent lawyer, was a graduate of Harvard, he sent his two eldest sons to the new Bowdoin College, at Brunswick, in 1822. Henry excelled and graduated in 1825 in the same class with Nathaniel Hawthorne. Already he had published serially both prose and verse, but his father was anxious that he should follow him into law. Longfellow was rescued from this programme when Bowdoin offered him the newly established professorship of modern languages. His translations had already attracted attention.

Before taking up the professorship, he went to Europe to complete his preparation. He visited France, Spain, Italy and Germany, and on his return wrote several text-books for his own use, as well as a number of new translations. He also contributed articles on literary and linguistic subjects to *The North American Review*.

In 1831, Longfellow married, and three years later he was offered the Smith Professorship of French and Spanish at Harvard. He went to Europe again with his wife. On the journey, his wife lost her child and died in Holland. Longfellow returned alone to Harvard, renting the spacious house he would occupy for the rest of his life – Craigie House – in Cambridge. There he composed the romance *Hyperion*, about a young man endeavouring to forget sorrow in travel. In 1839 his first collection of poems, *Voices of the Night*, appeared. It included his famous didactic exhortation, 'The Psalm of Life':

Tell me not in mournful numbers,
  Life is but an empty dream! –
For the soul is dead that slumbers,
  And things are not what they seem.

But of greater significance to Longfellow and his public
was *Ballads and Other Poems* published two years later.
The ballad form held a special fascination for him. He
had written, 'And now I long to try a loftier strain, the
sublimer Song whose broken melodies have for so many
years breathed through my soul in the better hours of
life, and which I trust and believe will ere long unite
themselves into a symphony not all unworthy the sublime
theme, but furnishing "some equivalent expression for
the trouble and wrath of life, for its sorrow and its
mystery".'

This collection supplied what the public wanted: 'It
was the schooner Hesperus,/That sailed the wintry sea',
and 'The Skeleton in Armour', 'The Village Blacksmith',
and 'Excelsior':

There in the twilight cold and gray,
Lifeless but beautiful he lay,
And from the sky, serene and far,
A voice fell, like a falling star,
    Excelsior!

No matter that a voice could not fall like a falling star:
this was story-telling of a high order. Much as Tennyson's
Idylls of the King were to do, it fed the public's hunger
for an idealized, heroic past – 'lifeless but beautiful'.

Longfellow visited Europe again, visiting London as
the guest of Dickens. On his homeward journey he wrote
his only political verse, *Poems on Slavery*. In 1843 he
married his second wife. Her father gave them Craigie
House, and there they raised their six children. Longfellow's verse drama, *The Spanish Student*, was published
in 1843, and in 1845 *The Belfry of Bruges and Other*

Poems. It includes 'The Old Clock on the Stairs' with its insistent refrain, 'Forever – never/Never – forever!', a technique of repetitions he often used, sometimes to good effect, as in 'My Lost Youth': 'A boy's will is the wind's will,/And the thoughts of youth are long, long thoughts.'

Longfellow was ceaselessly prolific. *Evangeline* – the first important long poem in American literature – was published in 1847. The use of English hexameters is strange and persistent. What the poem gains in melodiousness it loses in suppleness:

So came the autumn, and passed, and the winter, – yet Gabriel came not;
Blossomed the opening spring and the notes of the robin and bluebird
Sounded sweet upon the wold and in wood, yet Gabriel came not.
But on the breath of the Summer winds a rumour was wafted
Sweeter than song of bird, or hue or odour of blossom.

When Longfellow submitted it for publication, he pleaded, 'I hope you will not reject it on account of the metre. In fact, I could not write it *as it is* in any other; it would have changed its character entirely to have put it into different measure.' No doubt a change in the metre would have altered its character. It might have avoided the slowness of pace, the rhapsodic monotony. The metre is almost impossible to sustain over a long stretch. But Longfellow, undeterred, used it again in *The Courtship of Miles Standish*.

In 1849 he published his last prose book, *Kavanagh*, and a book of poems, *The Seaside and the Fireside*, followed in 1851 by *The Golden Legend* and in 1855 by his most quoted and parodied poem, *The Song of Hiawatha*. It develops American Indian legends, concentrating on the life and death of Hiawatha, in the verse patterns of the *Kalevala*, the national epic poem of Finland.

Then the little Hiawatha,
Learned of every bird its language,
Learned their names and all their secrets
How they built their nests in Summer,
Where they hid themselves in Winter.

The poem has proved popular despite the critics. A review in a Boston newspaper shortly after its publication was scathing about its 'silly legends of the aborigines. His poem does not awaken one sympathetic throb; it does not teach a single truth.' The critic pointed out both the strength and weakness of the poem. He complained that it was not didactic: this is its real virtue. But, more appositely, he observes the coldness of characterization. The reader does not identify with the characters of the poem. Longfellow seems to have hoped that by distancing action and character he could – with epic impersonality – evoke a strange, idealized native dignity.

Longfellow resigned his professorship in 1854 in order to have more time for writing. But this happy, prolific period of his life came to a sudden end with the tragic death of his second wife. She was sealing a letter when her dress caught fire from a wax taper. In an unsuccessful attempt to save her, Longfellow too suffered severe burns. He never fully recovered from the shock. Even his outward appearance changed. He was compelled to grow the beard – so familiar in portraits of him – to conceal the scars left by the burns.

During his recovery he began translating Dante's *Divine Comedy*, a task he completed in 1867. *Tales of a Wayside Inn*, too, was published (1863: first series; 1874: second series). It included 'Paul Revere's Ride':

Listen my children, and you shall hear
Of the midnight ride of Paul Revere ...

The poems were either for entertainment – *Tales* – or darkly didactic. In 1872 *Christus* appeared, a trilogy which the poet considered his outstanding achievement, and in 1875 the *Masque of Pandora* was published, including the ode 'Morituri Salutamus' and some fine sonnets. *Keramos and Other Poems* was issued in 1878, followed by *Ultima Thule* (1880) and the posthumous *In the Harbour* (1882).

In 1881 his health deteriorated rapidly, and in 1882 he died of peritonitis. His reputation during his life had been high throughout the world, particularly in England where he received Honorary Degrees from Oxford and Cambridge and had an audience with Queen Victoria. A greater honour was conferred two years after his death when a bust of him was unveiled in Poets' Corner in Westminster Abbey. He was the first American poet to be commemorated there.

The faults of Longfellow's verse are all too clear to modern readers, in particular his sentimentality and his sometimes excessive facility. And metaphor that weakens or demeans either of the elements compared falls readily into sentimentality. When he writes, 'Silently one by one, in the infinite meadows of heaven,/Blossomed the lovely stars, the forget-me-nots of the angels', the fanciful comparisons simplify, blur, instead of clarifying by adding depth to image and meaning. 'Meadows' and 'forget-me-nots' deny 'heaven' and 'stars' their natural qualities – even their colours. We are not surprised by the rightness of the metaphors but by their incongruity. In *Evangeline* the same fault is plain. '... On the river/Fell here and there through the branches a tremulous gleam of moonlight,/Like the sweet thoughts of love in a darkened and devious spirit.' The spineless simile again reduces the sense to vagueness. The rhapsodic metre seems to dictate word choice.

Another form of sentimentality is the appeal to the feelings only – without recourse to the reason, as in 'The Child Asleep':

Upon that tender eye, my little friends,
  Soft sleep shall come, that cometh not to me!
I watch to see thee, nourish thee, defend –
  'Tis sweet to watch for thee, – alone for thee!

At other times a vacuous, high-sounding metaphor destroys the moral tone:

Lives of great men all remind us
  We can make our lives sublime,
And, departing, leave behind us
  Footprints on the sands of time.

The sands are hardly a substance in which to leave marks for eternity. The poems appeal to that 'heart' he mentioned in an early poem, almost in despite of reason. On a larger scale, formally, too, Longfellow fails to surprise by rightness, relies on the seemingly-powerful rhetoric he over-mastered. In *Hiawatha* the Indians appear as on a tapestry. They do not develop. The action cannot move forward. In its hypnotic rhetoric, the poem falls into bathetic rhetoric, largely on account of the persistent repetitions:

Can it be the sun descending
O'er the level plain of water?
Or the Red Swan floating, flying,
Wounded by the magic arrow,
Staining all the waves with crimson,
With the crimson of its life-blood ... ?
Yes; it is the sun descending,
Sinking down into the water ...
No; it is the Red Swan floating
Diving down beneath the water ...

Longfellow is his own best parodist. He forgets his own dictum: 'One so often sees the muse painted up to her eyes and bedizened with false jewelry that it is a positive relief to meet her without her rouge and in simple attire.'

The distinction between clarity and simplicity is all too pertinent. Longfellow seldom wrote from direct experience: even his description of the Mississippi in *Evangeline* was 'copied' from a painting by Banvard, and the Hiawatha legends, even in their particulars, came from books. On those occasions when he does face his own particular reality he writes with authority. In 'The Cross of Snow', though the image was discovered in a picture-book, it fitted exactly the feeling he wished to convey about his wife's death. The poem was not published in his lifetime:

In the long, sleepless watches of the night,
    A gentle face – the face of one long dead –
    Looks at me from the wall, where round its head
    The night-lamp casts a halo of pale light.
Here in this room she died; and soul more white
    Never through martyrdom of fire was led
    To its repose; nor can in books be read
    The legend of a life more benedight.
There is a mountain in the distant West
    That, sun-defying, in its deep ravines
    Displays a cross of snow upon its side.
Such is the cross I wear upon my breast
    These eighteen years, through all the changing scenes
    And seasons, changeless since the day she died.

The sonnet form has its implicit laws. As a form, its first appeal is through the reason. The poem is simple, but the image is apposite and both intensifies and clarifies the poet's feelings. This is Longfellow at his elegiac best. But he could draw the reader into less intense experience as well. The movement of some of his narratives is at times irresistible. In *Keramos* he writes,

Thus sang the Potter at his task
Beneath the blossoming hawthorn-tree,
While o'er his features, like a mask,

The quilted sunshine and leafshade
Moved, as the boughs above him swayed,
And clothed him, till he seemed to be
A figure woven in a tapestry ...

The images develop with a sense of inevitability.

Amy Lowell was too harsh when she declared that one aspect of her mission was to rid the world of Longfellow. His influence on serious writers has been marginal. The parodists saw to that. And his best poems – including 'My Lost Youth', 'The Birds of Killingworth', 'Chaucer', 'Chimes', 'The Cross of Snow', 'The Monk of Casal-Maggiore', 'Daylight and Moonlight', 'Mezzo Camin' and the stories in *Tales of a Wayside Inn* – continue to attract even those readers who do not normally turn to poetry.

Edgar Allan Poe 1809–1849

Here comes Poe with his Raven, like Barnaby Rudge,
Three fifths of him genius, two fifths sheer fudge.

– James Russell Lowell

Poe's genius manifests itself not only in his creative
writing but in his constructive literary criticism. He was
able to define the function of poetry and to identify the
motives, techniques, and themes of his own writing. Facile
didacticism such as Longfellow's and the strong narrative
line in long poems seemed to him inimical to the true
art. Emerson and the Transcendentalists could never – to
his mind – achieve poetry, restricted as they were by their
ideas of constructive passivity, the unity of forms at the
heart of Nature, and the ready intercommunication with
the Over-Soul. For Poe the long poem does not exist,
poetry is not a vehicle for moral improvement or for
rhythmic story telling. The work of art is autonomous.
The natural, aesthetic and metaphysical orders are quite
distinct.

Poe's clarity of thought is the product of will rather
than the legacy of an orderly upbringing. Born in Boston
in 1809 of actor parents, he was an orphan before he was
three. His father – a heavy drinker and gambler – left
home for good shortly after his birth. His mother moved
to Richmond, Virginia, and soon died. Edgar was taken as

a foster-child into the childless home of a merchant from Scotland, John Allan – hence Edgar's middle name – and his wife. The Allans moved to England (1815–20) and Edgar went to school in Stoke Newington. On their return to Virginia, Edgar was unhappy. Though he did well at the local school, his foster-parents quarrelled interminably.

While at school Edgar fell in love with the mother of one of his schoolmates who eventually – according to Poe – inspired his poem 'To Helen' (1831):

Helen, thy beauty is to me
  Like those Nicéan barks of yore,
That gently, o'er a perfumed sea
  The weary, way-worn wanderer bore
  To his own native shore ...

Since Poe inherited his parents' acting spirit, we can seldom trust his autobiographical anecdotes. 'To Helen' explores, however, the central theme of much of his subsequent poetry: the search for the ideal, epitomized by the beautiful woman. Her death is the supreme subject. He wrote in 'The Philosophy of Composition', 'I asked myself – "Of all melancholy topics, what, according to the *universal* understanding of mankind, is the *most* melancholy?" Death – was the obvious reply. "And when," I said, "is this most melancholy of topics most poetical?" ... "When it most closely allies itself to *Beauty*": the death, then, of a beautiful woman is, unquestionably, the most poetical topic in the world.'

In the last stanza of 'To Helen' she becomes almost a statue: 'Lo! In yon brilliant window-niche/How statue-like I see thee stand.' She prefigures the 'placid bust' in his later poem, 'The Raven'. Purity, untouched, becomes the beloved of the soul and acquires symbolic status later (in 'The Raven', 'Lenore', 'To my Mother', and above all, in 'Ulalume').

At the age of seventeen Poe fell in love again, with Miss

Sarah Elmira Royster, and his love was reciprocated. But on his admission to the University of Virginia, her family intervened, and she married a Mr Shelton. In the last year of Poe's life, when she was widowed, he again asked her hand and was again denied.

At the University Poe excelled in Classics and French, but drink and gambling compelled him to withdraw in 1826. Details of his biography are unclear, because Poe bequeathed his literary estate to Rufus Griswold who maliciously rewrote the poet's life, forging letters and presenting the poet as entirely *maudit*. The legends still hold wide currency. It is true, however, that tensions increased between Poe and his step-father and that at the age of eighteen Poe ran away to Boston. There he arranged for the publication of his first book, *Tamerlane and Other Poems* (1827), while working as a clerk. The volume includes three characteristic poems, displaying already his hypnotic rhythm of loneliness and his concern with the hidden. '*All* that we see or seem/Is but a dream within a dream', he wrote. He carried the melancholy theme into 'A Dream' and into the tensions of 'The Lake'.

Poe joined the army under the name of Edgar A. Perry later in 1827, and when Mrs Allan died two years later he returned to Richmond and brought out his second book, *Al Aaraaf, Tamerlane and Minor Poems* (1829). With Mr Allan's help he entered the military college, West Point. When his new book attracted favourable reviews, he left West Point, partly to concentrate on writing, partly through lack of money. He began to suffer long depressions and resorted to drink.

In 1831 his third collection, *Poems: Second Edition*, was published, including a critical introduction in which at the age of twenty-two he developed a clear aesthetic to which he remained faithful throughout his career. It advocates a poetry characterized by three cardinal qualities: the indefinite, 'music', and symbolism. 'A poem, in my opinion, is opposed to a work of science by having, for its *immediate* object, pleasure, not truth; to romance, by having for its object an *indefinite* instead of a *definite* pleasure, being a poem only so far as this object is attained; romance presenting perceptible images with definite, poetry with *in*definite sensations, to which end music is an *essential*, since the comprehension of sweet sound is our most indefinite conception. Music, when combined with a pleasurable idea is poetry; music without the idea is simply music; the idea without the music is prose from its very definitiveness.'

The ideal of purity is a central theme of these poems, as in 'To Helen':

On desperate seas long wont to roam,
  Thy hyacinth hair, thy classic face,
Thy Naiad airs have brought me home
    To the glory that was Greece
    And the grandeur that was Rome.

In 'The Sleeper' the hypnotic music, redolent of the supernatural, is first seen in its mature rhythms, relying strongly on alliteration and echo:

At midnight in the month of June,
I stand beneath the mystic moon.
An opiate vapour, dewy, dim,
Exhumes from out her golden rim,
And, softly dripping, drop by drop,
Upon the quiet mountain top,
Steals drowsily and musically
Into the universal valley.

Poe is a poet of extremes. He looks always for the 'most intense', and his poems are contrived in their music. Though he does not insult the intellect, as Longfellow is inclined to do, he is often constrained by the music to insert merely musical words. Perhaps 'mystic' is such a word. And yet within so rigorous a sound structure the rightness of 'Exhumes' – in sense and sound – is undeniable. Poe's later poems take the assonance and alliteration further – in 'Ulalume' to best effect. There is too, in the later poems, a deft deployment of refrains and repetitions, either – as in 'The Raven' – confirming a total mood or – as in 'The Bells' – raising the pitch to near hysteria.

In 'The City in the Sea' the power of Poe's 'vagueness' is arresting. The development of the underwater setting, which recurs frequently in the poems, is here particularly impressive:

So blend the turrets and shadows there
That all seem pendulous in air,
While from a proud tower in the town
Death looks gigantically down.

The fusion of the abstract with the concrete world of images, giving concepts the qualities of *things*, is at the centre of Poe's art. In 'The Bells', 'merriness', 'happiness', 'terror', solemnity' and 'melancholy' find their music in the way the image of their bells is developed.

In the poem 'Israfel' Poe's opposition to Emerson's vision of universal oneness and natural symbolism becomes clear:

Yes, Heaven is thine; but this
  Is a world of sweets and sours;
  Our flowers are merely flowers,
And the shadow of thy perfect bliss
  Is the sunshine of ours.

The angel Israfel is from a completely *different* world, a world which reflects *on*, but is not reflected *in*, this world.

Poe was still unrecognized in 1832, working in poverty in Baltimore and living with his aunt, Mrs Clemm. His first stories were being published, and in 1833 he won the *Baltimore Saturday Visitor* competition with his story 'MS Found in a Bottle'. In 1836, the year in which he married his cousin Virginia, he became editor of the

Southern Literary Messenger in which several stories and two important poems – 'To One in Paradise' and 'The Coliseum' – appeared.

Perhaps because his pen was said to run with 'vitriol for ink', his critical writings began to be noticed. Though he was severe with the second rate, he was a powerful advocate of good work – Dickens's, for example. In 1837 he moved to Philadelphia to edit *Burton's Gentleman's Magazine* for a year, and some of his best stories, including 'The Fall of the House of Usher', were published; and, in 1840, 'Sonnet-Silence', a poem which confronts the theme of the haunting. In 1841 he edited *Graham's Magazine* and published his first detective story, 'The Murders in the Rue Morgue'.

His reputation grew, but he remained poor and his wife was dying. In 1844 he moved to New York and the following year his poem 'The Raven' appeared in the *Evening Mirror*. By the end of the year he had published 'Eulalie' and the collection *The Raven and Other Poems*, a book with the full authority of his maturity, each poem painstakingly made. But his critical writings sabotaged his growing reputation. Because of his attacks on Longfellow he became a subject of derision. He published his 'Philosophy of Composition', describing the creation of 'The Raven', but his reputation was damaged. His wife died in 1847, and he succumbed to drinking again.

The publication of 'Ulalume' in 1848 proved that his artistic integrity was not marred. It is arguably his masterpiece. But he was under considerable stress. He wrote to an acquaintance, 'I am constitutionally sensitive – nervous in a very unusual degree. I become insane, with long intervals of horrible sanity. During these fits of absolute unconsciousness I drink, God only knows how often or how much. As a matter of course, my enemies referred the insanity to the drink rather than the drink to the insanity.'

'Eureka: A Prose Poem' was the last of his work to be published in his lifetime. It is an attempt to explain the nature of the universe as a unity: not the oneness of Emerson's view, but the harmony of disparate elements. The natural universe, gradually contracting, moves in its harmony to extinction, which is identity with God. Again he stresses the distinction between the physical world and the metaphysical or divine. A 'reciprocity of adaptation' is essential for 'unity', and the unity of the world comes from the harmonious relationship of details *within itself*, dependent on no details *external* to itself.

His aesthetic beliefs are a continuation of this argument. In writing, 'We should aim at so arranging the incidents that we shall not be able to determine of any one of them, whether it depends from any one other or upholds it.' Equilibrium or harmony, this is the most important expression of his mature aesthetic. He wrote to Mrs Clemm that after 'Eureka' he was ready to die. And so he did, a year later.

In 1849 he wrote 'The Bells', 'Annabel Lee' and a second 'To Helen', dedicated to a second Helen. 'The Poetic Principle', developing his theory that the long poem cannot exist, was also written that year. He argues that 'a poem deserves its title only inasmuch as it excites by elevating the soul,' and a poem of any length cannot sustain that excitement. He also alludes to the 'heresy of *The Didactic*'. During the summer he lectured successfully on 'The Poetic Principle' and was returning to New York when he was discovered delirious in the street in Baltimore. He was taken to hospital where he died.

Poe did not leave a large collection of verse, but his influence was great, particularly in France, where his poems, stories and critical writings left a marked impression. His most important theory was that the poem is *itself*. It is not a didactic vehicle or indeed a vehicle for anything but itself. It cannot be paraphrased or finally analysed, for what it says is contained in *how* it is said. It is a self-contained unity, relying on no externals for its existence, its resonance, or its comprehension. Even the seemingly precise geographical details of a poem such as 'Ulalume' are unconnected with any *real* landscape.

Poe advocates 'originality', but not experimentation for its own sake. 'It is by no means a matter as some suppose of impulse or intuition ... In general, to be found, it must be elaborately sought, and although a positive merit of the highest class, demands in its attainment less of invention than negation.' Here, Poe's idea of 'originality' has been misinterpreted by his detractors and casual readers. He is in fact attempting to *extend* the application of principles of rhyme and alliteration, while they interpret him as advocating a rejection of those principles. The 'negation' to which he refers is the result of an extension rather than a repealing of those principles.

His scorn for allegory is a further aspect of his distaste for didactic literature. 'In defence of allegory (however, or for whatever object, employed) there is scarcely one respectable word to be said,' he writes in a review of Hawthorne's *Twice-Told Tales*. This extends his argument against 'externals'. For allegory presupposes interpretation in terms other than itself. The current of inner meaning in Poe's poetry – in 'The Raven', for example – must not be confused with allegory. For the symbol of the raven acquires meaning from its context, and retains its meaning only within that context. It is this quality that most attracted the French poets, Baudelaire in particular, and they used Poe as a model for their more programmatic poetic 'Symbolism', in which emotions and ideas are presented by suggestion rather than description, and symbolic content is found in the organization of images and even in the sounds of words.

Some readers have misread Poe's moral intentions in his quest for *poetic* truth and have, for their own purposes, called him 'evil', either applauding or condemning this quality. He illuminates dark corners of experience, but he does not invite us into them or lend them his *moral* approval. 'The Black Cat' has been seen as a story inviting destructive action, for, in 'the spirit of PER-VERSENESS' he cuts out the cat's eye. In 'The Imp of the Perverse', he writes, 'Though the promptings of perverseness we act without comprehensible object ... through its promptings we act, for the reason that we should not.' Baudelaire, Mallarmé, and above all Gide, admired Poe for this. Gide called it *acte gratuit*. But in reading Poe they seem to have ignored the powerful presence of *guilt*. Where a perverse act goes unpunished, an undercurrent of insanity, an inherent punishment, develops, as in 'The Tell-Tale Heart'.

Despite misreadings – perhaps because of them – Poe's influence has been wide and varied. Dostoievsky (whose wilful characters are nearer Poe's than those of Gide are), Conan Doyle, H. G. Wells, Chekhov, Debussy, Ravel, Beardsley, the Symbolist writers in France and elsewhere, and, by a weak shift of emphasis from 'autonomy of art' to 'art for art's sake', the Art Nouveau and Pre-Raphaelite movements in England, did not work in ignorance of his achievement. However we judge that influence, we can only agree with Poe's verdict on American literature, a literature he was instrumental in defining and to which he lent the authority of his genius: 'We have at length arrived at that epoch when our literature may and must stand on its own merits or fall through its own defects. We have snapped asunder the leading-strings of our British Grandmamma.'

Henry David Thoreau
1817–1862

The Poet March 3. He must be something more than natural
– even supernatural. Nature will not speak through but along
with him. His voice will not proceed from her midst, but,
breathing on her, will make her the expression of his thought.
He then poetizes when he takes a fact out of nature into spirit.
He speaks without reference to time or place. His thought is
one world, hers another. He is another Nature – Nature's
brother. Kindly offices do they perform for one another. Each
publishes the other's truth.

– Thoreau's *Journal* for 1839

Thoreau was born in Concord, Massachusetts, in 1817,
the son of a small farmer and artisan who kept a shop in
the village. His upbringing was puritanically strict, with
heavy stress laid upon duty and thrift. At Harvard, between the ages of sixteen and twenty, he developed an
intense interest in the classics and began a translation
of Aeschylus. His first book, *A Week on the Concord and
Merrimack Rivers*, records his devotion to the great
writers. In it he quotes from Homer, Virgil and Ovid,
from Gower, Shakespeare, Quarles and Milton, from
Byron, Emerson and Tennyson.

  After college, Thoreau briefly became a teacher but
with little success. Emerson – already a well-established
figure – invited the young man to join his household

when he discovered Thoreau wrote verse. He became Emerson's disciple and lived with him from 1841 to 1843. For a period, in manner and style, Thoreau imitated his master slavishly, but both men were finally too self-centred for such a situation to persist.

Thoreau's individualism took the form of radical opposition: to Puritanism, to the State, and to Society as it was then constituted. His attitude to the State is best expressed in his essay 'Civil Disobedience', his most influential prose work. 'That government is best which governs least ... I quietly declare war with the State after my fashion, though I will still make use and get what advantage of her I can, as is usual in such cases.' He contributed to the *Dial*, the magazine of the Transcendentalists, and in 1849 *A Week on the Concord* was published.

In 1845 he had begun an experiment in self-sufficiency and simple economy, living in a hut he erected on Emerson's land at Walden Pond. Out of this experience came his prose masterpiece, *Walden* (1854), an account of the two years spent there. During that period he went to jail, refusing to pay poll-tax to a government waging war against Mexico. His aunt Maria, much to his chagrin, bailed him out after one night's martyrdom.

Early in life he began suffering from tuberculosis. In 1860 he contracted a chill while surveying tree stumps. He never fully recovered. In 1862, after two abortive attempts to re-establish his health at Niagara and in the Mid-West, he died. His *Journals* were published posthumously, between 1884 and 1892, and a volume of *Poems of Nature* in 1895.

Thoreau's style is at its best in *Walden* – conversational, seasoned with metaphors. He moralizes without preaching. A fault of *A Week on the Concord* is that the descriptive and the moralistic passages are in conflict and work against the unity: 'We are bid to a river-party – not to be preached at,' James Russell Lowell wrote.

It is this fault that mars many of the poems, preventing them from achieving major success. The oracular and the descriptive clash rather than complement one another. When either the didactic or the descriptive voice dominates an entire poem, Thoreau achieves some successes. A bookish, unashamedly classical poem such as 'Smoke' is mysteriously rich in its dark, somewhat blurred imagery:

Light-winged Smoke, Icarian bird,
Melting thy pinions in thy upward flight,
Lark without song, and messenger of dawn,
Circling above the hamlets as thy nest;
Or else, departing dream, and shadowy form
Of midnight vision, gathering up thy skirts;
By night star-veiling, and by day
Darkening the light and blotting out the sun;
Go thou my incense upward from this hearth,
And ask the gods to pardon this clear flame.

Though the image of the nest may, in its excess, recall Longfellow, the controlled rhythm and the general dramatic appositeness of the imagery is notable. 'Winter Memories', on the other hand, relies simply on the poet's love of nature. He does not go in search of startling imagery but relies on a contemplative approach:

When in the still light of the cheerful moon,
On every twig and rail and jutting spout,
The icy spears were adding to their length
Against the arrows of the coming sun,
How in the shimmering noon of summer past
Some unrecorded beam slanted across
The upland pasture where the Johnswort grew ...

The 'spears' and 'arrows' are left suggestive, not forced into significance. The poem quietly contains, without asserting its meanings.

Thoreau fails when his efforts to startle are laboured, as in 'Haze':

Woof of the sun, ethereal gauze,
Woven of Nature's richest stuffs,
Visible heat, air-water, and dry sea,
Last conquest of the eye;
Toil of the day displayed, sun-dust,
Aerial surf upon the shores of earth,
Ethereal estuary, firth of light,
Breakers of air, billows of heat ...

The suspended rhythm, in which he attempts to penetrate the image from various sides, is admirable in the rugged effort it reveals. But he fails to touch the crowded, disparate imagery into unity. There is a better, roughly metaphysical striving in 'Sic Vita':

I am a parcel of vain strivings tied
    By a chance bond together,
Dangling this way and that, their links
    Were made so loose and wide,
      Methinks,
    For milder weather.

Effective use of an exacting form carries the poem through. But Thoreau senses his problem in the poem 'Inspiration':

If with light head erect I sing,
    Though all the muses lend their force,
From my poor love of anything,
    The verse is weak and shallow as its source.

But if with bended neck I grope,
    Listening behind me for my wit,
With faith superior to hope,
    More anxious to keep back than forward it,

Making my soul accomplice there
    Unto the flame my heart hath lit,
Then will the verse forever wear, –
    Time cannot bend the line which God hath writ.

The language he is forced to use and the received forms he puts it in are inadequate. He rejects facility, and in what must be his worst line of verse, 'But if with bended neck I grope', and the lines that follow, he suggests a cautious course in which he will attempt to discover a true and personal language which will prove durable. The quest did not prove entirely successful.

A striking individuality marks Thoreau's poetry, but it is finally the individuality of character and content rather than voice. His experiments often failed to find the right word for the right place, the correct rhythm and form for the experience. Emerson described his verse accurately. 'The gold does not yet flow pure, but is drossy and crude. The thyme and marjoram are not yet made into honey.'

Herman Melville 1819–1891

I am like one of those seeds taken out of the Egyptian pyra-
mids, which, after being three thousand years a seed, and
nothing but a seed, being planted in English soil it developed
itself, grew to greenness, and then fell to mould. So I. Until I
was twenty-five I had no development at all. From my twenty-
fifth year I date my life. Three weeks have scarcely passed at
any time between then and now, that I have not unfolded
within myself . . .

– Letter to Hawthorne, written during the composition of
Moby Dick.

Melville, one of America's great prose writers, was also a
prolific poet, though he is seldom considered for his
poetic achievements. His prose writings frequently achieve
in heightened passages the intensity of poetry, while the
poems themselves are not heightened in this sense. But,
like his prose writings, they often evoke the lived experiences – from the excitement of exploration and discovery
to a recognition of the corruption and corrupting influence of Western man and his religion, and eventually to
resigned pessimism or – occasionally – momentary recon-
ciliation. He is driven by a sense of urgency into argument with God and Society.

Melville was born in New York in 1819 of a well-to-do
merchant importer who went bankrupt and died insane

before the boy was thirteen, leaving a widow and eight children. Melville worked at various jobs early in life – clerking, teaching and farming among them. When he was eighteen he signed on as ship's boy and sailed to Liverpool. Later, after travelling in America, he became a member of the crew of the *Acushnet* and in 1842 deserted in the Marquesa Islands and lived among the cannibal islanders, the Typee. He escaped on board an Australian whaling vessel and was imprisoned in Tahiti for his part in a mutiny. After living in Hawaii and working in a bowling alley, he returned to Boston in 1844.

He married and settled in New York in 1847, where he was introduced into literary society by Evert Duyckinck, a well-connected man of letters. From Melville's varied travels came the books *Typee* (1846) and *Omoo* (1847). They were so successful that Melville complained to Hawthorne that he would be known only as 'a man who had lived among cannibals'. This apprehension was confirmed. His political and religious allegory *Mardi* (1849) was rejected. He returned to narrative in *Redburn* (1849) and *White-Jacket* (1850) in which he was able to expose the darker sides of naval law in sanctioning brutality.

In 1849, after moving to Pittsfield, Massachusetts, he completed the first draft of *Moby Dick*. When it was published in 1851, Melville's disillusion increased. The book was received with apathy. *Pierre* (1852), his only major novel set entirely on land, was rejected by the critics, and he turned to short story writing with *Piazza Tales* (1856). It included 'Benito Cereno', one of his best stories. The next year he published his bitter prose satire *The Confidence-Man*, displaying the deceit of commercial society.

The apathy with which his prose was greeted helped to turn Melville more towards verse writing. His visit to the Holy Land (1856–7) inspired his 18,000 line poem *Clarel*, written in octosyllabic couplets. In 1866, resigned to relative obscurity, he became a New York customs officer,

writing poetry which he published at his own expense –
Battle Pieces (1866), *Clarel* (1876), *John Marr and Other
Sailors* (1888), and 'Timoleon' (1891). He died in 1891
with the manuscript of the prose work *Billy Budd* completed but unpublished. His reputation was at such low
ebb that even this masterpiece was not published until
1924. More poems appeared in the same year and his
Journal up the Straits in 1935.

Much of the verse relates thematically to the novels and
is of interest on that count as well as intrinsically. Randall
Jarrell in his essay 'Some Lines from Whitman places
that intrinsic interest high. 'Whitman, Dickinson, and
Melville seem to me the best poets of the nineteenth
century here in America,' he wrote. 'Melville's poetry has
been grossly underestimated.'

Melville's attitude towards the composition of poetry
closely parallels his attitude towards prose composition.
The poem 'Art' is a clear exposition of his idea of artistic
creation:

In placid hours well-pleased we dream
Of many a brave unbodied scheme.
But form to lend, pulsed life create,
What unlike things must meet and mate:
A flame to melt – a wind to freeze;
Sad patience – joyous energies;
Humility – yet pride and scorn;
Instinct and study; love and hate;
Audacity – reverence. These must mate,
And fuse with Jacob's mystic heart,
To wrestle with the angel – Art.

The poem moves from passivity to action. The struggle
and victory resemble Jacob's. Jacob saw God face to face
and was preserved, but he was wounded in his struggle
with the angel ('and the hollow of Jacob's thigh was out
of joint', Genesis, XXXII, 25). Creation and destruction,
the discovery and the wound, are combined in one act,

like and unlike yoked in the act of making – instinct and study, content and form, Melville and his God. Contrasts and opposites are held in tension, in balance, within the poem. Melville's struggle is often with his medium. His energy finds itself too often constrained to verse forms unsuited to his theme. *Clarel*, an extended philosophical debate between faith and doubt, often succumbs to the exigencies of its form:

Yes, God is God, and men are men,
Forever and for aye. What then?
There's Circumstance – there's Time; and these
Are charged with store of latencies
Still working in to modify.
For mystic text that you recall,
Dilate upon, and e'en apply –
(Although I seek not to decry)
Theology's scarce practical.

Despite its flaws, the poem – twice the length of *Paradise Lost* – is often impressive. Melville's didacticism is particularly affecting because – unlike Longfellow and Emerson – he has no certainties to impart. His technique is Socratic, raising more questions than he can answer, so that we feel he too is under instruction, in doubt. The pilgrimage in *Clarel*, spiritual and geographical, of an American theological student in Palestine in quest of firm faith, fails to reach its goal. But the student joins the common throng on the Via Crucis, shouldering his own cross and vanishing 'in the obscurer town' in doubt. The 'Epilogue' reminds him that in his pilgrimage he has neglected the heart whose passions are paramount:

That like the crocus budding through the snow –
That like a swimmer rising from the deep –
That like a burning secret which doth go
Even from the bosom that would hoard and keep;
Emerge thou mayst from the last whelming sea
And prove that death but routs life into victory.

It recalls the ballad 'Billy in the Darbies', at the conclusion of *Billy Budd*:

But me they'll lash in hammock, drop me deep.
Fathoms down, fathoms down, how I'll dream fast asleep.
I feel it stealing now. Sentry, are you there?
Just ease these darbies at the wrist, and roll me over fair,
I am sleepy, and the oozy weeds about me twist.

What is lacking in *Clarel* is a sense of *living* cross-
bearers continuing on their individual courses. We sense
only an apprehension of the intellectual and emotional
inadequacy of the Christian myth. Billy is more convincing, the innocent Christ-like figure has been hanged and
in the ballad accepts the final sleep. His ascent is to the
scaffold. Afterwards, he is held below. The ballad provides
the intellectual climax of the prose work.

Melville's poems, even the most laboured, seem to rise
out of heightened experience. Some of them were suggested by phrases in his journal, others by Biblical passages. They are then worked at. This may be why they do
not burn on the page, however intense the experience or
theme. But the reality of the experience is generally
beyond doubt. 'The Portent', while it attests to his poetic
power, reveals his unsuccessful struggle *against* his medium. Each phrase is self-consciously gauged and worked.
The effect is a halting progression, intellectual and
rhythmical, the product of his attitude to the craft:

Hanging from the beam,
  Slowly swaying (such the law),
Gaunt the shadow on your green,
  Shenandoah!
The cut is on the crown
(Lo, John Brown),
And the stabs shall heal no more.

Hidden in the cap
  Is the anguish none can draw;
So your future veils its face,

Shenandoah!
But the streaming beard is shown
(Weird John Brown),
The meteor of the war.

It is thought intensity. The poem, one of his *Battle Pieces* about the Civil War, is ballad-like but more sophisticated, with balanced shifts from Shenandoah, the lush valley, to John Brown, the drying dead. John Brown's 'weirdness' is full of connotations: he is weird-looking with his white beard, and 'fateful' – 'wyrd' – with the portents of the meteor. The poem abounds in double meanings and degenerates at times into mere cleverness and verbal wit, losing the impulse of its experience. And yet Melville's seventy-two *Battle Pieces* include some of his best poems. Though he supported the North politically, he is nonpartisan on the issue of suffering. In 'Ball's Bluff' he watches men moving off to war:

They moved like Juny morning on the wave,
  Their hearts were fresh as clover in its prime
  (It was the breezy summer time),
    Life throbbed so strong,
How should they dream that Death in a rosy clime
  Would come to thin their shining throng?
Youth feels immortal, like the gods sublime.

Three of the best poems in *John Marr and Other Sailors* are 'The Tuft of Kelp', 'The Aeolian Harp', and 'The Haglets' (ie Hacklets or small seagulls). In each the form is more suited to the content than is usual in Melville and the final effect is more integrated. 'The Tuft of Kelp' is brief and to the point:

All dripping in tangles green,
  Cast up by a lonely sea,
If purer for that, O Weed,
  Bitterer, too, are ye?

The image is realized and then suggestively allegorized, but Melville does not work out the meaning.

In *Timoleon* the sea, which gives life to many of Melville's poems, is at ebb, and explicitly philosophical subjects dominate. In 'The Garden of Metrodorus', for example, he writes,

Here none come forth, here none go in,
Here silence strange, and dumb seclusion dwell:
  Content from loneness who may win?
  And is the stillness peace or sin
Which noteless thus apart can keep its dell?

Writing in neglect, the poet's idiom becomes more private. The images do not crystallize. Philosophical questions overwhelm the poetry.

The poems published posthumously under the title *Weeds and Wildings, with a Rose or Two* (1924) do little to extend our appreciation of his poetry. They rather confirm the tensions in the later books. But there is much throughout the *oeuvre* to admire. The philosophical dimension of his best poems adds a new dimension to his dominant theme, that of man struggling with all the will he has to *make* a faith by which to live. The moments of intellectual vividness draw us to the verse. It is to the prose we turn for richness of detail and imagery, and for his distinctive rhythms. But in the prose we are unlikely to find the rare sense of hope that sometimes enters the verse – a hope based on Nature rather than God, reminiscent of Emerson and the Transcendentalist optimists, as in 'Malvern Hill':

We elms of Malvern Hill
  Remember every thing:
But sap the twig will fill:
Wag the world how it will,
  Leaves must be green in Spring.

Walt Whitman 1819–1892

Walt Whitman, an American, one of the roughs, a kosmos,
Disorderly fleshy and sensual . . . eating drinking and breeding.

– *Leaves of Grass*

The greatness of Whitman is not in question. Yet it is
difficult to approach so large a figure. His *Leaves of Grass*
in its final form is vast. It might seem best to take its
title literally: blades of grass, implying spontaneity of
growth, each blade formed yet separate, and when taken
together forming a rough harmony. The work is then
admired for its best passages, seen not so much in their
interdependence as in their coexistence. But if we read
each section in sequence, we witness the progress of a
man's spirit, the magnitude of the journey, and the final,
completed vision of itself. The book grew with Whitman
from his thirty-sixth year, when he published the first
edition of *Song of Myself* (1855), until the year he died,
aged seventy-two, when the last edition was published.
Before the first edition there had been no suggestion of
Whitman's unique style, no indication of the originality
to come.

He was born in 1819 at West Hills, Long Island, of
farming stock. He turned to his mother for affection and
stability, since his father – a carpenter in what was then

the small town of Brooklyn – was given to outbursts of temper and fits of moroseness:

> The mother with mild words, clean her cap and gown, a wholesome odor falling off her person and clothes as she walks by,
> The father, strong, self-sufficient, manly, mean, anger'd, unjust,
> The blow, the quick loud word, the tight bargain, the crafty lure...

The letters exchanged between mother and son during the Civil War testify to their closeness.

Walt was apprenticed to a printer and founded his own newspaper, *Long Islander*, when he was nineteen. Then he taught in rural schools until 1841. He also wrote a temperance tract, *Franklin Evans: or, The Inebriate: A Tale of the Times*, which he described later as 'damned rot ... not insincere, perhaps, but rot'. He had also written some stories and conventional verse at this time and edited one or two newspapers from which he had been sacked for his radical views.

In 1848 he travelled to New Orleans to work on the *Crescent* newspapers. After this few months' journey his notebooks reveal a complete change in attitude. He had been a dandy moving in Bohemian company; but he returned as a prophet prepared to speak for all America, to write *Leaves of Grass*. Many explanations have been advanced for the so-called 'New Orleans experience'. The grandeur of the journey may have affected him, since he returned by way of the Great Lakes, Niagara and the Hudson. Some critics cite an intense affair with a woman, which could account for the passions of the 'Children of Adam' sequence in *Leaves of Grass*. Others insist on a shattering homosexual experience, which may be reflected in the 'Calamus' sequence. And a profound mystical experience has been suggested. Certainly *Leaves of Grass* is suffused with a joyful mysticism, involving Emerson's transcendentalism and yet including nothing of the Transcendentalist vision of blissful emptiness in space. Whitman's universe is crowded.

In the first edition of *Leaves of Grass* (1855), in place of the author's name Whitman had a daguerrotype of himself in workman's clothing. He designed the large page (8″ × 11″) to suit his long lines and employed neighbours to print the volume. About a thousand copies were printed and Fowler & Wells of New York and Boston were the only shop willing to stock it. Whitman reported that none of the edition sold, but copies were despatched to influential people, among them John Greenleaf Whittier and Emerson. Whittier is said to have burned his copy – hardly surprising, in view of such lines as:

Through me forbidden voices,
Voices of sexes and lusts ... voices veiled, and I remove the
    veil,
Voices indecent by me clarified and transfigured ...

Copulation is no more rank to me than death is.

The ungainly length of the unrhymed lines was enough to startle the reader, and the sensuous evocation of a woman watching men bathing might seem improper to a moralist:

The beards of the young men glistened with wet, it ran from
    their long hair,
Little streams passed all over their bodies.
An unseen hand also passed over their bodies,
It descended tremblingly from their temples and ribs ...

A memorable image of loneliness and frustration, spoken with sympathy, without sentimentality: 'They do not think whom they souse with spray.'

The book met generally with disregard, and this in spite of the powerful 'Preface', now considered a landmark in American literary criticism. It seems hastily written. It is immediate in appeal. 'The direct trial of him who would be the greatest poet is today. If he does not flood himself with the immediate age as with vast oceanic tides ... and if he does not attract his own land body and soul to himself and hang on its neck with incomparable love and plunge ...' It is the voice of his poetry. The forward thrust of Whitman himself shocks the first-time reader:

I celebrate myself,
And what I assume you shall assume,
For every atom belonging to me as good belongs to you.

It at once invites and repels. The assumed authority is clear in the 'Preface'. 'This is what you shall do: Love the earth and sun and the animals, despise riches, give alms to every one that asks ... read these leaves in the open air in every season of every year of your life ... dismiss whatever insults your own soul, and your very flesh shall be a great poem.'

Taken on its own terms the poem works. The long exhalation of the lines, the rhetorical catalogues and repetitions that achieve something like ritualistic rhythms, bring to mind the Psalms. Indeed, the 'Preface' calls the work 'the great psalm of the republic'. Later, in *A Backward Glance over Travelled Roads* (1889), Whitman wrote that the profoundest service poems could perform, more than merely satisfying the reader's intellect, was to 'fill him with vigorous and clean manliness, religiousness, and give him good heart as a radical possession and habit.' *Leaves of Grass* succeeds with that kind of sweep. As Emerson wrote when he received a copy, 'I am not blind to the worth of the wonderful gift of *Leaves of Grass*. I find it the most extraordinary piece of wit and wisdom that America has yet contributed ... I find incomparable things said incomparably well, as they must be. I find the courage of treatment which so delights us, and which large perceptions only can inspire ...'

A second edition was prepared (1856) with a preface calling upon America to cast off its literary ties with Europe and to let its own literature flow forth. It urged writers to protest against the taboo on sex as a literary subject. A third edition in 1860 added the 'Children of Adam' and the 'Calamus' sequences and the original *Leaves of Grass* became *Song of Myself*. Emerson urged Whitman to restrain himself in the 1860 edition, but he failed. The book was banned in Boston. Whitman lost his job. An edition was prepared in London omitting the offensive poems.

For Whitman the great sobering experience was the Civil War. It broke before he had completed the collection of new poems for the fourth edition of *Leaves*. He did not himself serve, but when he heard that his brother had been wounded, he went in search of him. *Specimen Days and Collect* (1882), a prose work, gives an account of the experience. *Drum Taps* and *Sequel to Drum Taps*, included in later editions of *Leaves*, evoke his reaction in verse. First there was exhilaration:

Beat! beat! drums – blow! bugles! blow!
Through the windows – through doors – burst like a ruthless
    force
Into the solemn church, and scatter the congregation,
Into the school where the scholar is studying ...

But as he relates in *Backward Glance*, he went to the battlefields and 'partook of all the fluctuations, gloom, despair, hopes again arous'd, courage evoked – death readily risked ...' He stayed in Washington to help in the wards and his exhilaration gave way to compassion, as lines from 'The Wound-Dresser' show:

An old man bending I come among new faces ...
An attendant follows holding a tray, he carries a refuse pail,
Soon to be fill'd with clotted rags and blood, emptied, and
    fill'd again ...

(Come sweet death! be persuaded O beautiful death!
In mercy come quickly.)

The contrast with the earlier flood of spontaneous health
is revealing:

Spontaneous me, Nature,
The loving day, the mounting sun, the friend I am happy with,
The arm of my friend hanging idly over my shoulder ...

One of Whitman's best-known poems is in the Civil
War sequence:

When lilacs last in the dooryard bloom'd,
And the great star early droop'd in the western sky at night,
I mourn'd, and yet shall mourn with the ever-returning spring.

Written in memory of Lincoln in the weeks after his
assassination, it becomes a threnody powerfully affirming
regeneration through the force of nature. Swinburne
called it 'the most sweet and sonorous nocturne ever
chanted in the church of the world.' Whitman's real and
ideal worlds here come together. It is the centre of *Leaves
of Grass*. It does not elegize, it celebrates.

From 1865 to 1873 Whitman worked as a government
clerk in Washington. In 1873 he suffered a stroke, however, and moved to Camden, New Jersey. Three years
later another edition of *Leaves* was ready, containing a
new sequence called 'Passage to India' which commem-
orates three great engineering feats of the 1860s: the
Atlantic Cable, the Suez Canal, and the Union Pacific
Railroad. Whitman's ready combining of the material
and spiritual worlds is again notable. The new poems
included the passages set by Vaughan Williams in his
Sea Symphony, 'O we can wait no longer,/We too take
ship O soul'. There were two further editions, one in 1889
which added 'November Boughs', and another in 1891
with 'Sands at Seventy' and 'Goodbye My Fancy'. The
overall pattern is clear. In the early poems the pre-

occupation is with self. The intensely compassionate focal middle section of poems relating to the Civil War follows, and the final section is composed of more solemnly meditative poems. Whitman stressed his preference for the final 1891 edition which included all.

Whitman's influence has been wide-reaching and it is still felt, although many poets have strenuously, if unconvincingly, denied any technical influence. Eliot, Pound, D. H. Lawrence, and the Imagists learned from him. Thomas Mann called the book 'a great, important, indeed holy gift'. Turgenev contemplated translating sections of it into Russian. Delius made a memorable setting of the 'Sea Drift' sequence. The revolutionary and religious aspects of the writings have affected all manner of liberal, political, sociological and religious movements. William Carlos Williams referred to *Leaves of Grass* as 'a book as important as we are likely to see in the next thousand years'. Federigo García Lorca wrote in his 'Ode to Walt Whitman', 'Not for one moment, beautiful aged Walt Whitman/have I failed to see your beard full of butterflies.' Allen Ginsberg's references to his master are numerous. Even Pound, who resented Whitman's powerful effect on him, felt constrained to write:

I make a pact with you, Walt Whitman –
I have detested you long enough ...
It was you that broke new wood,
Now it is a time for carving ...

Perhaps the best advocate of Whitman was Randall Jarrell who wrote in his essay 'Some Lines from Whitman', 'It is only a list – but what a list! And how delicately, in what different ways – likeness and opposition and continuation and climax and anti-climax – the transitions are managed, whenever Whitman wants to manage them ...' Jarrell's comment on a single passage applies to the whole of *Leaves of Grass*.

Emily Dickinson 1830–1886

Pardon my sanity in a world insane.

– One of Emily Dickinson's *Letters*

Emily Dickinson is one of the finest and most prolific American poets. She composed over 1,750 poems, hundreds of them attesting to her idiosyncratic genius. Her life was poor in incident, characterized instead by intellectual and imaginative intensities. The poems reveal a full and strong-willed personality. Most of her critics have examined her persistent references to Life, Time, Nature and Eternity, all have laid stress on her solitariness, but few acknowledge the part her conscious will played in determining her life and her profoundly original work. Few, too, take into account the prevalent attitudes to women – particularly spinsters – in the second half of the nineteenth century. Emily Dickinson's life and art developed within certain defined borders, certain conscious preferences and imposed social forms. Her imagination was paradoxically freed and forwarded by those limitations, predispositions, habits and choices.

In one poem, she writes,

My life closed twice before its close –
It yet remains to see
If Immortality unveil
A third event to me

So huge, so hopeless to conceive
As these that twice befell.
Parting is all we know of heaven,
And all we need of hell.

Positive resignation is expressed in such a poem. In a real sense she *decided* to lead no life after the harrowing 'closing' alluded to in this poem and elsewhere. The resignation suggests a religious analogy, not only in the abstractions she uses but in the verb 'unveil' as well. She elected to write a poetry of powerful wit, in the fullest sense of the word. She knew the power of her art. Her poems often take epigrammatic form, develop a paradox, or suggest their subject in the manner of a riddle:

His Bill and Auger is
His head, a Cap and Frill
He laboreth at every Tree
A Worm, His utmost Goal.

The bird is evoked with conscious artifice. Emily Dickinson was aware of her skill and its limits. Often, she strains after strangeness:

Bee! I'm expecting you!
Was saying Yesterday
To Somebody you know
That you were due –

The Frogs got Home last Week...

The poem is signed, 'Yours, Fly.' It has more the quality of a unique speaking voice than an epistle.

Emily Dickinson was born in the village of Amherst, Massachusetts, in 1830. Apart from a brief period at Mount Holyoake Female Seminary, a trip to Washington and Philadelphia, and a stay in Boston for eye treatment, all her life was spent in the village. 'I don't go from home,' she wrote, 'unless emergency leads me by the hand.' She studied at Amherst Academy and spent a normal childhood. But during her seventeenth year, at Mount Holyoake, the evangelical movement reached the village and seminary. Many of her fellow students committed themselves to the evangelists. Emily held back, even when her family gave way to the fervour of the moment. When she was twenty-four, she refused to become a member of the church, though she still attended services sporadically. It was a major decision for her, and an expression of her integrity and strong will. She distrusted the lasting value of emotional conversion. Freedom of spirit was of paramount importance to her. Yet the magnitude of the decision is reflected in the poems and their idiom, for she remained deeply religious – in her own way – throughout her life. Religious themes constantly preoccupy her. 'You mention Immortality!' she wrote in a letter, 'That is the Flood subject.'

Positive doubt characterized her religion: she could find no convincing proof or disproof of immortality or of the existence of God in received religion, nor could she follow the materialist into the world of unbelief. Her preference seems to have been for a vision of imminent heaven, the present natural sacrament, rather than for one too remote to hold. It is a faith reminiscent of Emerson's – the world takes on a symbolic quality. 'And God at every gate', she writes in one poem:

Oh Sacrament of summer days,
Oh Last Communion in the Haze –
Permit a child to join.

Thy sacred emblems to partake –
Thy consecrated bread to take
And thine immortal wine!

In another poem, she says,

There came a Day at Summer's full,
Entirely for me –
I thought that such were for the Saints,
Where Resurrections – be – ...

Her vision aspires to the mystical, but her images and metaphors are of this world. She discovers God in earthly analogies – when she senses him he has an almost physical habitation, a visible nature:

I never saw a Moor –
I never saw the Sea –
Yet I know how the Heather looks
And what a Billow be.

I never spoke with God
Nor visited in Heaven –
Yet certain am I of the spot
As if the Checks were given –

She approaches him as she approaches those things in nature which she has not seen, through imagination, if not through final faith.

Another decision crucial to her writing was her withdrawal from the world. Various explanations for this have been advanced. The most popular assumes a broken love-affair. Several beaux have been suggested, though none can be confidently verified. She began a partial withdrawal when she started writing poetry more frequently. Yet the attractive legend of the woman in white – a wedding dress? – gliding through the garden and occasionally glimpsed upon the stair has been overemphasized. Too little attention has been given to the fact that she could not – even had she wished – retire to some hut as Thoreau had done. She was a woman. It was not uncommon for maiden ladies to stay closely at home: if it had been, Emily's sister would seem almost as mysterious as the poet herself.

But what is remarkable is that her withdrawal, although it began gradually, eventually became as total as a religious renunciation. And it is not an impossible hypothesis that the beloved whose departure she mourns may be not a particular man but Christ, the loss of religious certainty, the Soul's lover. Her poetry mirrors the withdrawal:

The Soul selects her own Society –
Then – shuts the Door –
To her divine Majority –
Present no more –

At times her isolation is despairing:

Had I not seen the Sun
I could have borne the shade
But Light a newer Wilderness
My Wilderness has made –

At other times, her solitude is her strength:

We learn in the Retreating
How vast an one
Was recently among us –
A Perished Sun

Endear in the departure
How doubly more
Than all the Golden presence
It was – before –

A third important decision was made in 1862, when Emily wrote to Thomas Wentworth Higginson. She was thirty-two. Although she had written over three hundred poems, she had not considered publishing them. Indeed, in her lifetime only seven of the poems appeared in print. But she had admired Higginson's 'Letter to a Young Contributor' in the *Atlantic Monthly* – an article advising aspiring writers. She knew his reputation as a lecturer interested in the status of women writers, and she felt a need for criticism.

She wrote sending her poems. 'Are you too deeply occupied to say if my verse is alive? ... The mind is so near itself it cannot see distinctly, and I have none to

ask.' Higginson did not understand her work. His predispositions were those of a Victorian. He urged her to
tidy the 'irregularity' of her verses, presumably to bring
them into line with the hymn metres which they closely
resembled. But she had been offended to see her printed
poems tidied up in this fashion, and Higginson's advice
further confirmed her in the idiosyncratic individuality
of her work – the very quality that most recommends her.

Her poems are punctuated in manuscript by frequent
dashes that indicate voice pauses. The metrical variations
and half-rhymes surprise certain passages into sharp
definition. But her withdrawal from 'constructive' criticism leads her to occasional obscurities, at times whimsical
and coy. Her rhythms, though, remain alert at all times.
Her best poems focus through an observed and deftly
articulated image on timeless concepts, relating her
doubts about physical and metaphysical fulfilment:

There's a certain Slant of light
Winter Afternoons –
That oppresses, like the Heft
Of Cathedral Tunes –

Heavenly Hurt, it give us –
We can find no scar,
But internal difference,
Where the Meanings, are –

None may teach it – Any –
'Tis the Seal Despair . . .

Sometimes her homely allusions recall Anne Bradstreet,
her eccentricities come from the same source as Edward
Taylor's. 'The Day undressed – Herself –' she writes, 'Her
Garter – was of Gold . . .' In another poem,

Till Seraphs swing their snowy Hats –
And Saints – to windows run –
To see the Little Tippler
Leaning against the – Sun . . .

Yet her subtleties are far greater than theirs. She understands not only the niceties of vocabulary and rhythm. She is deft in her dramatic handling of syntax. In many poems she sets the scene with syntactically separated and short lines, and then – when the storm breaks or the bird flies – she develops an eloquent, integrated syntax stretching over a stanza or two, fusing the elements disparately presented in the opening passage.

It is difficult to trace literary influences on Emily Dickinson, for her sensibility and craft conspire in her powerful individual alchemy. 'For several years,' she wrote, 'my Lexicon – was my only creation,' but the Bible and the plays of Shakespeare were clearly of great influence. Emerson, too, who visited the Dickinsons' house, Thoreau – and George Eliot, the Brontës and the Brownings, may have affected her. The English Metaphysical poets are closer to her than the Romantics, however, particularly Herbert and Vaughan, and we hear echoes of Sir Thomas Browne.

After Emily Dickinson's death, her sister found a box containing nine hundred poems 'tied together with twine' in 'sixty volumes'. Mabel Loomis Todd and Higginson undertook to edit and publish them. A hundred and fifteen were prepared with Higginson's 'corrections' of rhymes, punctuation, and metre, the metaphors rendered 'sensible'. The publication in 1890 was a success, and the next year a hundred and sixty-six more were published, as well as the letters, and further poems edited by Todd in 1896. An edition by Emily's niece and heir Martha Dickinson Bianchi came out in 1914 under the title *The Single Hound*. The text was based more closely on the original manuscripts. Editions in 1929, 1935, 1945 and finally 1955 collected all the extant poems. The last edition was prepared by Thomas H. Johnson, who gave variant readings and fragments and reproduced closely the original punctuation.

The range of Emily Dickinson's sensibility, her power to renew language and ideas, the fusion she achieved between startling metaphor, rich vocabulary, and true emotion, the accuracy with which she evoked natural detail, characterize her best poems, and very few of the poems are entirely without interest. At her best she touches elemental mysteries deftly and individually:

I've seen a Dying Eye
Run round and round a Room –
In search of Something – as it seemed –
Then Cloudier become –
And then – obscure with Fog –
And then be soldered down
Without disclosing what it be
'Twere blessed to have seen –

Edwin Arlington Robinson
1869–1935

Miniver sighed for what was not ...

– 'Miniver Cheevy'

Robinson is usually regarded as a transitional figure
between nineteenth- and twentieth-century American
poetry. This, and the fact that his name is often bracketed
with Robert Frost's, his contemporary and fellow New
Englander, have been unfortunate stigmas to his reputation. There is little ground for the comparison with Frost
except, in Frost's words, that both 'stayed with the old-
fashioned way to be new', revitalizing established poetic
forms with new rhythms and attitudes. There is nothing
modish about either of them. But Robinson's view of
New England is distinctly his own, 'Here where the wind
is always north-north-east/And children learn to walk on
frozen toes ...'

Robinson's dominant theme is the tragic disparity
between what *is* and what might have been. He does not
generally idealize the past but, as Hardy does, shows it as
unrealized in the present. He invented a town, Tilbury,
in New England and peopled it with voices. In dramatic
monologues reminiscent of Browning's, the citizens express their unfulfilment. But it is Robinson who talks
to himself through his characters, just as old Eben Flood
does in 'Mr Flood's Party':

Well, Mr. Flood, we have the harvest moon
Again, and we may not have many more;
The bird is on the wing, the poet says,
And you and I have said it here before.
Drink to the bird.

In the words, 'The bird is on the wing', Robinson nods
in passing at Browning.

Robinson's concern with the unhappiness of people
who live 'Like a dry fish flung inland from the shore'
('Lost Anchors'), or those who like his 'Flying Dutchman'
seek – with little hope of finding – the 'Vanished Land',
is often poignant. His theme draws him into the past,
particularly in his ambitious narrative trilogy: *Merlin*
(1917), *Launcelot* (1927) and *Tristram* (1927); or on a
smaller and more convincing scale in 'Miniver Cheevy':

Miniver loved the days of old
    When swords were bright and steeds were prancing;
The vision of a warrior bold
    Would set him dancing.

Miniver sighed for what was not,
    And dreamed and rested from his labors;
He dreamed of Thebes and Camelot,
    And Priam's neighbors.

In his long poem 'Isaac and Archibald' a small boy
observes the lives of two old men, 'And wondered with
all comfort what might come/To me, and what might
never come to me ...'

Born in Head Tide, Maine, in 1869, Robinson was
raised in the nearby town of Gardiner – the 'Tilbury' of
his poems. He regarded himself as 'a tragedy from the
beginning'. He never felt part of the family. His parents
were no longer young when he was born. They did not
understand him. His brothers were willing to follow his
father in the way of business. He was precocious and
delicate, but his early literary interests were not encouraged. He got to Harvard but after two years was

recalled because of his father's ill health and the decline in the family's fortunes.

From an early age he suffered acute pain from ear infections and feared subsequent brain damage. He fell in love with Emma Shepherd in 1888 but she rejected him and married his brother Herman. When Herman died in 1909, she still repulsed his advances. Both his brothers died and his mother (a descendant of Anne Bradstreet) fell victim of black diphtheria. It is no wonder that he described his early and middle years as a 'living hell'. Unencouraged, unhealthy, unfulfilled, he avoided self-pity in his best poems by channelling his emotions through fictional speakers who, though they reflect aspects of his character, are dramatically individuated.

By the time he was twenty-five he had written a number of poems. Having done some tutoring to earn money, he published his first book at his own expense in 1896, *The Torrent and the Night Before*. This he revised and published, again at his own expense, in 1897 as *The Children of Night*. In 1898 Robinson moved to New York and lived there – with brief intervals away – almost destitute and in near isolation. He became a heavy drinker.

In 1902, with financial help from a group of friends, he published his long verse novel, *Captain Craig*. It earned him some recognition. Theodore Roosevelt, who had admired *The Children of Night*, as a token of his admiration secured for Robinson the post of clerk in the New York Custom House in 1905. In the two years previous he had worked in the New York Subway and in advertising.

His first commercially published book, *The Town Down the River*, appeared in 1910. In the same year he began regular summer visits to the MacDowell Colony – a writers' residence established by the widow of the composer Edward MacDowell. This was his occasional refuge until his death.

In 1916 his collection *The Man Against the Sky* finally

established him as a poet of standing, and the two volumes *Collected Poems* (1921) and *The Man Who Died Twice* (1924) were rewarded with Pulitzer Prizes. His three Arthurian romances brought him further popularity and the third, *Tristram*, became both a best seller and a Pulitzer Prize winner. Six books followed in the next five years. He died – an alcoholic – of cancer in New York in 1935, after completing *King Jasper*, published posthumously in 1935, with an introduction by Robert Frost.

The last book refines his vision of the tragedy implicit in the condition of human existence. 'His theme was unhappiness,' Frost wrote, and the destiny of his characters always remains in question. In *The Man Against the Sky* the emblematic man – Everyman – stands alone on a burning hill:

With nothing on it for the flames to kill
Save one who moved and was alone up there
To loom before the chaos and the glare
As if he were the last god going home
Unto his last desire.

Why, Robinson asks, has he not committed suicide?

'Twere sure but weaklings' vain distress
To suffer dungeons where so many doors
Will open on the cold eternal shores
That look sheer down
To the dark tideless floods of Nothingness
Where all who know may drown.

It is a portentous poem, and Robinson's explanation of the theme underlines its weakness: the ideas have overwhelmed the poetry. 'I meant merely through what I supposed to be an obviously ironic medium, to carry materialism to its logical end and to indicate its futility as an explanation or justification of existence.' The poem is restricted by its philosophical premise. The meanings do not emanate from the experience – rather, the meanings come first, the experience is contrived for them.

Robinson is more successful in shorter poems where, as Frost said, he can indulge in 'a revel in the felicities of language'. He constantly attempted to contemporize traditional forms with colloquial language, but in the best poems he balances the archaic and colloquial to reveal subtle ironies in both theme and character. In 'Miniver Cheevy' he speaks of 'Priam's neighbors'; Priam becomes a distinguished citizen of Tilbury. In 'Mr Flood's Party', Eben Flood drinks,

Alone, as if enduring to the end
A valiant armor of scarred hopes outworn,
He stood there in the middle of the road
Like Roland's ghost winding a silent horn.
Below him, in the town among the trees,
Where friends of other days had honored him,
A phantom salutation of the dead
Rang thinly till old Eben's eyes were dim.

And in 'Richard Cory' Robinson writes,

So on we worked, and waited for the light,
And went without the meat, and cursed the bread;
And Richard Cory, one calm summer night,
Went home and put a bullet through his head.

The small-town tragedies, dramatically evoked, reveal an acute understanding of isolation and unfulfilment. Robinson's own fears are projected vividly into his characters, and the clarity of his forms has an individual authority. One of his best effects is to break open an essentially literary experience with a live one – Richard Cory's suicide, for instance. His longer narrative poems, in a more open style based on conventional blank verse lines, develop with ease, but they do not possess the illuminating irony of the shorter poems, which generate the dry wit necessary to point the futility:

Miniver scorned the gold he sought,
  But sore annoyed was he without it;
Miniver thought, and thought, and thought,
  And thought about it.

Miniver Cheevy, born too late,
  Scratched his head and kept on thinking;
Miniver coughed, and called it fate,
  And kept on drinking.

Edgar Lee Masters 1869–1950

I was one of you, Spoon River, in all fellowship ...

– *Spoon River Anthology*

Edgar Lee Masters is remembered for one book of the fifty he wrote: *Spoon River Anthology*. It was widely read, even by those not normally drawn to poetry, for its bitter honesty and direct presentation of ordinary people and their intrigues. His other books of poetry, fiction, biography and autobiography, have been generally forgotten.

Born in Garnett, Kansas, in 1869, Masters was raised in rural Illinois, and by the time he was sixteen he was making a living at odd jobs. He attended Knox College and at twenty-two became a lawyer in Chicago where he worked for twenty-five years.

His early poems – he had written about four hundred by the time he was twenty-four – show the influence of his mentors all too clearly. Poe, Whitman, Shelley and Swinburne primarily drew him in different directions. After several collections of poetry and one verse drama, in 1915 he suddenly found his own style in *Spoon River Anthology*. He began to use the deceptively casual free-verse unrhymed lines of Whitman, but in concise forms, attempting the epigrammatic quality we associate with poems in the *Greek Anthology*. The collection includes over two hundred epitaphs spoken by the dead from their graves in the imaginary mid-Western town of Spoon River. Together, they form an astringent commentary on life in a decaying community, revealing its destructive hypocrisy, its ability to corrupt the decent and honest. Disgust and pity inform the poems, which are tempered with an ironic humour.

The prologue opens with a parody of Villon's line, 'Where are the snows of yester-year?':

Where are Elmer, Herman, Bert, Tom and Charley,
The weak of will, the strong of arm, the clown, the boozer, the
    fighter?
All, all are sleeping on the hill.

One passed in a fever,
One was burned in a mine,
One was killed in a brawl ...

Any element of rural romance is exiled from Master's vision:

One died in shameful child-birth,
One of thwarted love,
One at the hands of a brute in a brothel ...

The granite pedestal marking Knowlt Hoheimer's grave bears the words *'Pro Patria'*. Hoheimer mutters, 'What do they mean anyway?' For him the war was folly:

When I felt the bullet enter my heart
I wished I had stayed at home and gone to jail
For stealing the hogs of Curl Trenary,
Instead of running away and joining the army.

The verse seems to be spoken without literary nicety. There is little that is poetical in the voices from the graveyard. Each speaker finds his own rhythm and voice.

The dead turn for comfort to the dead priest, but:

You are over there, Father Malloy,
Where holy ground is, and the cross marks every grave,
Not here with us on the hill ...

You were so human, Father Malloy,
Taking a friendly glass sometimes with us,
Siding with us who would rescue Spoon River
From the coldness and the dreariness of village morality ...

Some of us almost came to you, Father Malloy ...

As they speak for Masters, the dead come alive, particularly when they rouse his forthright anger – anger at their situations, their frustrations, and their inconsiderate treatment of one another, which perpetuates the corruption of which they are themselves victims. His sympathy, too, is directly and unsentimentally expressed, as with Lucinda Matlock, the busy housewife, whom he seems to admire:

I spun, I wove, I kept the house, I nursed the sick,
I made the garden, and for holiday
Rambled over the fields where sang the larks ...

At ninety-six I had lived enough, that is all ...

He sympathizes too with the dry humour of Cassius Hueffer whose epitaph reads: 'His life was gentle, and the elements so mixed in him/That nature might stand up and say to all the world,/This was a man.'

Those who knew me smile
As they read this empty rhetoric.
My epitaph should have been:
'Life was not gentle to him,
And the elements so mixed in him
That he made warfare on life,
In the which he was slain.'
While I lived I could not cope with slanderous tongues,
Now that I am dead I must submit to an epitaph
Graven by a fool!

There is the sad futility of Petit, the poet, whose rhythms Masters evokes through parody:

Triolets, villanelles, rondels, rondeaus,
Seeds in a dry pod, tick, tick, tick,
Tick, tick, tick, what little iambics,
While Homer and Whitman roared in the pines?

Petit, at least in death, recognizes his failure. Masters is less gentle with Editor Whedon, one of those journalists who 'pervert truth' and use 'great feelings' for 'base designs', whose work is 'To scratch dirt over scandal for money,/And exhume it to the winds of revenge ...':

To be an editor, as I was.
Then to lie close by the river over the place
Where the sewage flows from the village,
And the empty cans and garbage are dumped,
And abortions are hidden.

Masters gloats over this citizen's distaste. He takes his revenge on the muck-raker, reducing him to his own element.

The total ingenuity of the *Anthology* can be appreciated only as the interaction of the various characters is revealed, working against the fate that brought them all to live and die in Spoon River. The tragic irony is complete.

The irony for Masters was that he could not repeat the style or success of this book. In 1924 he tried again with *The New Spoon River*, a fierce attack on American urbanization, but bitterness and anger overwhelmed his human insights. His bitterness at the neglect of the books that followed *Spoon River Anthology* affected his other writings, particularly his series of belittling biographies, including *Lincoln, The Man* (1931). During the twenties and thirties he wrote five novels, verse plays, and his autobiography, *Across Spoon River* (1936). He died in 1950, having dispelled, with one book at least, the sentimental notion that village life was uncomplicated, fulfilling, and humane.

Stephen Crane 1871–1900

God is cold...

– refrain of a poem found among Crane's papers twenty-eight years after his death

In the nineteenth-century context, Stephen Crane's poetry is disconcerting in its stark directness. He did not wish to be called a poet, despite the intensely personal nature of his verse. He is better known as the author of *The Red Badge of Courage*, one of his six novels. He also wrote many short stories and two volumes of verse before he died of tuberculosis in a German sanatorium at the age of twenty-nine.

Born in 1871, the youngest of fourteen children, his father – a Methodist minister in New Jersey – died when Stephen was eight. He studied at a military academy, Lafayette College, and Syracuse University, New York. He was drawn to journalism as a career, and while working as a freelance reporter in New York, following newspaper stories into the Bowery slums, he completed the first draft of his novel, *Maggie*. It was completed and brought out with borrowed money under a pseudonym in 1893. Its full title is *Maggie: A Girl of the Streets*, a sordidly realistic tale told with a strong current of pessimistic determinism. Few readers bought the book, but Crane sent a copy to the writer Hamlin Garland, whom he had admired as a lecturer. He inscribed in the copy, 'It is inevitable that you be greatly shocked by this book but continue, please, with all possible courage to the end. For it tries to show that environment is a tremendous thing in the world and frequently shapes lives regardless. If one proves that theory, one makes room in Heaven for all sorts of souls (notably an occasional street girl) who are not confidently expected to be there by many excellent people.' The reaction against his own solidly Protestant background is evident in the dedication.

When Garland met him, he asked if he could look over some papers poking out of Crane's pockets. Garland describes the episode. 'Upon unrolling the manuscript, I found it to be a sheaf of poems written in blue ink upon single sheets of legal cap paper, each poem without blot or correction, almost without punctuation, all beautifully legible, exact and orderly in arrangement.' Crane touched his head and said he had more 'up here all in a little row'. They were 'on tap', he said, and he could draw them off complete. Shortly afterwards he produced his first volume of poems, published in 1895 by Copeland and Day under the title, *Black Riders*.

Perhaps they were accepted for publication because of his growing success after the appearance in the same year of *The Red Badge of Courage*. The novel, set on Civil War battlefields, provides a strong impression of the plight of an individual trapped in a machine-like struggle. Crane had not experienced war first hand, but he was fascinated by the reactions of men in the grip of it. When researching for the book among the memoirs of soldiers, he said to a friend, 'I wonder that *some* of those fellows don't tell how they *felt* in those scraps! They spout eternally of what they *did*, but they are as emotionless as rocks!' It is this that intrigued him – it gives the book its distinct power. The general omission of proper names for the greater part of the book takes its relevance beyond the immediate subject of the Civil War.

Crane went on to write several short stories. His persistent rebellion against the morality of the day made him so unpopular in New York that he moved to Florida. There he met Cora Taylor, the madam of a Jacksonville brothel. He brought her to England in 1897, shortly before his death, to settle at Brede Place in Sussex. He had spent some time before gun-running in Cuba, and as war correspondent in the Greco-Turkish war, experiences which provided the background for some of his other writings. A second volume of poems, *War is Kind*, was brought out in the last year of his life.

His prose works were highly praised by Conrad, Henry James, and H. G. Wells, principally for their irony and their subtle, subdued symbolism. But his poems have only latterly come in for extensive study. A notable contributor to the criticism was John Berryman.

The poems, like the prose works, depend on irony; and Crane's bitterness can be devastating. The dates of composition are impossible to establish. Many of the poems seem more the product of this century than the last:

I walked in a desert.
And I cried,
'Ah. God, take me from this place!'
A voice said, 'It is no desert.'
I cried, 'Well, but –
The sand, the heat, the vacant horizon.'
A voice said, 'It is no desert.'

On first reading, it is dry. On second reading, it is chilling. One is reminded of Crane's words, 'environment is a tremendous thing.'

Some critics have described the poems as an amalgam of Whitman and Dickinson, presumably because of the free verse style on the one hand and the fact that Crane was inspired to write poetry after hearing some of Emily Dickinson's poems read aloud on the other. But his poetry possesses none of Whitman's prophetic authority and scope, none of the linguistic tensions and verbal surprises of Dickinson.

Berryman has written that he 'was not only a man with truths to tell, but an interested listener to this man. His poetry has the inimitable sincerity of a frightened savage anxious to learn what his dreams mean.' He not only experiences – he observes himself experiencing. There is a strong element of fatalism and fear in most of the poems:

'Have you ever made a just man?'
'Oh, I have made three,' answered God,
'But two of them are dead,
And the third –
Listen! Listen!
And you will hear the thud of his defeat.'

The poems demand to be read on their own terms. In *The Red Badge of Courage* Crane took the romance out of war; in *Maggie* he took the sentimentalism out of city life; and in the poems he reduced life to a sequence of bitter ironies united by a cold symbolism:

Many workmen
Built a huge ball of masonry
Upon a mountain-top.
Then they went to the valley below,
And turned to behold their work.
'It is grand,' they said:
They loved the thing.

Of a sudden, it moved:
It came upon them swiftly:
It crushed them all to blood.
But some had opportunity to squeak.

If there is a chilling sameness, a metaphorical and linguistic thinness about the poems, if they repeat the same theme without significantly developing it, they nonetheless confirm the reality of the bitterness.

Robert Frost 1874–1963

Not a heavenly dog made manifest,
But an earthly dog of the carriage breed.

– 'One More Brevity'

Robert Frost was a late beginner. He travelled to England
when he was thirty-eight with no books published and
few poems written. He returned two years later to popular
and critical acclaim. His early life had been full of frustrations, and even his great success in later years did not
assuage the doubts and fears produced by his early
failures.

He was born in San Francisco in 1874 of a New England
father and a Scots mother. When he was eleven – at his
father's death – he was taken to New England. Later he
attended Dartmouth College, but so disliked the academic
world that he left to work at a mill. He tried the academic
life again at Harvard (1897–99). Then he drifted from
shoe-making to teaching to editing a country newspaper
and, finally, to farming. In 1912 he arrived in England
with his wife and four children on a poetry-or-nothing
gamble. He took a house in Beaconsfield.

There he struck up a friendship with Edward Thomas,
whom he encouraged to write verse, and in 1913 offered
a volume of his own poems, *A Boy's Will*, to an English
publisher. It was accepted and published. At first glance

the book seems quite conventional – composed primarily
of brief lyrics, traditional in diction and syntax: 'A
stranger came to the door at eve/And he spoke the
bridegroom fair', or 'She talks and I am fain to list'. But
there was a new rhythm underlying the surface conven-
tionality which Edward Thomas, reviewing the book,
described in these terms: 'These poems are revolutionary
because they lack the exaggeration of rhetoric ... Many,
if not most of the separate lines and separate sentences
are plain and in themselves nothing. But they are bound
together and made elements of beauty by a calm eagerness
of emotion.' Despite the archaisms, there is already a
conversational tone and the aphoristic authority of
phrase which characterizes his best work: ' "Men work
together," I told him from the heart,/"Whether they
work together or apart." ' Some of Frost's later aphorisms have entered the language. 'Something there is that
doesn't love a wall', 'Good fences make good neighbours'.
They have the authority of folk sayings.

A pervading sense of insecurity and uncertainty imparts a double edge to the homeliest phrases:

One of my wishes is that those dark trees,
So old and firm they scarcely show the breeze,
Were not, as 'twere, the merest mask of gloom,
But stretched away unto the edge of doom.

Frost confirmed this latent uncertainty in a letter written
in 1917: 'The conviction closes in on me that I was cast
for gloom as the sparks fly upward.' Even in 'Mowing',
one of the finest poems in the first collection, there is an
indecision. The poem – a sonnet with an unusual
rhyme scheme and a finely varied iambic rhythm – in its
sensuous response to the subject, goes beyond the immediate subject, hinting at the 'otherworldliness' that in
later poems becomes a dominant tension. 'My long scythe
whispered and left the hay to make,' he wrote. The act
of mowing is somehow isolated from the process of hay-

making. It becomes in the poem an end in itself.

By the time Frost – still in England – had published his second book, *North of Boston* (1914), his style was more or less complete. He did not alter it radically, though with increasing skill he gradually achieved a freer expression of mood by subtle manipulation of rhythm. Monologue and dialogue are his dominant forms in *North of Boston*, which includes one of his most famous poems, 'Mending Wall'. The language of most of the poems is slow and ruminative, spoken; the tone is conversational. Frost concentrates on New Englanders. The book is seasoned with aphorisms, wise, cynical, or homely.

Nine further collections were published. Four of them were awarded Pulitzer Prizes. Frost accumulated forty-four honorary degrees and met with other forms of acclaim. And yet, despite the accolade, the poet never came to write without thematic indecision, even unease. Constantly he was aware of the dark side of experience, the contradiction implicit in the seemingly true statement. ' "Out, Out" –' a poem in his third collection, *Mountain Interval* – is a brief narrative about a village boy who severs his hand while sawing wood. The setting is characteristic: 'Five mountain ranges one behind the other/ Under the sunset far into Vermont'. The language is conversational: 'His sister stood beside them in her apron/To tell them "Supper".' These are Frost's New Englanders in their daily routines. The saw slips, the hand is cut. When the doctor arrives, the boy cries, 'Don't let him cut my hand off—'. But, 'in the dark ether', the boy dies. After a brief interruption, the village resumes its routine:

... They listened at his heart.
Little – less – nothing! – and that ended it.
No more to build on there. And they, since they
Were not the one dead, turned to their affairs.

It is a frightening, inexorably bitter pattern of acceptance. In 'Home Burial' the conversations are full of suppressed tension:

'There's something I should like to ask you, dear.'
'You don't know how to ask it.'
                    'Help me then.'
... 'I don't know how to speak of anything
So as to please you.'

Frost's letters echo the experience of the poems. His loneliness and fear of insanity – his sister in fact died in a mental hospital – are clear in them, and his inclination to suicide. His outbursts of rage and jealousy, followed by self-recrimination for his selfishness, are also revealed. Guilt is an overwhelming passion. The actual Robert Frost and his public image of home-spun philosopher grow more remote from each other as we read the letters; and yet the poet and his poems seem closer. His farmers, mowers, hirelings and apple-pickers appear as beings in isolation, or at best in tightly knit, exclusive groups, not in rural *community*. Competitive, mistrustful, they remain obstinately individuated.

But the image of Frost as the farmer-poet, the warm contemplative, was sustained by his public, and he himself fostered it. The verse is hardly warm. It builds on the tensions of uncertainty, the poet torn between his function as observer – recording things as they are – and as artist, perfecting them. There is a lack of decision which gives the writing a strange power. The meanings remain ambiguous as his uncertainty. As a result there are few concrete images, there is a sense of contrast never finally resolved.

The skill with which Frost isolates his characters and then surrounds them with doubts imparts to them a mystery. The man 'Stopping by Woods on a Snowy Evening', for instance, says,

My little horse must think it queer
To stop without a farmhouse near
Between the woods and frozen lake
The darkest evening of the year.

Frost arrests man and horse in a kind of preternatural ritual of contemplation which neither understands, though they enact it. Frost does not intellectualize or impose meanings. Whatever significance there is is latent in the experience. In his essay 'The Figure a Poem Makes' he wrote that a poem 'begins in delight and ends in wisdom', but the wisdom is either aphoristic or unparaphrasably implicit in the poem. The moments of wisdom relate to specific incidents and do not add up to a vital philosophy. In 'One More Brevity', for instance, a dog follows a man into his cottage one evening. It stays the night and asks to be let out next morning:

I opened the door and he was gone ...
He might have been the dream of a ghost
In spite of the way his tail had smacked
My floor so hard and matter-of-fact ...

The speaker is almost convinced it was Sirius, the dog-star, but,

A symbol was all he could hope to convey,
An intimation, a shot of ray,
A meaning I was supposed to seek,
And finding, wasn't disposed to speak.

Frost is reluctant to put the meaning of the experience in terms other than those *of* the experience.

The black resignation of Frost's later poems was admirably described by Randall Jarrell in *The Other Frost*. Frost wrote poems, he says, 'which express an attitude that at its most extreme, makes pessimism seem a hopeful evasion'.

One can do nothing against evil in the world – if there

were anything, 'would *you* ever do it?' Resignation has altered the aphoristic Frost. His style perfectly suits his later attitude. Melancholy, flatness, and calm desperation require what Frost called in a letter in 1913, 'a language absolutely unliterary', the language he was working towards at the time in *North of Boston*. The irony and tension of his poetry come from the contrast between lofty ambition and flatness of speech. The language should be that *heard today* in conversation: 'The living part of a poem is the intonation', and his success or otherwise in achieving such a language determines the quality of the finished poem. The art in the poem 'Birches' is in the apparent ease and naturalness of style: the simple narrative contains a parable of human aspiration, evolving through a progression of metaphors so apparently inevitable to the mind and ear that the poem has done its work before one is conscious of it:

And so I dream of going back to be.
It's when I'm weary of considerations,
And life is too much like a pathless wood
Where your face burns and tickles with the cobwebs
Broken across it, and one eye is weeping
From a twig's having lashed across it open.
I'd like to get away from earth awhile
And then come back to it and begin over ...
One could do worse than be a swinger of birches.

In 1936 Frost was asked to name some of his favourite books. '*Robinson Crusoe,*' he said, 'is never quite out of my mind. I never tire of being shown how the limited can make snug in the limitless. *Walden* has the same fascination. Crusoe was cast away: Thoreau was self-cast away. Both found themselves sufficient.' The will to be sufficient in himself was strong in Frost; his poems reveal the impossibility of that will ever being finally expressed in action. His letters confirm his restlessness and unease, his self-centredness, a trait that has been amply documented by his critics and biographers since his death in 1963. In many poems, 'Provide, Provide' for example, bitterly and uncompromisingly he confronts himself with himself and his disillusion:

No memory of having starred
Atones for later disregard
Or keeps the end from being hard.

Better to go down dignified
With boughten friendship at your side
Than none at all. Provide, provide!

Carl Sandburg 1878–1967

I am the grass; I cover all.

– 'Grass'

Carl Sandburg, born in 1878, was fortunate to find his poetic powers when he did – around 1910 – for the modern movement in poetry was against received tradition and the Jazz Age was at its full, echoing the variety of American popular speech. Sandburg saw himself as a radical, in poetry and in politics. He was fortunate, too, in being born far from New England and its values, in Galesburg, Illinois. His spirit was against the academies, at home in the Mississippi Valley. In this he was like Vachel Lindsay and Edgar Lee Masters, fellow Illinoisans, who shared with Sandburg a common hero in Abraham Lincoln. Sandburg wrote a masterly six-volume life of Lincoln, portraying him as the epitome of the American man of the people. But for that robust talent at displaying the age and its moods, Sandburg would have been without strong motive in his poetry. He attempts to make the ordinary seem extraordinary. The driving impulse of his work is anger – not despair – at unhappiness and ugliness. His anger seldom rises to sustained satire; it is tempered by a general tenderness, even sentimentality, towards humanity.

In one poem he calls Chicago the 'Hog Butcher for the World':

City of the Big Shoulders:
They tell me you are wicked and I believe them, for I have
  seen your painted women under the gas lamps luring the
  farm boys.
And they tell me you are crooked and I answer: Yes, it is true
  I have seen the gunman kill and go free to kill again.
And they tell me you are brutal and my reply is . . .

This Whitmanesque poem was first published in *Poetry*
(Chicago), a magazine newly founded by Harriet Monroe,
and won for Sandburg a literary prize in 1914. It was his
first taste of recognition – at the age of thirty-six.

He had left school at thirteen to work as a labourer
and travelled to Kansas, Nebraska and Colorado before
returning to Galesburg in 1898 to work as a house
painter. He enlisted and served in the Sixth Illinois
Infantry in Puerto Rico during the Spanish-American
War, returning after eight months to work his way
through the local Lombard College. Between 1902 and
1910 he wandered again, eventually finding himself
secretary to the first socialist mayor of Milwaukee, Wisconsin. He became an organizer for the Social Democratic
Party, editorial writer for the Chicago *Daily News,* and
published his *Chicago Poems* (1916). This was his second
collection – there had been an undistinguished pamphlet,
In Reckless Ecstasy, in 1904. It was in *Chicago Poems*
and *Cornhuskers* (1918) that his style flourished. It
changed very little over the half century of his creative
life, though later it resembles Whitman less, becomes
repetitive, incantatory, and often mechanical. The titles
of his volumes are startling: *Smoke and Steel* (1920),
Slabs of the Sunburnt West (1922), *Good Morning,
America* (1928) and *The People, Yes* (1936).

Sandburg unfortunately allowed everything that he
saw to dictate its own terms to him. Instead of control,
selection, *forming,* he made his poems signify by forcing
objects, happenings, people, by sheer weight of number,

into meaning. He was always compromised by his subject matter. Whitman's imagination was poetically inclusive – he suggested, without exhaustively listing, the scope of his subject. His catalogues are lucid and selective. Sandburg's are cluttered.

The early poems were influenced by Imagism, a contemporary movement which directed the poet to the object observed, without moralizing it. This drew from Sandburg small exact poems such as 'Fog' from *Chicago Poems*, which in its short lines pinpoints subject and atmosphere. The fog is a cat:

It sits looking
over harbor and city
on silent haunches
and then moves on.

Sandburg's style ranges from this to the massive, rhetorical *The People, Yes*, with its sections of virtual prose:

Who made Paul Bunyan, who gave him birth as a myth, who joked him into life as the Master Lumberjack, who fashioned him forth as an apparition easing the hours of men amid axes and trees, saws and lumber? The people, the bookless people, they made Paul and had him alive long before he got into the books for those who read. He grew up in shanties, around the hot stoves of winter, among socks and mittens drying, in the smell of tobacco smoke and the roar of laughter mocking the outside weather.

A vivid and individual style it is, though at length it becomes dull and dulling. It is Sandburg's adaptation of Whitman's style that predominates, however, 'I am the people – the mob – the crowd – the mass':

My love is a yellow hammer spinning circles in Ohio, Indiana. My love is a redbird shooting flights in straight lines in Kentucky and Tennessee. My love is an early robin flaming an ember of copper on her shoulders in March and April.

My love is a graybird living in the eaves of a Michigan house all winter. Why is my love always a crying thing of wings?

There is much energy, many points of vividness. And yet Sandburg dissipates them.

The poetry, journeying through many places and incidents, reflects Sandburg's life. He had a subsidiary career as a lecturer which began in 1908 with, significantly, 'Walt Whitman, an American Vagabond'. A few years later he became a folk singer and toured the country collecting songs for *The American Songbag* (1927) and *The New American Songbag* (1950). As he collected and recorded folk songs, so in his poems he recorded sights and happenings in their own terms, without shaping them, though he often concentrated on points of decay and the ephemeral:

In the darkness with a great bundle of grief
    the people march.
In the night, and overhead a shovel of stars for
    keeps, the people march:
        'Where to? what next?!

The persistency of Sandburg's style proves monotonous. There is little variety of rhythm even between lines of different length. Occasionally, with an ear to common speech, he achieves a momentary, aphoristic intensity:

If you got enough money
you can buy anything
except ... you got to die.

But in general, unlike Whitman, Sandburg lacks the power to engage the reader in the central themes of his poems. They remain two-dimensional.

William Carlos Williams, reviewing Sandburg's *Complete Poems*, described this impression. 'Search as we will among them we must say at once that technically the poems reveal no initiative whatever other than their formlessness; there is no motivating spirit held in the front of the mind to control them. And without a theory, as Pasteur once said, to unify it, a man's life becomes little more than an aimless series of random and repetitious gestures. In the poem a rebellion against older forms means nothing unless, finally, we have a new form to substitute for that which has become empty from the exhaustion of its means ... The drive for a new form seemed to be lacking in Sandburg.' Williams points out that Sandburg abandoned his art in order to expose rhetorically the rot at the heart of official democracy. He becomes so involved subjectively in the content of the poem that he forfeits perspective. Hence, Williams says, 'the poems show no development of thought ... The same manner of using the words, of presenting the image is followed in the first poem and the last.' This is telling criticism of a poet who still commands a large popular audience, particularly in the United States. But Williams is right: to read Sandburg at length – as some of the poems demand – is to watch a slow, at times a *very* slow, procession pass by. The poems do not force us to question, do not engage us, do not confront us with sudden truths. We see without *vision*. Fortunately some of the poems, brief and accurate, stand out against the vast monotony. One such poem is 'Theme in Yellow':

I spot the hills
With yellow balls in autumn.
I light the prairie cornfields
Orange and tawny gold clusters
And I am called pumpkins.
On the last of October
When dusk is fallen
Children join hands
And circle round me
Singing ghost songs

And love to the harvest moon;
I am a jack-o'-lantern
With terrible teeth
And the children know
I am fooling.

Wallace Stevens 1879–1955

... Things as they are
Are changed upon the blue guitar.

– 'The Man with the Blue Guitar'

A difficult, attractive and rewarding poet, Wallace Stevens is regarded by several critics to be as fine a poet as Eliot or Pound, yet he commands a far smaller audience than theirs. Stevens tempts us to misread him in two ways. The verbal richness and rhythmic beauty can become a pleasant end in itself, leading to a sterile, subjective satisfaction. On the other hand, one can contend with the complexities of thought, attempting to extract meanings in paraphrasable form, forgetting the poetry, concluding that the ideas are somehow less significant than the words had suggested.

A balanced approach is best. For Stevens's poetry is fully meaningful, and the meanings are contained in the way they are expressed. The best poems elude paraphrase, can be analysed as rhythmic or image patterns, but cannot be reduced to simple statements.

Stevens's life had no direct effect on his style of writing or his subject matter. He was born in Reading, Pennsylvania, in 1879. He studied at Harvard (1897–1900) and at the New York Law School and was admitted to the bar in 1904. He practised law in New York, married in 1909, then joined the legal staff of the Hartford (Connecticut) Accident and Indemnity Company in 1916. He became a vice-president in 1934, and remained in Hartford until his death in 1955.

He began writing poetry when he was nineteen but wasn't published until Harriet Monroe took an interest in his work and published the first version of 'Sunday Morning' in *Poetry* (Chicago) in 1915. He was forty-four when his first collection, *Harmonium* (1923), was published. Twelve years later his second book, *Ideas of Order* (1935) appeared. Then, in more rapid succession, followed: *Owl's Clover* (1936), *The Man with the Blue Guitar* (1937), *Parts of a World* (1942), *Notes towards a Supreme Fiction* (1942), *Esthétique du Mal* (1945), *Transport to Summer* (1947), *The Auroras of Autumn* (1950), and finally *Collected Poems* (1954). His essays – originally lectures given between 1942 and 1951 – were published as *The Necessary Angel: Essays on Reality and the Imagination* (1951). *Opus Posthumous* (1957) includes more poems, two plays, some miscellaneous prose works, and *Adagia*, a selection of aphoristic writings.

The world of business, the everyday world, does not obtrude itself on his writing. Indeed, the fact that his poetry is *apart* is crucial, the key to his idea of the poet, one who 'still dwells in an ivory tower, but who insists that life there would be intolerable except for the fact that one has, from the top, such an exceptional view of the public dump and the advertising signs.' The poet remains above the 'dump' only so long as he is emotionally aware of its presence there below him.

Poetry has a high purpose to fulfil, Stevens believes. 'After one has abandoned belief in God,' Stevens writes in *Adagia*, 'poetry is that essence which takes its place as life's redemption.' For him, poetry is the 'Supreme Fiction'. The poet, from the perspective of his tower, can see life, or reality, more fully, can create the necessary art to fulfil that reality. 'I am the necessary angel of earth,/Since, in my sight, you see the earth again', he writes. Reason will not suffice. 'As the reason destroys, the poet must create.' He works, as it were, against reason.

The scene would be bleak indeed without the 'Supreme Fiction':

... How cold the vacancy
When the phantoms are gone and the shaken realist
First sees reality.

To complete and raise up reality, the poet creates an exotic vision,

Ach, Mutter
This old, black dress,
I have been embroidering
French flowers on it.

He obeys the romantic impulse: man himself is responsible for creating. With Coleridge, he believes that 'in our life alone does nature live'. The rhythms of the poems must be heightened, artificial, at a remove from speech, subtly regularized often to a melodious, sometimes a monotonous, iambic pattern. Stevens does not approximate poetic with speech rhythms.

Many poems develop this basic theme, and all of them relate to it:

She sang beyond the genius of the sea ...
She was the single artificer of the world
In which she sang. And when she sang, the sea,
Whatever self it had, became the self
That was her song, for she was the maker ...

Embellishment *and* self-creation: this dual approach is evoked in 'The Man with the Blue Guitar':

The earth, for us, is flat and bare.
There are no shadows. Poetry

Exceeding music must take the place
Of empty heaven and its hymns,

Ourselves in poetry must take their place,
Even in the chattering of your guitar.

vi

A tune beyond us as we are,
Yet nothing changed by the blue guitar

Ourselves in the tune as if in space ...

Stevens, who learned many lessons from the French symbolist poets, here and elsewhere develops a symbolic vocabulary. 'Blue' is used in referring to the imaginative flight that is, or is moving towards, the 'Supreme Fiction'; 'green' is a colour referring to things natural, untransmuted. Thus, before the flight, in the unchanged world, we find:

The man bent over his guitar,
A shearsman of sorts. The day was green.

They said, 'You have a blue guitar,
You do not play things as they are.'

The man replied, 'Things as they are
Are changed upon the blue guitar.'

And they said then, 'But play, you must,
A tune beyond us, yet ourselves ...'

In order to get at the actual nature of objects, Stevens reveals them in terms of something else. 'Reality is a cliché from which we escape by metaphor,' he writes in *Adagia*. Metaphor is not mere embellishment – it is the substance of poetry. His style depends on analogy and interaction of images. New dimensions are discovered through analogy, which enhances mere reality, providing a *poetic* reality. The interplay between bare factual reality and poetic reality is central to his writing. 'Poetry is the subject of the poem,' he says. The poems expand the idea:

The central poem is the poem of the whole,
The poem of the composition of the whole,
The composition of blue sea and of green,
Of blue light and of green, as lesser poems ...
The roundness that pulls tight the final ring.

In a few poems, such as 'Not Ideas about the Thing but the Thing Itself', Stevens finds a poetic analogy that illuminates simple fact, transforming it into a poetic reality. At dawn he hears a bird's cry:

The scrawny cry – it was
A chorister whose 'c' preceded the choir.
It was part of the colossal sun.

Surrounded by its choral rings,
Still far away. It was like
A new knowledge of reality.

This was Stevens's highest ambition – to bring the process full circle, to find in fact itself the poetic reality. The cyclic movement is confirmed in the image of the seasons, in the circular structures and recurrences within a poem. In 'The Ordinary Women' Stevens begins,

Then from their poverty they rose,
From dry catarrhs, and to guitars
They flitted
Through the palace walls.

The poem concludes,

Then from their poverty they rose,
From dry guitars, and to catarrhs
They flitted
Through the palace walls.

The echoed words, their order reversed, are emblematic of the world of fact and the imaginative world.

As with the Symbolists, with Stevens the image of

music and musical terminology is frequent. It comes into the titles of many poems; it supplies the imagery. Or, as in 'Peter Quince at the Clavier', the sound of music evokes a world beyond the world of fact, a world rich in legend and sensuous promise. So, too, the poems allude to the other arts, to painting for example.

Titles such as 'Landscape with Boat', or 'Woman Looking at a Vase of Flowers', suggest paintings. The poem is suggesting a world, a rhythm, a harmony beyond language, something which the senses apprehend but cannot paraphrase, something in which response is pure, unreasoned.

Stevens, in quest of a harmony between the individual and the world in which he exists, suggests that without the harmony there is only bleakness, poverty; where the harmony is so perfect that factual and poetic reality are one, the cycle is complete:

I was the world in which I walked, and what I saw
Or heard or felt came not but from myself;
And there I found myself more truly and more strange.

Out of the flowing impermanence of factual reality, Stevens selects the patterns of his poetry; heightening them, he discovers analogies, a wider pattern. There are many related modes of order; there are 'Thirteen Ways of Looking at a Blackbird'.

William Carlos Williams
1883–1963

... I must
find my meaning and lay it, white
beside the sliding water ...

– *Paterson*

Popular anthology poems have obscured the fact that
William Carlos Williams is a poet of considerable substance and variety. Along with his poems, novels, criticism
and plays, he fortunately left an *Autobiography*, an
engaging book called *I Wanted To Write A Poem*, and
several illuminating letters. These books and documents
confirm the stature and the integrity of the poet.

He practised medicine in the town where he was born
in 1883 – Rutherford, New Jersey. He studied at the
University of Pennsylvania, where he met H.D. (Hilda
Doolittle) and began a lifelong friendship with Ezra
Pound. 'Before meeting Ezra Pound,' he wrote, 'is like
B.C. and A.D.' He worked his internship – specializing in
pediatrics – at hospitals in New York, where he came
into contact with Wallace Stevens. In London in 1909, he
stayed with Pound and met Yeats.

He found life in Europe intensely 'literary' but completely alien to his temperament. On his return to
America, he took up residence in Rutherford and, in
1912, married Florence Herman, the 'Flossie' of the

poems. His first collection, *Poems*, he published privately in 1909. Later he described it as 'bad Keats' nothing else – oh, well, bad Whitman, too.' His dependence on past models declined, partly in response to the criticism of friends – Pound, H.D. and Marianne Moore in particular, who were themselves working towards a dry, objective poetry, stripped of poetic embellishment and easy rhetoric, and unmoralized. Imagism was coming into being.

His second volume, *The Tempers* (1913), reflects the change. Pound included his poems in his 1914 anthology, *Des Imagistes*, and Williams was briefly associated with strict imagism. He also responded to the painters of the day, in particular to the exhibition in New York in 1913 of work by Cézanne, Matisse, and Picasso. At the same time he realized his own *American* responsibility and destiny: 'From the beginning I felt I was *not* English. If poetry had to be written I had to do it my own way,' and he vowed that he would 'create somehow by an intense, individual effort, a new – an American – poetic language.'

The lessons he learned from the Cubists and Surrealists affected two of his books, *Kora in Hell* (1920) and *Spring and All* (1923). *Spring and All* originally consisted, in Williams's words, 'of poems interspersed with prose ... It was written when the world was going crazy about typographical form and is really a travesty on the idea. Chapter headings are printed upside down on purpose, the chapters are numbered all out of order ...' The surrealism is a momentary affectation, thin and clearly imitative.

In 1931, more fruitfully, he joined with Charles Reznikoff, Louis Zukofsky and George Oppen in the 'Objectivist' movement whose aims were, as Williams says in his *Autobiography*, to treat the poem as 'an object that in itself formally presents its case and its meaning by the very form it assumes ... the poem being an object (like a symphony or a cubist painting) it must be the purpose of the poet to make of his words a new form: to invent, that is, an object consonant with his day.' This was largely Williams's motive throughout his mature creative life.

In 1950 he won the National Book Award and in 1952 the Bollingen Prize. He was appointed to the Chair of Poetry at the Library of Congress, an honour that was withdrawn during the McCarthy era – he was alleged to be a leftist, and he was a friend of Ezra Pound's. At this time, Williams suffered a series of strokes, but kept on writing. He died at the age of seventy-nine and was posthumously awarded the Pulitzer Prize and the Gold Medal for Poetry.

His most original poem was *Paterson* – four 'books' with a fifth in note form, written between 1946 and 1951. It set out to be an *American* epic. In it he related the geography of the Passaic River to the history and society of the New Jersey city of Paterson, concentrating on a set of characters. It is the poem 'of a man identified with a city'. Williams uses lyrics, prose, documentary and letters, and the poem's appeal lies in the sense of authority and inevitable rightness the poet brings to his collage style of juxtaposing texts and modes.

Among his many prose works is a novel trilogy, *White Mule, In the Money*, and *The Build-Up*; and his major critical work, *In the American Grain* (1925). Here he explores the American-ness of America through the works of writers and the lives of explorers. He describes the book as an attempt 'to re-name the things seen'. This is what he was attempting in his poetry, too, to 'make it new' by seeing it with fresh eyes and expressing it in a new way. His last collection of poems was *Pictures from Brueghel* (1962).

The clarity of Williams's shorter poems is their most immediate appeal. Words name and evoke what he sees through a window or in the breakfast-room. There are no abstractions, no inexactitudes, no moral conclusions. The poems are imagistic in accuracy:

Cattail fluff
blows in
at the bank door...

or,

As the cat
climbed over
the top of

the jamcloset...

They illuminate his dictum in *Paterson*, 'no ideas, but
in things'. But in themselves they are insufficient. 'A
poem is a small (or large) machine made of words as he
finds them inter-related about him and composes them –
without distortion which would mar their exact significance – into an intense expression of his preoccupations
and ardors that they may constitute a revelation in the
speech that he uses. It isn't what he *says* that counts as a
work of art, it's what he makes, with such intensity of
perception that it lives with an intrinsic movement of its
own to verify its authenticity.' Both of the images quoted
above are perceptions, expressed in the speech that he
uses, but as yet they have no 'intrinsic movement', no
context, nor the 'intense expression' he advocates. They
lack what Pound – in defining the image – called 'the
precise moment when a thing outward and objective
transforms itself, or darts into a thing inward and subjective.'

Williams's skill as a poet is in his ability subtly to
work this transformation. His best short poems are not
merely descriptions: they shift emphasis from action to
reaction, from perception to sympathy, from object to
subject. Complex response, delight at the discovery of
relationship between action and reaction, characterize
his best work:

Flowers through the window –
lavender and yellow

changed by white curtains –
Smell of cleanliness –

Sunshine of late afternoon –
On the glass tray

a glass pitcher, the tumbler
turned down, by which

a key is lying – And the
immaculate white bed

The shift is gradual, from the perception to the subjective
response to smell, leading to a tenuous personal nostalgia.
He is able, after the transition, to return to perception,
but the objects seen – tray, pitcher, tumbler, key and
bed – now have in their stillness subtle subjective overtones. The poem is resonant not in any assumed rhetoric
but in its 'intrinsic movement'.

In 'Iris', too, there is a shift to an 'intensity of perception', a spoken tension generated by the pauses at the
line endings. The tension is released by the transition.
The poet and his wife notice a strong scent as they come
down for breakfast:

we searched through the
rooms for
that

sweetest odor and at
first could not
find its

source then a blue as
of the sea
struck

startling us from among
those trumpeting
petals

In 'The Red Wheelbarrow' the complex emotion which colours the rest of the poem is present in the opening lines: 'so much depends/on'. The brief description that follows is resonant because of them. Sometimes the shift of emphasis or tone is so rapid, contains such complex suggestions, that the poem becomes a collage of perceptions rather than a concentration of a central subjective response. 'An Elegy for D. H. Lawrence' glances over Lawrence's work: the elegiac note is below the surface:

Flood waters rise, and will rise,
rip the quiet valley
trap the gypsy and the girl
She clings drowning to
a bush in flower.

In *Paterson* the collage technique is fully developed. Prose appears abruptly after lyric passages; dry versification is interrupted by a laundry list. The poem sets out to illustrate 'that a man in himself is a city, beginning, seeking, achieving and concluding his life in ways which the various aspects of the city may embody'. The poem must be inclusive, even of the pollution of the river, which mirrors the corruption in man. A work of such length, so large in conception, necessarily has lapses. But when the collage technique works richly, the lyric passages provide contemplative pauses, and Williams works fine effects:

The rose is green and will bloom,
overtopping you, green, livid
green when you shall no more speak, or
taste, or even be. My whole life
has hung too long upon a partial victory ...

Only the first book is fully sustained. In the three completed books that follow, the reader experiences only moments of satisfaction.

In *I Wanted To Write A Poem* Williams describes his

search for technique. 'I didn't go for long lines because of my nervous nature. I couldn't. The rhythmic pace was the pace of speech, an excited pace because I was excited when I wrote. I was discovering ...' Each poem possesses this sense of breathless discovery. The petunia, for instance:

Purple!
for months unknown
but for
the barren sky ...

He struggled against what he saw as restrictive traditional forms – the sonnet, iambic pentameter. And yet 'Free verse was not the answer. From the beginning I knew that the American language must shape the pattern.' In 1948 he wrote *Paterson, Book II,* and suddenly understood his particular style:

The descent beckons
   as the ascent beckoned
      Memory is a kind
of accomplishment
   a sort of renewal
      even ...

A letter to Richard Eberhart explains his discovery of the 'variable foot'. A poem takes the music of one line as its rhythmic basis, not the stress pattern of a word nor a predetermined number of syllables. A single beat is to be counted to each line: 'Over the whole poem it gives a pattern to the metre that can be felt as a new measure. It gives resources to the ear which result in a language which we hear spoken about us every day.' He thus released his verse from the short breathless line, giving it scope for sustained lyricism:

Of asphodel, that greeny flower,
   like a buttercup
      upon its branching stem –

save that it's green and wooden –
> I come, my sweet,
>> to sing to you.

Williams felt a personal animosity towards T. S. Eliot; but it was bolstered up by a critical animosity as well, particularly towards *The Waste Land*. Eliot, he felt, 'returned us to the classroom, just at the moment when I felt we were on the point of an escape to matters much closer to the essence of a new art form itself – rooted in the locality which should give it fruit.' Eliot's literary collage was anathema to Williams, in search for a technique he finally mastered in *Paterson*:

> I cannot stay here
to spend my life looking into the past:

the future's no answer. I must
find my meaning and lay it, white,
beside the sliding water: myself –
comb out the language – or succumb

– whatever the complexion.

Ezra Pound 1885–1972

> But the beauty is not the madness
> Tho' my errors and wrecks lie about me.
> And I am not a demigod,
> I cannot make it cohere.
> If love be not in the house there is nothing

– Canto CXVI

Ezra Pound was born in Hailey, Idaho, in 1885. He grew up in Wyncote, Pennsylvania, and became a student of Romance Languages at Hamilton College and later at the University of Pennsylvania, where William Carlos Williams and Hilda Doolittle became his friends. After receiving his degree in 1906, he lectured briefly in French and Spanish at Wabash College (1907) but was dismissed for his bohemian behaviour.

At this time he was writing verse translations in the tradition of Swinburne and Rossetti and had a lively interest in Whitman's poetry and Browning's dramatic monologues. His first collection, *A Lume Spento*, he published at his own expense in Venice – where he went after leaving Wabash College – in 1908. The book contains much that is Browningesque, and the collections that came shortly afterwards took their models from the past, recalling the troubadors of the Middle Ages, the world of Provence and the Anglo-Saxon world. His translation, from the Anglo-Saxon, of 'The Seafarer' in *Ripostes* (1912) is one of his first major poems, imitating the alliterative stress patterns of the original:

> Days little durable,
> And all arrogance of earthen riches,
> There come now no kings nor Caesars
> Nor gold-giving lords like those gone.

Ripostes came after *Personae* (1909) and *Canzoni* (1911). The poet who wrote it was twenty-seven, already well advanced towards his mature style, though all the early poems seem, in retrospect, apprentice-work for his great project, the *Cantos*.

Ripostes included a supplement, the 'complete poems' of T. E. Hulme, whom Pound had met in London and whose work and conversation he admired. He suggested to Pound the possibility of short, objective, classical poems, without didactic purpose, purged of excess verbiage. A group of poets who shared Pound's interests gathered into a group calling themselves Imagists. Pound described their objectives: 'Direct treatment of the "thing" whether objective or subjective; to use absolutely no word that did not contribute to the presentation: as regarding rhythm, to compose in sequence of the musical phrase, not in sequence of a metronome.' Pound submitted the poems of H.D. and Richard Aldington to *Poetry* (Chicago), for which he acted as foreign correspondent, and prepared the anthology *Des Imagistes* (1914), which included Pound's own poems as well as work by H.D. (Hilda Doolittle), Aldington, F. S. Flint, William Carlos Williams, Amy Lowell, Ford Madox Hueffer and James Joyce. Pound had published in *Poetry* the year before his 'essay' 'A Few Don'ts by an Imagist', which set down the rules: 'Use no superfluous word, no adjective which does not reveal something ... Go in fear of abstractions ... Don't chop your stuff into separate iambs. Don't make each line stop dead at the end and then begin every next line with a heave ...' Pound's contributions to *Des Imagistes* included poems based on Chinese models:

O fan of white silk
  clear as frost on the grass-blade
You also are laid aside.

An extreme example of this strictly pared style is 'In the Station of the Metro'. In first draft it was thirty-one lines long. Pound rejected this version as of 'second intensity'. He cut it to fifteen lines, and a year later to two:

The apparition of these faces in the crowd;
Petals on a wet, black bough.

As Imagism began to concentrate more on *vers libre*, Pound evolved with Wyndham Lewis a new strategy, a stricter, more dynamic form of the original imagism embracing the other arts as well: Vorticism. Together Pound and Lewis produced two issues of the magazine *Blast*, to which Pound contributed some mediocre poems. Though his relations with both movements were short-lived, they clarified for him disciplines and techniques which his later poems developed.

Ernest Fenollosa's widow, noting Pound's interest in Chinese culture, gave her husband's notes on Chinese culture to him. Fenollosa's reading of Chinese, inaccurate though it may have been, stimulated Pound, and he edited Fenollosa's *The Chinese Written Character as a Medium for Poetry*. The Chinese elements in his verse increased, particularly in *Cathay* (1915) which includes a number of free translations which catch the Chinese tone and atmosphere evocatively:

By the North Gate, the wind blows full of sand,
Lonely from the beginning of time until now!
Trees fall, the grass goes yellow with autumn.
I climb the towers and towers
          to watch out the barbarous land ...

Oriental literature and philosophy held a lifelong fascination for him. His is not affected Edwardian 'chinoiserie' but something distinctly new in English. He translated *Certain Noble Plays of Japan* (1916), prepared *Ta Hio: The Great Learning* (1928), *Confucius: The Unwobbling Pivot and the Great Digest* (1947), and Chinese material enriches the *Cantos*.

His interest in a wide range of literary cultures early in his creative life determined him in an ambition to find common ground between the writings of apparently alien cultures. From Imagism he learned about objective clarity; from Vorticism he discovered how to juxtapose contrasting images, matter from different planes of relationship. Chinese writing suggested to him the ideal of image and idea fused in concrete form: the pictograph.

When he wrote *Homage to Sextus Propertius* (1917) he was not yet prepared to break into his own idiom and retained certain rhetorical trappings out of habit rather than necessity. The *Homage* is more imitation than translation. In *Hugh Selwyn Mauberley* (1920), however, Pound purged his style of inessential matter and the last dross of aestheticism. T. S. Eliot saw 'Mauberley' as 'a great poem' and 'a document of an epoch'. It marks the point in Pound's career when his previous experiments and experiences fused, intensified by the recent, dislocating experience of World War I. Mauberley surveys decadent and moribund English culture and society. With detached irony Pound can speak through his creature:

For three years, out of key with the time,
He strove to resuscitate the dead art
Of poetry; to maintain 'the sublime'
In the old sense. Wrong from the start –

The decisive opening sets an authoritatively ironic tone: 'Better mendacities/Than the classics in paraphrase!' Of the Great War, with telling bitterness, he writes,

There died a myriad,
And of the best, among them,
For an old bitch gone in the teeth,
For a botched civilization ...

The poem shares thematic material with Eliot's *The Waste Land*. Eliot called Pound '*il miglior fabbro*' – 'the better craftsman'.

In *Mauberley* Pound stigmatizes the religion of material profit, where beauty is 'Decreed in the market place' and we have 'the Press for wafer; Franchise for circumcision'. The men who survived the War came home to the old deceit, to 'usury age-old and age-thick / And liars in public places'. It was the first time he had, with such power and acid emphasis, evoked the theme which became central to the *Cantos*.

In 1920 he and his wife – Dorothy Shakespear, whom he married in 1914 – moved to Paris, and on to Italy in 1924, where they settled in Rapallo. In London Pound had begun the *Cantos*, which already seemed to be developing towards a long poem. The War and *Mauberley* intervened, but in Italy he revised and published *A Draft of XVI Cantos* (1925). It was followed over the years by *A Draft of XXX Cantos* (1930), *Eleven New Cantos* (1934), *Fifth Decade of Cantos* (1937), *Cantos LII-LXXI* (1940), *The Pisan Cantos* (1948), *Section: Rock-Drill, Cantos 85-95* (1955), *Thrones, Cantos 96-109* (1959) and *Drafts and Fragments of Cantos CX-CXVII* (1968). This large body of poetry was supplemented with critical books, polemics, and essays – notably *How to Read, ABC of Economics, ABC of Reading, Make it New, What is Money For?* – work which occupied him until his death in 1972.

As Pound's life changed, as his thought became more disciplined and intense, so the *Cantos* developed and evolved. His sympathies became strong and produced in him an acute anger at social evils which seemed to him to stem from international usury – often in Pound's mind equated with the capitalist profit motive and with Zionist conspirators. His anti-semitism – a product of his muddled economic theories – grew strident. Living in Italy during the thirties, he became convinced that Mussolini's programme of reform was the right one to reduce poverty and disease, that he would ensure equitable distribution of resources. During World War II Pound remained in Italy and was given radio time to lecture to America. He urged his countrymen not to fight for the capitalists.

When the Americans took Italy, Pound was arrested (1944) and kept alone in a cage in a detention compound in Pisa. The *Pisan Cantos* were the painful distillation of this experience. He was taken back to the United States, tried for treason, declared insane, and detained in St Elizabeth's Hospital near Washington. It was there that he completed the *Pisan Cantos*, wrote the *Rock-Drill Cantos*, and finished his translation of *The Classic Anthology Defined by Confucius* (1954). In 1958 he was released, after considerable pressure had been exerted by friends – Frost and Carlos Williams among them – and was allowed to return to Italy where he lived in Merano and Venice, revising and adding to the *Cantos*.

Several critics have suggested skeletal 'structures' underlying the *Cantos*, coordinating them. Pound himself was annoyed by such theories. They falsify the nature of the work. It is not an 'intelligible' or paraphrasable work in the sense the analytical critics would wish, but rather a complex juxtaposition of images and ideas, of literature and history, punctuated by satirical, elegiac and prophetic admonitions at a world in which money is used to get *money*, and little else. Yeats wrote in 1936, 'Ezra Pound has made flux his theme; plot, characterization, logical discourse, seem to him abstractions unsuitable to a man of his generation.' The variety of style and allusion preempts an over-all structure. Homer and the alliterative style of Anglo-Saxon poetry in 'Canto I', for instance, fuse in an entirely new language:

Dark blood flowed in the fosse,
Souls out of Erebus, cadaverous dead, of brides
Of youths and of the old who had borne much;
Souls stained with recent tears, girls tender,
Men many ...

In 'Canto II' there is a sudden change of tone and mode:

Hang it all, Robert Browning,
        there can be but the one 'Sordello'.
But Sordello, and my Sordello?

Pound suggested that readers perplexed by the *Cantos* should study Browning's 'Sordello'. It is like Beethoven's hint that, to understand one of his Sonatas, we should read Shakespeare's *The Tempest*. Pound's hint sends us to the theme, not the form.

In 'Canto XIII' the style shifts again:

Kung walked
        by the dynastic temple
        and into the cedar grove ...

and on to ('Canto LXXVII')

And this day Abner lifted a shovel ...
        instead of watchin' it to see if it would
        take action ...

Various planes of thought cross and recross. Language in all its registers, from the most colloquial varieties of English to the most literary, is employed; and various languages come into play. Passages deal with various parallel worlds: the ancient world, the world of the Renaissance, the modern world, a permanent plane of gods, a plain of archetypal figures, real and fictional, including Confucius and Odysseus, and a plain of accidental figures such as Malatesta. The worlds coexist and interpenetrate. The poet's reactions to his various reading – of Remy de Gourmont, Homer, Ovid, Browning, and others – are recorded. So, too, we read of his reactions to economists and political leaders, of his own memories of Paris and London, of the painters who saw the world fresh – particularly Wyndham Lewis and Picasso. All are juxtaposed in contrasting passages or adjacent memories: a tree suggests Daphne; a new literary acquaintance emerges from an old myth; Eleanor of Aquitaine becomes Helen of Troy.

A characteristic point of composition occurred in 1923 when Pound toured the Italian battlefields with Hemingway, who explained to the poet the history of the Renaissance soldier of fortune, Sigismundo de Malatesta, who contested with Pius II in political battles. A warrior and a lover of beauty, Malatesta for Pound became emblematic as builder of the beautiful Tempio. He appears often in the *Cantos*. Another recurrent figure is C. H. Douglas whose *Economic Democracy* was published in 1919 and affected Pound so strongly that he revised his drafts of the early *Cantos*.

William Carlos Williams likened the *Cantos* to an 'impressive monument which Pound is building against our time.' 'Against' is the operative word, for Pound is a poet in opposition, with an obsessive social vision and the rancour of a prophet rather than a satirist – though his satire is stinging. Monumental though they are, the *Cantos* include contemplative passages which, however bitter their nostalgia, remain intensely personal and restorative:

Tudor indeed is gone and every rose,
Blood-red, blanch-white that in the sunset glows
Cries: 'Blood, Blood, Blood!' against the gothic stone
Of England, as the Howard or Boleyn knows.

Nor seeks the carmine petal to infer;
Nor is the white bud Time's inquisitor
Probing to know if its new-gnarled root
Twists from York's head or belly of Lancaster;

Or if a rational soul should stir, perchance,
Within the stem or summer shoot to advance
Contrition's utmost throw, seeking in thee
But oblivion, not thy forgiveness, FRANCE.

as the young lizard extends his leopard spots
  along the grass-blade seeking the green midge half an ant-
  size
and the Serpentine will look just the same
and the gulls be as neat on the pond
and the sunken garden unchanged
and God knows what else is left of our London
      my London, your London
and if her green elegance
  remains on this side of my rain ditch
  puss lizard will lunch on some other T-bone

sunset grand couturier.

– 'Canto LXXX'

T. S. Eliot wrote in preface to his translation of St-John Perse's *Anabase* of the technique: 'Any obscurity of the poem, on first readings, is due to the suppression of "links in the chain", of explanatory and connecting matter, and not to incoherence or to love of cryptogram ... The reader has to allow the images to fall into his memory without questioning the reasonableness of each at the moment; so that, at the end, a total effect is produced. Such selection of a sequence of images and ideas has nothing chaotic about it. There is a logic of the imagination as well as a logic of concepts.' The description illuminates Pound's technique as well.

H.D. (Hilda Doolittle) 1886–1961

H.D. once said 'serenitas'

– Ezra Pound, 'Canto CXIII'

Since 1920, H.D.'s poetry has attracted facile critical epithets: 'the perfect Imagist' who produced 'miniature gems'. Her later and most distinctive work betrays such classification. Much of it has remained out of print and unread until recently. Her early imagist poems are good apprentice work; it is in her later poems and prose that her originality and greatness lie: *The Walls Do Not Fall* (1944), *Tribute to the Angels* (1945), *The Flowering of the Rod* (1946) – published together as *Trilogy* (1973) – and *Hermetic Definition*, published in 1972.

Hilda Doolittle was born in Bethlehem, Pennsylvania, in 1886. When Hilda was eight, her family moved to Philadelphia where her father was appointed director of the Flower Astronomical Observatory at the University of Pennsylvania. She befriended Ezra Pound – to whom she was for a time engaged – and William Carlos Williams in her late teens. In 1904 she entered Bryn Mawr College where she began translating Latin poetry and seriously writing her own.

She first appeared in print as a writer of children's stories in a local paper. Many years later she published a children's book, *The Hedgehog* (1936). By the time she sailed for Europe, she was already writing poems in her individual free-verse style. She settled in London and married the English poet, novelist, and critic Richard Aldington. Pound accepted poetry by both of them for *Poetry* (Chicago). He was attracted to H.D.'s poetry because, as he wrote to Harriet Monroe, editor of *Poetry*, it was 'Objective – no slither –; direct – no excessive use of adjectives, no metaphors that won't permit examination. It's straight talk, straight as the Greek!'

These were qualities central to the Imagist movement, set in motion by Pound to bring poetry back from the tired rhetoric of the nineties to hard, uncluttered images, *vers libre*, 'absolutely accurate presentation and no verbiage'. Poetic ideas were rendered through concrete objects. H.D.'s three poems in *Poetry* appeared signed, at Pound's insistence, 'H.D. Imagiste' – the French ending was to link the group with the modern French school. Her work appeared in Pound's anthology *Des Imagistes* (1914). H.D.'s poems were praised for their 'Hellenic hardness', though the anthology was generally disliked. H.D., Amy Lowell and Richard Aldington edited three further anthologies of Imagist poetry and wrote a manifesto describing their aims: exactness of vocabulary and meaning, new rhythms to suit new ideas, total freedom of choice of subject matter, hard and clear poetry. Above all, concentration was the essence of Imagist poetry.

H.D. did not need to conform to these precepts – for her, this was a natural way to write. She achieved what F. S. Flint called 'accurate mystery'. Much has been made of her classical background, her debts to Euripides, Sappho, Homer, and the *Greek Anthology*. More important is the undecorated hardness, the product of acute precision, characteristic of her best work. A flower in her poetry is seldom just a flower: it is a 'sea poppy', a 'rose', a 'spice-rose', a 'white hyacinth', a 'Sitalkas', a 'hypatica'. The simple, precise naming lends authority to the chaste poems:

Along the yellow sand
above the rocks
the laurel-bushes stand.

Against the shimmering heat,
each separate leaf
is bright and cold,
and through the bronze
of shining bark and wood,
run the fine threads of gold.

In 'Sea Rose' she writes,

Stunted, with small leaf,
you are flung on the sands,
you are lifted
in the crisp sand
that drives in the wind.

Accurate evocation, not analytical description; the
mystery is in the object and therefore in the poem that
renders the object. Her evocative skill makes it possible
for her to fuse disparate images with a sense of rightness,
as she does in the poem Pound held up as the ideal
Imagist example, 'Oread':

Whirl up, sea –
Whirl your pointed pines,
Splash your great pines
On our rocks,
Hurl your green over us,
Cover us with your pools of fir.

She does not draw a visual analogy but fuses 'sea' and
'firs'. The image becomes, not merely a vehicle for trans-
scribing a sensation: it presents the sensation itself. The
words are individually simple and direct, their organization is complex. A sensed analogy inspires the poem which
begins from the point where the images fuse. The move-

ment is neither narrative nor descriptive but organic to the poem itself. No external reference is required.

H.D.'s poems also appeared in the periodical *Egoist*, the Imagists' platform, which she edited with Aldington and, during World War One, with T. S. Eliot. A series of personal tragedies occurred during this period. She had a miscarriage. Her favourite brother was killed in France, and her father died from shock. Aldington took a mistress and her marriage came to an end. In 1919, pregnant again and seriously ill, she was discovered in an advanced state of double pneumonia by her friend Bryher, the novelist. The child, Perdita, was born, but the various tensions led to a nervous breakdown.

At the time, only one collection of H.D.'s poetry, *Seagarden* (1916) had appeared. *Hymen* was published later, in 1921, and *Heliodora* in 1924. Her *Collected Poems* (1925) included eighty-four poems and three translations from the Greek. It is on the basis of this book that H.D.'s reputation as a miniaturist is based.

But the turning point in her creative life came shortly after. Bryher took her, to recover from her nervous breakdown, to Corfu. There she suffered hallucinations. On the wall of the hotel room she saw Helios, the sun god, and Nike, goddess of victory. When, years later, she underwent psychoanalysis with Freud in Vienna and London (1933-4), she came to understand the vision and wrote her seminal prose work, *Tribute to Freud*. He enabled her to see that the whole of her life had been a quest, that her personal dream, her memories of childhood, her close affiliation with the Moravian religion, her constant movement between various cultures, and her attraction to the clarity of Greek metaphor, related integrally to archetypal myths. Freud helped her discover the connection between her childhood and the present woman she was, and related her hallucinations to an attempt to make the abstract quest symbolically concrete. Through Freud she found a universal myth and learned of the parallel archetypal images present in her. This recognition played a vital role in her later poetry.

The only books she published between the *Collected Poems* and her psychoanalysis were a verse drama, *Hippolytus Temporizes* (1927) and the poems in *Red Roses for Bronze* (1931), still essentially imagistic. In 1937 her translation of Euripides's *Ion* was published, and a new and significantly more mature imagination is at work. H.D. wrote, 'Without the analysis and the illuminating doctrine or philosophy of Sigmund Freud, I would hardly have found the clue or the bridge between the child-life, the memories of peaceful Bethlehem [her birthplace] and the orgy of destruction, later to be witnessed and lived through in London. That outer threat and constant reminder of death drove me inward ...' The Second World War stimulated her new period of creativity. Seeing London devastated, she remembered other broken cities. London was now open to the sky – she recalled the temple of Amen-Ra and the ruined cities of Egypt.

Her *Trilogy* is a quest through desolation towards regeneration, rebirth. It opens in a freer, more flexible and personal style:

An incident here and there,
and rails gone (for guns)
from your (and my) old town square ...

She sets London and Luxor side by side:

there, as here, ruin opens
the tomb, the temple; enter,
there as here, there are no doors:

the shrine lies open to the sky,
the rain falls, here, there
sand drifts; eternity endures ...

She can speak of eternity as a *fact*. The analogies she

draws are more ambitious, revealing archetypal figures and experiences. 'Thoth, Hermes, the stylus,/the palette, the pen, the quill endure'. She returns home where canals:

flow
between iris-banks:
where the heron
has her nest...

and at times approaches the core of meanings, the underlying unity, 'where all lights become one'. Her search for the still, generative centre resembles Eliot's in that other major civilian war poem, *Four Quartets*. And when 'we gain/the arc of perfection,/we are satisfied, we are happy,/we begin again.'

we are voyagers, discoverers
of the not-known,

the unrecorded;
we have no map;

possibly we will reach haven,
heaven.

She discovers her own map as she advances, sometimes taking the variation in meaning of words, or etymology, or homonymous qualities as a guide: 'mer, mere, mère, mater, Maia, Mary/Star of the Sea,/Mother.' With the three wise men she arrives at last at the Mother of God – 'she was shy and simple and young'. *Trilogy* is a highly complex structure of juxtapositions of myths, legends, experiences. The three poems are a major unified work.

H.D. retired to Switzerland. At the age of seventy-one she fell ill. She was unable to walk without a cane. She settled at a clinic near Zurich, but in 1960 returned briefly to the United States to receive the Award of Merit Medal for Poetry – the first woman to be thus honoured.

Back in Switzerland, she completed *Helen in Egypt*, a poem of considerable length. Again a quest is the central theme. Legends suggested that the real Helen lived in Egypt, that Helen of Troy was an illusion. H.D., identifying with Helen, undertakes a search for the self. Three analogous stories are superimposed, one on the other, in the manner of a palimpsest. The freer verse style is interspersed with prose; the passages of poetry concentrate on the central theme contemplatively:

> things remembered, forgotten,
> remembered again, assembled
> and re-assembled in different order
> as thought and emotions ...

The interweaving of dream and reality and the need to disentangle the dream is the theme of her novels, too – particularly *Bid Me To Live* (1960).

H.D. died of a heart attack in 1961. Some of her best poetry was published posthumously in *Hermetic Definition* (1972). A long poem in three sections, the title poem is a variation on her persistent theme: the quest. H.D. writes as an old woman, confined to bed by a broken hip. Burning resin and pine cone scent her isolation and free her mind to associations:

> Why did you come
> to trouble my decline?
> I am old (I was old till you came);
>
> the reddest rose unfolds,
> (which is ridiculous
> in this time, this place ...)

Turning to her past, she looks again at her early achievements, finally expressing the theme of death and rebirth in one of her finest passages. The wheel comes full circle in the last section of the poem, 'Star of Day':

It was April that we met,
and once in May;
I did not realize my state of mind,

my 'condition' you might say,
until August when I wrote,
the reddest rose unfolds ...

In another poem in the volume, 'Sagesse', H.D. lies alone, counting the hours of the night and day. A picture of an owl suggests a sequence of thoughts in which she tells the hours by the angels that traditionally preside over them. Herself confined, she remembers Pound constrained in his cage at Pisa. She sees children watching the owl and her own childhood comes back to her:

I wish I'd kept my half-bun,

not crumbled it for the pelicans – birds, too?
I'd like to feel his tongue upon my hand ...

In the final section Venus strikes the hour of eight: the poem ends in celebration:

... laugh the world away,
laugh, laugh and place your flowers

on the shrine of Teut, Agad, Hana, Sila
who share your name, *Soleil.*

She had confronted her guardian angels.

The last poem in the volume is 'Winter Love'. The poet searches for herself as Helen in old age: 'the Sun goes into the dark,/the Gods decree/that Helen is deserted utterly.'

Grande Dame, I will carry your crutch for you,
you needn't hobble, hobble any more,
you will tell me what was true,

what wasn't true,
we will walk miles over the sand ...

Later in the poem, subjective longing is replaced by a willingness to be sacrificed in order for life to be renewed:

Espérance, O golden bee,
take life afresh and if you must,
so slay me.

Hermetic Definition is the climax of her later style, a rare achievement. With intimacy and directness she writes of age, loss, and the necessary pattern of rebirth, even if that pattern includes her own death. She does not accept or find easily: she is on a quest:

     – take the Child away;
cruel, cruel is Hope,
terrible the weight of honey and of milk ...

Most remarkable is her ability to sustain such large and urgent themes on such a scale.

Robinson Jeffers 1887–1962

Give him a blood-trail to follow,
That's all he wants for Christmas.

– 'Thurso's Landing'

Robinson Jeffers was born in Pittsburgh, Pennsylvania,
in 1887. As a child he was tutored by his father, a Presbyterian minister and professor of Old Testament literature. At the age of five he was learning Greek. His
education continued in Switzerland, Germany and the
United States. In 1903 his parents moved to California
and that remained Jeffers's permanent home. He studied
medicine at Occidental College, California, and later
forestry, graduating in 1905. By means of a legacy in 1912
he became financially independent and in 1913 married
Una Call Kuster, a woman of considerable vitality whom
he had pursued for eight years. She has been described as
hawk-like, an admirable complement to his own fierce
austerity.

They went to Carmel on the coast at Monterey, California, and there, quarrying the granite and raising the
stones with his own hands, he built a house with a stone
tower overlooking the barbaric cliffs and coastline backed
by mountains. He took Emersonian individualism to
startling lengths. The isolated tower came to represent for
him a self-reliance that in turn led to misanthropy on a
grand scale.

His first two volumes of poetry, in 1912 and 1916, were undistinguished, and Jeffers omitted them entirely from his *Selected Poetry* (1938). *Tamar and Other Poems* (1924) was another matter: it brought Jeffers rapid popular acclaim. The poem 'Tamar' is his first long narrative, prefiguring the strengths and weaknesses of much of his later poetry. The power and rapidity of narrative is there, and also the obsessive themes of incest, cursed heredity and doom-laden lust. The story derives from Shelley's *The Cenci* and from the Biblical book of Samuel, II,13. Jeffers's penchant for the over-reaching phrase mars the poem, a tendency to trust the rhetorical gesture that proves finally sentimental, blurring rather than clarifying the theme:

> She pressed her mouth
> Between the muscles of his breast: 'I want you and want you.
> You didn't know that a clean girl could want a man.
> Now you will take me and use me and throw me away
> And I've ... earned it.'

With such blatant overwriting, the poem's immediate success is hard to comprehend. But there is something naïve in his attempt to describe incestuous seduction in a genteel fashion.

The outspoken cruelty of some passages disturbingly prefigures Jeffers's later work. It is powerful, certainly, but exaggerated, too. The fire of Judgment comes:

> the gasp
> That followed on a cry drew down a sword
> Of flame to her lungs, pain ceased, and thinking, 'Father',
> She dropped herself into the arms of the fire ...

There are more extreme passages which exceed melo-drama:

> Will Andrews
> Struggled to rise and like a gopher-snake that a child

Has mashed the head of with a stone, he waggled
The blood-clot of his head over the floor ...

Blood, guts and bones colour the later narratives. When –
in another best-seller, *Roan Stallion* (1925) – a man is
killed by his own horse, we read: 'hooves left nothing
alive but teeth tore up the remnant'. In *Thurso's Landing*
(1932) a character speaks of a buck hit in the lung who:

'Coughed up a froth of blood and ran down hill.
I have to get him.' 'It looks like a red toadstool:
Red scum on rotten wood. Does it make you sick?'
'Not a bit: it makes you happy.'

Disgust with the human being and its acts, expressed in
delight at human pain, dismemberment, mangling, is part
of Jeffers's world-view: men, creatures, and incidents are
expressed in terms of the archetypal tragic myths. When
they first appeared, the narratives were considered to have
something of the power of Aeschylus or Sophocles. Indeed, *The Tower Beyond Tragedy* is concerned with the
theme of the Oresteia.

Possibly his best work is the free adaptation of
Euripides's *Medea*, made in 1946 for a stage appearance
of the actress Judith Anderson. But overstatement is self-
defeating, overstated emotion devolves into sentimentality – in Jeffers's case a sentimentality of violence. His
misanthropy found expression in a vision of the in-
significance of man in the cosmos, a philosophy of what
he called 'inhumanism', involving an infatuation with
death. Incest was for him a symbol of human self-regard,
human blindness to the consequence of action.

The fifteen volumes of Jeffers's poems develop the same
themes. Perhaps the most positive collection was *Give
your Heart to the Hawks and Other Poems* (1933) in
which he urged men to emulate the qualities of rocks,
the solitude of the hawks, in order to endure their con-

dition. In extreme form, his misanthropic vision is expressed in these terms:

This is the human dawn. As for me, I would rather
Be a worm in a wild apple than a son of man ...

In 'Hurt Hawks' he writes, 'I'd sooner, except the penalties, kill a man than a hawk.' A few fine, hard lines recall the more balanced power of Ted Hughes: 'I lie and hear/dark rain beat the roof, and the blind wind', or 'The broken pillar of the wing jags from the clotted shoulder/The wing trails like a banner in defeat ...'

Most sustained are the poems that put by the long, loose, Whitmanesque lines, choosing a shorter and less rhetorical measure:

No vulture is here, hardly a hawk,
Could long wings or great eyes fly
Under this low-lidded soft sky?

But something at the heart of the verse eventually undermines it, a wilful blindness to developments in modern poetry and modern thought. He would not countenance the moderns' search for new forms, new idioms. In an introduction to his *Selected Poetry* he wrote, 'It became evident to me that poetry – if it was to survive at all – must reclaim some of the power and reality that it was so hastily surrendering to prose ... [Poetry] was becoming slight and fantastic, abstract, unreal, eccentric ... It must reclaim substance and sense, and physical and psychological reality ... It led me to write narrative poetry, and to draw subjects from contemporary life ... and to attempt the expression of philosophic and scientific ideas in verse.' Such an ambition, understandable in itself, is hardly borne out in the poems which are fantastic, eccentric, unreal. He added, 'I decided not to tell lies in verse. Not to feign any emotion that I did not feel.'

The latent flaw in his ambition is in the word 'lies'. He had been obsessed since late adolescence with Nietzsche's words, 'The poets? The poets lie too much.' Jeffers seems to take 'truth' as entirely subjective. He does not allow for 'imagination' in his description of the 'lie'. Imaginative insight – as opposed to imaginative projection – requires a strong impulse that takes with it both a lie and a burning desire for truth. Otherwise the truth will find expression as truism, ending in sentimentality or cliché. Jeffers, always implicitly or explicitly illustrating his philosophy, looking at the world only in order to confirm his beliefs, not to test them, does not permit the reader to take the imaginative leap, to experience insight. In trying to win back some of the ground that prose had taken – as he believed – from verse, his technique becomes prosaic. Mistrust of the 'lie' leads him to mar fine poems by overexposition. 'The Purse-Seine' lucidly evokes the catching of sardines – they:

> ... wildly beat from one wall to the other of their closing
> destiny the phosphorescent
> Water to a pool of flame ...

But, wary of too broad an interpretation, he explains the meaning of his image lest we misconstrue it. The net he compares to a city and, 'we and our children/Must watch the net draw narrower, government take all powers – or revolution ...'

Strait-jacketed in a prose meaning, the evocative description is reduced to parable. Fear of misinterpretation also leads Jeffers to over-particularize in his descriptions – the superfluity of detail becomes inessential.

Misanthropy introduced him to a cast of self-destroying characters, characters who win through to his brand of heroism only by intensity of will-power. Sometimes they achieve super-human qualities, but often they remain detailed descriptions of deformity – moral and physical. Men drag their lameness through the narratives. A woman becomes 'a crippled hawk in a cage', the landscape becomes 'a perfect arena for man's cruelty'. There is a wilful misreading of Nietzsche in much of his work, a considerable power of expression used to develop themes morally and politically repugnant. Turning his back on his fellow men, from his tower he faced a view of the sea which he described characteristically in his 'Apology for Bad Dreams': 'This coast crying out for tragedy like all beautiful places.' His poetry occupies a world of cruel escapism.

Marianne Moore 1887–1972

it is not the atmosphere of ingenuity,
the otter, the beaver, the puma skins
without shooting irons or dogs;
it is not the plunder,
but 'accessibility to experience.'

– 'New York'

Marianne Moore was born in St Louis, Missouri, in 1887,
and brought up in the household of her grandfather, a
Presbyterian minister. He imbued her with a strong moral
conscience and a sense of the importance of the individual.
She attended the Metzger Institute in Carlisle, Pennsylvania, and then went to Bryn Mawr College, where she
was a classmate of H.D. (Hilda Doolittle). She graduated
in 1909 and taught stenography for five years.

At this time, the Imagists were active in London.
Though she denies that their work influenced her directly,
she believed as they did in precision and impersonality of
expression. Some of her early poems appeared in the
Imagists' periodical, *Egoist*, and H.D. and her friend
Bryher published Marianne Moore's first book, *Poems*
(1921). These twenty-four poems were reprinted with
additions as *Observations* (1924). By that time she was
working as an assistant at the New York Public Library.

Between 1926 and 1929 she edited the *Dial*, a fortnightly review which attracted contributions from Conrad Aiken, Thomas Mann, T. S. Eliot and others. Her work received various awards – the *Dial* Award (1924), the Levinson Prize (1935), the Harstock Prize (1935), the Bollingen Award (1951), and the Pulitzer Prize (1952).

In 1935 her *Selected Poems* appeared with an introduction by Eliot. He wrote that in the poems, 'an original sensibility and alert intelligence and deep feeling have been engaged in maintaining the life of the English language.' Other collections followed: *The Pangolin and Other Verse* (1936), *What are Years?* (1941), *Nevertheless* (1944) and *Collected Poems* (1951), again with an introduction by Eliot. She received the Gold Medal for Poetry in 1953 and in 1955 published a volume of essays on some of her favourite authors, *Predilections*. Her last major work was *Fables of La Fontaine* (1954), a book on which she spent nine years. There were, too, more collections of poetry: *Like a Bulwark* (1956), *O To Be A Dragon* (1959), *The Arctic Fox* (1964), *Tell Me, Tell Me* (1966) and *Complete Poems* (1967). In the *Complete Poems* she pruned a number of her best poems to a bare minimum. 'Poetry', for instance, which originally had five stanzas and thirty lines, including her best-known line, 'imaginary gardens with real toads in them', became three lines only:

I, too, dislike it.
    Reading it, however, with a perfect contempt for it, one discovers in it, after all, a place for the genuine.

A few more poems appeared before her death in 1972.

Her later work was little different in technique and intensity from the early poems, with their precise logic of detail. Her mind, trained to accuracy, is directed towards an examination of objects and scenes, not towards contemplation. The poems are recommended by more than mere surface glitter. Levels of experience and meaning are suggested by her pattern of line-endings, intricate rhymes and near-rhymes, assonance and alliteration, vocabulary and exquisitely developed syntax, as well as the odd facts and ideas that find themselves held together in the poems.

One of Marianne Moore's chief skills is in her management of the reader's attention, the way she surprises, creating at once fascination and uncertainty. For instance, she may open a poem with a line which is rhythmically end-stopped, but unpunctuated, as in 'The Steeple-Jack'. Each line that follows takes the syntax, suspended in the line before, in an unexpected direction, so that the poem is never arrested at a statement, it evolves as a process, an evocation:

Dürer would have seen a reason for living
    in a town like this, with eight stranded whales
to look at; with the sweet sea air coming into your house
on a fine day, from water etched
    with waves as formal as the scales
on a fish.

The stanza is carefully integrated through internal rhyme. The last, suspended three-syllable line leads into the next stanza.

The poems depend on these nicely measured effects, subtle and engaging. Her approach to technique turns the actual mechanics of verse-making into poetry: we applaud an enjambment, she draws our attention to patterned alliterations.

Most frequently she uses syllabic form – one of the most mechanical and restrictive of verse techniques. The length of the lines in each stanza is governed by a predetermined number of syllables rather than stresses, metrical feet, or free cadence. The visual pattern of the stanza is established by indenting the shorter lines to a predetermined degree. On the surface, it appears merely arbitrary to choose such a technique. But, in the case of Marianne Moore, it was the technique that chose the poet. The style is not only natural to her: after reading even a few of her poems, it is difficult to imagine her writing in any other way. Given the skeletal, mathematically regular form, she can develop her own speech rhythms in it. The brilliant ease with which she deploys her measured lines often achieves dramatic effect, especially when, deliberately, she departs from her prescriptive norm to convey a change of mood or tone. We are reminded by her various devices of Alban Berg's self-consciously precise, emotionally exact handling of the twelve tone row in music.

England's pioneer syllabic poet, Elizabeth Daryush, who began developing the technique around the time Marianne Moore did, has stressed the *natural* possibilities of regular syllabics and their variants. But she points out that they are 'the instinctively chosen instruments of the poet whose ear is attuned to their possibilities.' Syllabics offer the poet a rhythmic freedom, but an altogether new set of disciplines and problems to resolve. True syllabic verse is not merely chopped-up prose. Usually it rhymes, and it has a clear, though a more subtle, rhythmic pattern as metrical verse.

Marianne Moore's poem 'Bird-Witted' appears on analysis to have a ridiculous syllabic scheme: six ten-line stanzas with a firm rhyme scheme (ababcadefc), the lines of each stanza with, respectively, nine, eight, six, four, seven, three, six, three, seven and four syllables. Yet the poem develops naturally, the form does not brake it:

With innocent wide penguin eyes, three
   large fledgling mockingbirds below
the pussy-willow tree,
   stand in a row,
wings touching, feebly solemn,
will they see
   their no longer larger
   mother bringing
something which will partially
feed one of them.

Toward the high-keyed intermittent squeak
  of broken carriage springs, made by
the three similar meek-
    coated bird's-eye
freckled forms she comes ...

The syllabics lend a precision, impose a logic on each
line, stanza, and poem. When Marianne Moore was asked
if she found her biology course at Bryn Mawr valuable to
her as a poet, she replied, 'I found the biology course
exhilarating ... precision, economy of statement, logic
employed to ends that are disinterested, drawing and
identifying, liberate – at least have some bearing on – the
imagination, it seems to me.' The matter-of-fact elegance
of her style suggests *manner* rather than *tone*, for the
manner remains constant while the tone varies, as sup-
plely as the images and their attendant ideas and moods.

In an interview in *Paris Review* she suggested that, for
her, the stanza rather than the line was the poetic unit.
Though she hazarded hyphens at the end of lines, she
found readers were 'distracted from the content by them,
so I try not to use them.' Technique should not distract
the reader – and yet, in her poems it often does, delight-
fully, though it delays the full impact of the poem.

Her range of reference is wide; she perceives her chosen
images coolly, from an adequate distance to supply them
with a context in which to act. 'The Steeple-Jack' is a
good example. In some places, to name is enough:

cattails, flags, blueberries and spiderwort,
    striped grass, lichens, sunflowers, asters, daisies –
yellow and crab-claw ragged sailors with green bracts – toad-
    plant,
petunias, ferns; pink lilies, blue
    ones, tigers; poppies; black sweet-peas.

Her perspective is shared with the Steeple-Jack. Sometimes, as in 'The Jerboa', aspects of a single image are
vividly set down:

the pig-tailed monkey on
slab hands, with arched-up slack-slung gait, and the brown
    dandy looked at the jasmine two-leafed twig
    and bud, cactus pads, and fig.

A disturbing aspect of her exoticism is that at first reading they sometimes appear inexact. On re-reading they imprint themselves on the mind, somewhat fantastically, as right. Of elephants' trunks she writes,

Uplifted and waved till immobilized
wistaria-like, the opposing opposed
mouse-gray twined proboscises' trunk formed by two
trunks, fights itself to a spiraled inter-nosed

deadlock of dyke-enforced massiveness ...

But 'wistaria-like'? 'mouse-gray'? The mouse-colour brings in the contrast in size and hints at the elephant's traditional fear of mice. The delicate tendrils of wistaria contrast with the power of the elephants, and yet take their conflict beyond the immediate image.
    Later in the poem the elephants become 'knowers' who:

      'arouse the feeling that they are
allied to man' and can change roles with their trustees.

The quote in the poem is from Cicero. Many of Marianne Moore's poems contain quotations from other sources, though occasionally she encloses a phrase in quotes simply to emphasize it.
    The notes she supplied for the poems are almost as rich as the poems themselves. Of the poem 'Elephants' she writes, 'Data utilized in these stanzas, from a lecture-film entitled *Ceylon, the Wondrous Isle* by Charles Brooke Elliott. And Cicero deploring the sacrifice of elephants in the Roman Games, said they "aroused both pity and a feeling that the elephant was somehow allied to man." George Jennison, *Animals for Show and Pleasure in Ancient Rome* p. 52'.
    The notes as much as the poems suggest an omnivorous

reader, assimilating what would be for many people 'unconsidered trifles' – from the *National Geographical Magazine*, the *New York Times*, the *New Yorker*, the *Illustrated London News*, and innumerable other sources. She included in her poems a menagerie of beasts. Many put in a vivid appearance in her translation of La Fontaine's fables: 'A serpent has mobility/Which can shatter intrepidity.'

Of La Fontaine, she reports, 'I fell a prey to that surgical kind of courtesy of his.' We fall prey to the same quality in her work. La Fontaine was one of many influences. Among her favourite prose stylists were Dr Johnson, Edmund Burke, Sir Thomas Browne, Sir Francis Bacon, Caesar, Xenophon, Cellini, and Henry James in his letters and essays. The style she developed, sometimes retaining traces of the work of her masters, is undoubtedly her own.

One of her admirers, Randall Jarrell, described her in an essay: 'She not only can, but must, make poetry out of everything and anything: she is like Midas, or like Mozart chosing unpromising themes for the fun of it, or like one of those princesses whom wizards force to manufacture sheets out of nettles.' And yet, in her words, 'there are things that are important beyond all this fiddle.' The poetry fails if the reader's appreciation is arrested by the surface brilliance, the 'atmosphere of ingenuity'. The reader who persists beyond that point finds eventually a unique 'accessibility to experience'.

John Crowe Ransom 1888–1974

Then he sat upon a hill and bowed his head
As under a riddle ...

– 'Necrological'

In his poetry – most of which was written between 1922
and 1926 – John Crowe Ransom attempted to clarify
certain disturbing, unresolved paradoxes, aspects of the
disparity between the actual and the ideal. His influential
critical writing developed from the experience he gained
as a poet. His major critical work began with *God Without Thunder* (1930) and spanned the period of his editorship of the *Kenyon Review*, from 1939 until his retirement in 1959. His pioneering work *The New Criticism*
(1941) has remained his most provocative book. His
period of poetic activity was relatively brief, and of his
poems he wished to preserve only forty-four in his
Selected Poems (1955), suppressing altogether the collection *Poems About God* (1919).

He was born in 1888 in Pulaski, Tennessee, son of a
Methodist minister. At fifteen he entered Vanderbilt
University in Nashville, Tennessee, to study classics and
philosophy. He was awarded a Rhodes Scholarship to
study at Christ Church, Oxford (1910–13). In England he
became deeply interested in modern poetry, participating
in discussion groups organized by another American

student, Christopher Morley. Oxford further confirmed his Southern traditionalism, and he became 'in manners aristocratic; in religion, ritualistic; in art, traditional.'

Modern poetry did not incite him to experiment. It excited him by its concreteness; it was an antidote to the abstractions of his philosophical studies. A vacancy for an English tutor at Vanderbilt tempted him. He applied and was appointed. Apart from a period abroad as an artillery officer in World War I, he remained at Vanderbilt from 1914 to 1937.

This was the period of the 'Southern Renaissance' when a group of important writers emerged in the South: Ransom, William Faulkner, Katherine Anne Porter, Allen Tate, Thomas Wolfe and Robert Penn Warren among them. All shared in varying forms certain Southern characteristics and traditions and a fighting individualism. In Ransom, literary individualism took the form of relentless fury against abstraction, coupled with an elaborate style, full of archaisms and marked by unusual diction, and resolutely traditional formalism. In his first collection, *Poems About God*, published during his early years at Vanderbilt, the obscurities of diction and tonal uncertainties gave little indication of the individuality he would achieve.

Young poets at the University formed a discussion group, and *The Fugitive*, a magazine of verse, was founded in 1922. It was in this context that Ransom's idiosyncratic style matured. Allen Tate and Robert Penn Warren joined the group, which became known as the Fugitive Group. After nineteen issues, *The Fugitive* ceased publication in 1925. Most of Ransom's best poems had appeared in its pages. He published them, with a sonnet sequence, as *Chills and Fevers* (1924) and *Two Gentlemen in Bonds* (1927). Only four poems appeared after this. His attention turned to criticism. He omitted his sonnet sequence from a selection of forty-two poems in 1945. The 1955 selection adds only two more poems to the total.

Ransom's first book of criticism was written in nine weeks. Its full title was *God Without Thunder: An Unorthodox Defense of Orthodoxy*. It attacks those liberal elements in religion that would destroy ritual, that pattern which offers a stability within the fluidity of life. He defends ceremony, myth, codes of conduct: in short, the *forms*. His search is for a poetry that will fulfil a ritualistic function – creating a point of stability within the flux – and at the same time provide an analogy with man's experience. Science cannot do this: it denies the pluralism of poetic possibilities, the ability within one experience to contain contrasts, opposites, or contradictions without casting doubt on the validity of the statement. Science explores our natural context: it is the function of poetry to define its own context, within which each poem is self-sufficient.

The 'myth', Ransom suggests, survives best in an agrarian culture. Industrial society deprives man of his myths. And myths, like rituals, are stable forms. He develops his argument further in his essay in a symposium of work by twelve Southerners, *I'll Take My Stand: The South and the Agrarian Tradition* (1930). Some of the poems, 'Antique Harvesters' in particular, look nostalgically to the South's pre-war agrarian economy.

In 1938 *The World's Body*, another book of criticism, appeared, followed by *The New Criticism*. Together, the books are the kernel of his critical thought, concerned primarily with ontology and poetry – the reality of a poem's existence. In an essay called 'Poetry: A Note on Ontology' he distinguishes between *Physical Poetry* – the concrete nature of true images, sustained by formal techniques but destroyed by abstraction – and *Platonic Poetry* – characterized by allegory, discursiveness, ideas, moralizing. He stresses the value of *Metaphysical Poetry* which assumes a magic by reason of extended metaphor.

The 'new criticism' he formulated treats the poem as an object with an existence beyond its historical context, beyond any context external to itself. The critical approach is to the poem on its own terms and involves close textual study, distinguishing between the poem's structure and texture. Structure is the argument and technical grammar; texture is the imagery, vocabulary and diction. Ransom emphasizes the value of concrete presentation. He distrusts abstraction. His practical criticism eliminates subjective response from the assessment of the poem and admits no moral or political judgement: the achieved work of art is seen to possess its own integrity. The critics's task is essentially descriptive.

This critical approach was exemplified in Ransom's *Kenyon Review*. He left Vanderbilt in 1937 for Kenyon College in Gambier, Ohio, where he founded the review in 1939. He gathered an impressive list of essayists who supported the 'new criticism': Tate, R. P. Blackmur, Kenneth Burke, William Empson, and others. It proved a seminal critical and creative journal.

It is the very act of objectifying a poem, removing the subjective matter to facilitate critical access, that characterizes Ransom's own poetry. Many of the poems could be used to illustrate his critical theories. They are attempts to establish an equilibrium between extremes of paradox: Christ and Antichrist, youth and age, and so forth. The resolute composure of the poems makes the *poet* anonymous; his voice speaks the poem, but does not impose a personality upon it. The poem exists whole, self-contained, final.

Sentimentality is a subjective response – Ransom gently ridicules it. In 'Janet Waking', for example, a little girl wakes and kisses the members of her family. It is a subject ripe for sentiment:

One kiss she gave her mother.
Only a small one gave she to her daddy
Who would have kissed each curl of his shining baby;
No kiss at all for her brother.

Then she goes to wake Chucky, her chicken, 'But alas,/

Her Chucky had died.' For Janet the tragedy is considerable:

And weeping fast as she had breath
Janet implored us, 'Wake her from her sleep!'
And would not be instructed in how deep
Was the forgetful kingdom of death.

The chicken died from a bee sting. With ironic understatement the poem develops the paradox of innocence and knowledge, simple joy and sorrow. The chicken was 'Translated far beyond the daughters of man.' The murderous insect was a 'transmogrifying bee'.

Ransom's essential subtlety is suggested in 'transmogrifying'. To transmogrify is to effect a change, to transform. Sentimental joy has changed to a sorrow beyond sentimentality. Chicken and child are transmogrified. The word is a curious one. It is the fulcrum of the poem.

Unusual diction is a regular feature of Ransom's style. In 'Philomela' he writes, 'I pernoctated with the Oxford students once,' and continues:

And in the quadrangles, in the cloisters, on the Cher,
Precociously knocked at antique doors ajar,
Fatuously touched the hems of the hierophants,
Sick of my dissonance.

But for the ironic tone, the touch of archaism is half-way to raising the subject to myth. Hierophants were originally official expounders of sacred mysteries. The young man's fatuity reduces the experience.

The poem begins with a characteristic paradox between the ideal and the actual: the nightingale is addressed by all her liquid names, the beauty of her song 'recited in the classic numbers'. The poet continues, 'Ah, but our numbers are not felicitous,/It goes not liquidly for us.' The ideal is for others: 'Unto more beautiful, persistently more young,/Thy fabulous provinces belong.'

So carefully completed are his poems that we accept the archaic, 'Thy fabulous provinces' without questioning. Their correct, courtly formality makes them haunting and memorable. They possess that 'miraculism' he defines in an essay: 'scientific predication concludes an act of attention but miraculism initiates one' and 'myths are conceits born of metaphors'. By means of metaphor the poems discover among concrete detail the universals they seek. Even the simple dog who, 'bored beyond his tongue's poor skill to tell,/Rehearses his pink paradigm, To yap' assumes an archetypal role when, after terrifying a herd of cows, he retreats whipped to kennel.

> God's peace betide the souls
> Of the pure in heart! But in the box that fennel
> Grows round, are two red eyes that stare like coals.

Perhaps Ransom's best exposition of the sadness of the unresolvable paradox is his sonnet 'Piazza Piece'. An old man desires a young lady. The young lady romantically expects a young man. She is shocked by the sight of the old man. He, outside, looks in at the unattainable; she, within, denying him, awaits the unlikely. The setting is formal, ironically courtly, with vines, trellises and roses. 'I am a gentleman in a dustcoat trying/To make you hear ...' 'I am a lady young in beauty waiting/Until my truelove comes ...' Half to himself, half to her, the old man murmurs,

> 'But see the roses on your trellis dying
> And hear the spectral singing of the moon;
> For I must have my lovely lady soon ...'

She finds his words 'dry and faint as in a dream'. The formal accomplishment is such that the poet is entirely absent, except as a voice, from the poem. The balanced stanzas and argument are so controlled that the implications are vividly clear, showing the 'pluralism of poetry' Ransom often described, as opposed to the monism of scientific exposition. The lady waits for love – and old age, too. The old man longs for youth, and woman too. The imagined incident exists as a fable.

Critics have complained of the emotional meagreness of the poems. But Ransom would not have us easily involved; he does not wish to play with our most accessible emotions, to side-track us on to subjective response. The poem should go whole into our subconscious. The drama of the poems is observed, not participated in. The girls in the poem 'Blue Girls' seems to exist in tapestry – they are distanced: 'Twirling your blue skirts, travelling the sward/Under the towers of your seminary ...'

Tie the white fillets then about your hair
And think no more of what will come to pass
Than bluebirds that go walking on the grass
And chattering on the air.

Innocence is again half the paradox: 'Practise your beauty, blue girls, before it fail ...'

In 'Lady Lost' a bird 'This afternoon, knocked on our windowpane/To be let in from the rain'. It assumes the mysterious quality of the 'lost one':

           has anybody
Injured some fine woman in some dark way
Last night, or yesterday?

Fear illuminates the poems as the ideal subsides and the actual becomes clear, though the ideal hovers always near, making the real more poignant, as in 'Two in August':

In the long ditch of darkness the man walked
Under the hackberry trees where the birds talked
With words too sad and strange to syllable.

Ransom is able, with his prodigious technique, to

syllable those words, or to generate an experience that suggests them. Always present is the sad paradox:

Why should two lovers go frozen apart in fear?
And yet they were, they were.

Thomas Stearns Eliot 1888–1965

Teach us to sit still
Even among these rocks

– 'Ash Wednesday'

The Complete Poems and Plays reveal Eliot's continuity
of development. The persistent, related themes of time,
isolation and quest, expressed through images of sea,
garden, rock, rose and fire, which reflect alienation in a
material desert and desire for regeneration, impress in
their total pattern. A highly personal vision seeking expression in a highly purposed impersonal style produced
Eliot's major poetry. His critical works explore the same
vision. In describing the Metaphysical poets he could be
writing of his own work: 'the poet must become more
and more comprehensive, more allusive, more indirect,
in order to force, to dislocate if necessary, language and
its meaning ...' His vision demanded a radical approach
to the forms and language of poetry. His practice in *The
Waste Land* is mirrored in the introduction to his translation of St-John Perse's *Anabase* (see page 142). Much of
the authority of Eliot's writing is due to his consistency,
the clarity of his development.

Though Eliot spent most of his life in England and
became a British subject, he never ceased to regard himself as an American poet. Interviewed in 1959, he said,

'my poetry has obviously more in common with my distinguished contemporaries in America than with anything written in my generation in England.' The vital influences of his early thought were American: notably Irving Babbitt and George Santayana, two of his tutors at Harvard. From Babbitt he learned that the past can be used not only to discipline the present but also to enrich it. If the technical influences on his early poems were French, the content was in no sense derivative: it reflected a particular experience in a particular American social milieu.

Eliot was born in St Louis, Missouri, the youngest of seven children, and there attended the Smith Academy from 1898 to 1905. He went for one year to Milton Academy, near Boston, and on to Harvard from 1906 to 1910 to study philosophy. From the age of fourteen he had been composing poems 'under the inspiration of Fitzgerald's *Omar Khayyam*', he wrote later; 'very gloomy, and atheistical and despairing quatrains.'

At Harvard he came across Arthur Symons's *The Symbolist Movement in French Literature* which inspired him to read the poems of Jules Laforgue. Laforgue's work helped Eliot to clarify his own style, especially the French poet's particular brand of *vers libre*. Eliot describes it as 'rhyming lines of irregular length, with the rhymes coming in irregular places'. He saw too that Laforgue's loose blank verse resembled that of late Shakespeare, Tourner and Webster. Laforgue's consciously ironic manner suggested to Eliot a tone that served him well:

Now that lilacs are in bloom
She has a bowl of lilacs in her room
And twists one in her fingers while she talks.
'Ah, my friend, you do not know, you do not know
What life is, you who hold it in your hands';
(Slowly twisting the lilac stalks)
'You let it flow from you, you let it flow ...'

Eliot spent a year in Paris at the Sorbonne, studying philosophy, then returned to Harvard from 1911–14. His PhD dissertation was on the philosopher F. H. Bradley and Meinong's *Gegenstandtheorie*. In 1914 he went to Oxford to continue studies, and in 1915 married Vivien Haigh-Wood. For two years he taught in High Wycombe and Highgate.

In 1917 his first book, *Prufrock and Other Observations*, was published by the Egoist Press. Working with H.D. (Hilda Doolittle) as editor of the *Egoist*, he was friendly with the Imagists, and though he did not join the group, he was in sympathy with their attempts to depersonalize the poetic voice, a theme recurrent in his criticism. In *Tradition and the Individual Talent* he wrote, 'The progress of an artist is a continual self-sacrifice, a continual extinction of personality'. The idea of the impersonal was most clearly expressed in his essay on *Hamlet* (1919): 'The only way of expressing emotion in the form of art is by finding an "objective correlative"; in other words, a set of objects, a situation, a chain of events which shall be the formula of that *particular* emotion; such that when the external facts, which must terminate in sensory experience, are given, the emotion is imediately evoked.' In this sense the character of Prufrock is an 'objective correlative' for Eliot's own emotions – though not for Eliot *himself*.

In 1920, for reasons of health, Eliot travelled to Lausanne where he began the first draft of *The Waste Land* (1922), and from 1922 to 1929 he edited the *Criterion* in which that poem first appeared. In 1925 he joined the publishing firm of Faber and Gwyer (later Faber and Faber) and in the same year his first *Collected Poems* appeared.

The year 1927 proved a turning point for Eliot: he became a British subject and was confirmed as a member of the Church of England. His poetry before this time had evoked the sterility of the material desert. After his confirmation, his distaste for the material world was expressed in his writing as ascetic withdrawal, a disencumbering, in order to approach the spiritual quest undiminished. This was the period of *Ash Wednesday* (1930), and as his faith became more firm, so his approach became more didactic, as in the plays *Murder in the Cathedral* (1935), *Family Reunion* (1939), *The Cocktail Party* (1950), and his last major poem, *Four Quartets* (published complete in 1944).

He returned to the United States in 1932 to deliver the Charles Eliot Norton Lectures at Harvard. He was awarded the Nobel Prize for Literature and the Order of Merit in 1948. After the death of his first wife he married Valerie Fletcher in 1957. In his last years, he produced no further major literary works. He died in 1965.

Six years after his death, Valerie Eliot's edition of the *Facsimile and Transcript of the Original Draft of The Waste Land* was published. For years it had been assumed that Eliot's friend Ezra Pound had radically pruned and revised the poem, with Eliot's permission. In fact, the changes Pound introduced were not major, though they were significant. The structure of the poem he left unaltered, advising on specific passages, and Eliot was selective in the advice he took. Eliot called *The Waste Land* 'just a piece of rhythmical grumbling' – a lighthearted dismissal of the greatest poem of its period. The description loosely fits much of the poetry that preceded *The Waste Land*, 'The Love Song of J. Alfred Prufrock' (1915), 'Portrait of a Lady' (1915), 'Gerontion' (1920), the 'Sweeney' poems (1918–20) and other work collected with them. One theme is the sterility of bourgeois culture. But the controlled decorum of the speaking voice takes the poems well beyond local satire. They articulate states of mind, evoke characters determined by, even as they recoil from, the society which encases them. 'I keep my countenance,/I remain self-possessed', a character says in 'Portrait of a Lady'. The speaker, bitterly resigned, is himself one of those he despises. And in 'Gerontion' the old man says:

I have lost my passion: why should I need to keep it
Since what is kept must be adulterated?
I have lost my sight, smell, hearing, taste and touch:
How should I use them for your closer contact?

In 'Morning at the Window' Eliot writes, 'I am aware of
the damp souls of housemaids/Sprouting despondently at
area gates,' and persists in his attempts to evoke this
despondency. The words Prufrock mutters, not expecting
a reply, fall just short of asking the crucial question he
cannot articulate. He wants to ask, but does not know
what or how. It is an aspect of his despondency:

And would it have been worth it, after all
Would it have been worth while,
After the sunsets and the dooryards and the sprinkled streets,
After the novels, after the teacups, after the skirts that trail
        along the floor –
And this, and so much more? –
It is impossible to say just what I mean!

Prufrock, though he cannot escape the sterility, senses the
possibility of escape. 'I have heard the mermaids singing
each to each' – but only momentarily, and he is excluded.
They do not sing for him, and besides, 'human voices
wake us, and we drown.' The world as it is and as the
imagination would have it are different worlds. Occasionally the one suggests the other, but only to emphasize the
inexorability of the world as it is:

I remain self-possessed
Except when a street piano, mechanical and tired
Reiterates some worn-out common song
With the smell of hyacinths across the garden
Recalling things that other people have desired ...

The garden here, as elsewhere, is Eliot's image of the
ideal. But in the early poems there is no accessible garden,
only 'The thousand sordid images/Of which your soul
was constituted'.

Some of the poems written after this period are in formal rhyming quatrains, far from Laforgue's *vers libre*. The influence was Theophile Gautier's and Pound's, for Eliot and Pound reacted together against the extremes to which *vers libre* had been taken. Although the formal poems retain impersonality and irony, Eliot's personal distaste is paradoxically more exposed in the strict style which inhibits the fluidity of his imagery but intensifies the bitterness of his wit:

Sweeney addressed full length to shave
  Broadbottomed, pink from nape to base,
Knows the female temperament
  And wipes the suds around his face.

(The lengthened shadow of a man
  Is history, said Emerson
Who had not seen the silhouette
  Of Sweeney straddled in the sun.)

The apposite reference to Emerson's *Self Reliance* is characteristic of Eliot. It occurs naturally. The context supplies the information we need, in the event that we do not know the source. Eliot frequently and subtly integrated lines and references from other writers in his work, often with such rightness that, when we come across the original source of the quotation, it seems to be borrowed from Eliot rather than the reverse. The notes to *The Waste Land* direct us to various sources – yet the poem supplies an adequate context for the allusions.

The Waste Land is the climax of Eliot's poetry. In five sections, without narrative, it expresses a movement from aridity – literal and metaphorical – towards possible regeneration and peace. It begins in Spring, a time of promise: 'What are the roots that clutch, what branches grow/Out of this stony rubbish?' The city reminds us of Dante's Hell:

Unreal City
Under the brown fog of a winter dawn,
A crowd flowed over London Bridge, so many,
I had not thought death had undone so many.

Futility, ennui are evoked: 'Are you alive, or not? Is there nothing in your head? ... What shall I do now? What shall I do?' Spring has failed in this context. In Autumn the Thames is dreary, stagnant: 'A rat crept softly through the vegetation/Dragging its slimy belly on the bank.' A seduction, without love or even strong lust, mechanical, habitual – is further evidence of sterility:

She turns and looks a moment in the glass,
Hardly aware of her departed lover;
Her brain allows one half-formed thought to pass:
Well now that's done; and I'm glad it's over.'

In the final section of the poem, a literal desert dominates:

If there were water we should stop and drink
Amongst the rock one cannot stop or think
Sweat is dry and feet are in the sand
If there were only water amongst the rock ...

Hope is suggested in a ghostly figure recalling Christ on the road to Emmaeus; but it is a fleeting hope. Cities fragment with the utter dryness:

Falling towers
Jerusalem Athens Alexandria
Vienna London

In an empty broken chapel in the desert, a flash of lightning is seen, 'Then a damp gust/Bringing rain ...' The poem concludes with a Sanskrit prayer.

A general description of the poem is necessarily inadequate. It is not discursive. The meaning cannot be paraphrased or divorced from the expression itself. The best commentary on it are the poems Eliot wrote before it, particularly the *Prufrock* poems, and 'The Hollow Men', written shortly after from rejected portions of *The Waste Land*. Undoubtedly Eliot's masterpiece, *The Waste Land* invites many different readings, as a quest poem, a social document, a vivid evocation of sterility illuminated by faint hope, or an exploration of an inner landscape, a mind:

> I have heard the key
> Turn in the door once and turn once only
> We think of the key, each in his prison
> Thinking of the key, each confirms a prison ...

'The Hollow Men' presented another image of the barren failure of that communication that gives meaning to existence:

> In this last of meeting places
> We grope together
> And avoid speech
> Gathered on this beach of the tumid river.

But Eliot's acceptance of the Anglican faith is reflected in the poem that followed. Spiritual potential is not in this world:

> The right time and the right place are not here
> No place of grace for those who avoid the face
> No time to rejoice for those who walk among noise and deny
>   the voice ...

If in *The Waste Land* Eliot could 'connect nothing with nothing', now he senses a purpose – not yet firmly grasped as faith – in a universal plan. Rejection of the material world brings the spiritual world nearer, the death of the one is the birth of the other. In 'Journey of the Magi' Christ's death and birth are one, the poem ends, 'I should be glad of another death.' 'Ash Wednesday' ends, 'Suffer

me not to be separated/And let my cry come unto Thee.'
In the *Quartets* he writes, 'In my beginning is my end.'

Eliot's style advances towards meditation. There is less
emphasis on impersonality, less reliance on the frightening images of the early poems, and a more direct attempt
to engage the reader. The poet becomes didactic, and with
this more rhetorical:

So here I am, in the middle way, having had twenty years –
Twenty years largely wasted, the years of *l'entre deux guerres* –
Trying to learn to use words ...

Eliot's simplification of style, his desire to communicate
ideas more directly, was an aspect of his attempts to write
verse drama. *Murder in the Cathedral* was written for
Canterbury Cathedral, the theme was the murder of
Thomas à Becket. The play adapts the highly poetic
mode of Greek drama and was written for a particular
audience. With his first commercial play, *The Family
Reunion*, Eliot tried to project his ideas to a wider
audience. It is his most ambitious play and includes some
fine poetry. He presents several plains of characters, each
with its own tone and register of language, from the
ordinary household to characters on a quest, potential
saints:

I only looked through the little door
When the sun was shining on the rose-garden
And heard in the distance tiny voices
And then a black raven flew over.

Yet the play has structural faults, partly because it ad-
heres too closely to its Greek model, *The Eumenides*. A
second play in this ambitious medium might have proved
an ideal vehicle for Eliot's ideas. Instead, he chose to
flatten his dramatic verse almost to prose and set his next
play – *The Cocktail Party*, based on the Greek theme of
Alcestis – as a drawing-room comedy with strong philosophical and religious overtones. The poetic language was
simplified – almost forfeited – in the service of complex

ideas. Spiritual fulfilment – on various levels, from the social to the religious, including martyrdom – is the theme.

If the verse was flattened in *The Cocktail Party*, the intellectual content was simplified in Eliot's last two plays. He nods in the direction of religion in *The Confidential Clerk* and *The Elder Statesman*. The poetry and the suggestive ideas are gone.

Four Quartets was Eliot's last major work of poetry. He regarded them as his finest, 'and I'd like to feel they get better as they go on.' Eliot's technical control is masterly – so evidently secure that we become aware of it, of the present artificer with his didactic burden, and of the finally arbitrary structure. It is as if, having constructed a philosophy, he now constructs a poetic framework to put it in and is convincing himself that the philosophy and the poetry fit together. They do – but at the cost of the intensity that pervaded his earlier poetry. The *Quartets* present meditations and variations on the movement of time, the ephemerality of the material world, the need to go beyond it, to achieve a spiritual and artistic unity through intercession. Each *Quartet* is associated with an element: air, earth, water and fire; and the five movements of each *Quartet* express, on a musical principle, parallels with the other quartets. The first 'movements' explore aspects of time, death and rebirth within time; the second suggest the vain ephemerality of the material world; the third begin journeys or quests; the fourth, in the manner of scherzos, are lyrical intercessions; and the last movements record achieved goals. Such a schematic presentation of the overall structure is of course inadequate. Considerable subtlety and variation are brought to bear. Fine passages occur, particularly in the lyrical movements. In 'Burnt Norton' Eliot writes.

Time and the bell have buried the day
The black cloud carries the sun away.

Will the sunflower turn to us, will the clematis
Stray down, bend to us: tendril and spray
Clutch and cling?

In 'Little Gidding', the second section includes the lines:

Ash on an old man's sleeve
Is all the ash burnt roses leave.
Dust in air suspended
Marks the place where a story ended ...

But Eliot's desire to communicate finished ideas of some complexity leads him into prosaic, explanatory verse. A disarming didactic tone prevents the *poetry* from containing his meanings: rather, the poetry decorates the meaning, and Eliot apologizes for it:

That was a way of putting it – not very satisfactory:
A periphrastic study in a worn-out poetical fashion,
Leaving one still with the intolerable wrestle
With words and meanings. The poetry does not matter.

But it does: and the devil has the best tunes in *The Waste Land*, where the intolerable wrestle is not with local words and meanings but with an intractable vision, surprising, shocking, painful, but poetically vivid:

A woman drew her long black hair out tight
And fiddled whisper music on those strings
And bats with baby faces in the violet light
Whistled, and beat their wings ...

This is the power on which, securely, Eliot's greatness rests.

Conrad Aiken 1889–1974

Or say that in the middle comes a music
Suddenly out of silence, and delight
Brings all that chaos to one mood of wonder;
A seed of fire, fallen in a tinder world;
And instantly the whirling darkness fills
With conflagration ...

– *Preludes for Memnon*

In a radio talk, Conrad Aiken spoke of poetry 'as the vanguard of man's consciousness, as it always has been, once again, by trial and loss, finding out its own way, or trying to, to bring into consciousness every scrap of knowledge, from whatever field, and no matter how uncompromisingly unpoetic or antipoetic it might seem to be.' He was describing the inclusive ambitions of his own poetry. Glancing through Aiken's *Selected Poems*, we are not surprised by variety of mood, form or style – and yet there is a gradual and clear progression towards the sort of poetry he wished to write. He took the solipsistic course: as his *own* realm of consciousness expanded, so did the themes of his poetry. This was the natural development for his imagination. Liberal thought and an early interest in the 'new psychology' of Freud were in his background. This, and a belief in the high purpose of poetry – 'no mere decorative toy, no amusement ... the advance guard in man's quest for the knowable' – produced a poetry of high integrity, not diminished by its persistent subjectivity.

Aiken's grandfather was William James Potter, one of the great liberal Unitarians of the nineteenth century who had readily assimilated Darwin's *The Origin of Species* and adjusted his conscience accordingly. He was a founder of the Free Religious Association. Conrad, born in 1889, was raised, he tells us, 'with no beliefs, or none of a dogmatic sort. Wasn't it enough that the world was beautiful, terrible, astonishing, even incredible?' He certainly experienced the terrible aspects early in his life: his father killed his mother, then committed suicide. Conrad was moved from Savannah, Georgia, his birthplace, to live with relatives in New Bedford, Massachusetts.

He went to Harvard and was in the class which included T. S. Eliot, Walter Lippmann, and Van Wyck Brooks. He graduated in 1912. From 1915 onwards he became what he describes as 'a regular and pretty energetic critic of American poetry ... contributing editor of *The Dial*, American correspondent for the *Athenaeum* in London and *The London Mercury*.' His first volume of criticism, *Scepticisms* (1919), included his notable preface 'Apologia Pro Specie Sua' in which he argued that dispassionate judgement was a chimera in literary appreciation because the various writers of the new American poetry – Frost, Robinson, Masters, the Imagists, Pound, Eliot and the others – were urging poetry, by way of polemic and example, to develop in their own particular preferred direction. Aiken's regular reviews and articles about American poetry led both Marianne Moore and I. A. Richards to agree that he was the most perceptive reviewer of new poetry in the English language to have emerged in the twentieth century.

He moved to England for a time, living in 1923 in Rye, Sussex, where he taught creative arts, but later he returned to America, drawn by what he called 'ancestral roots'. His awareness of the heritage of Whitman, Melville, Dickinson, Twain, Emerson, Thoreau, Hawthorne, Poe and Henry James sharpened. Critically, he 'discovered' Emily Dickinson in an introductory essay to his selection of her poems in 1924. Aiken reported that Pound and Eliot both disapproved.

Important in Aiken's own creative development was Trumbull Stickney (1874–1904), an American poet whose style he saw as the link between Whitman and the fragmented vision of the modernists: 'the first sounding of the "modern note", the abandonment of the oratorical or grandiose for a more flexible and colloquial tone of voice, which, nevertheless, when occasion demanded, could rise to the full *vox humana* of the highest poetic speech', he wrote. He also acknowledged his debt to John Masefield and Francis Thompson. Perhaps Aiken was equally indebted to music and the lessons it taught him by its analogy to poetry. He had an intense love of music, and many of his early works aspired to its effects – there were 'Tone-Poems' and 'Symphonies' which were later gathered in his book *The Divine Pilgrim*. Aiken developed a highly flexible style in which the form follows from the theme without conscious effort or adjustment. Lines, images, and words flow together and apart with a gentle fluidity – like a stream following the poet's consciousness – a consciousness which widened impressively through his fifty years as a poet.

George Santayana's lectures at Harvard left a deep mark on Aiken, especially the series on 'Three Philosophical Poets' – Lucretius, Dante and Goethe. This, and his interest in the psychologists Freud, Jung and Adler, led him to treat human consciousness, in particular his own, with great attention. The fragmentation of the mind is dealt with in the final section of *The Divine Pilgrim* in particular. It is the general purpose of his writing to bring 'all that chaos to one mood of wonder.'

In his 'Palimpsest: The Deceitful Portrait', for example, he writes with some awe:

We move in crowds, we flow and talk together,
Seeing so many eyes and hands and faces,
So many mouths, and all with secret meanings, –
Yet know so little of them; only seeing
The small bright circle of our consciousness,
Beyond which lies the dark ...

He is curious 'To learn what ghosts are there'. In 'No, I Shall Not Say' he hints at ways of telling the 'secret meanings':

... if I tell at all, I shall tell in silence.
I'll say – my childhood broke through chords of music
– Or were they chords of sun? – wherein fell shadows,
Or silences ...

The vagaries of the mind offer no certainties, no points of rest: they only hint at their deeper content. Aiken is a master of those vagaries. His *Preludes* are the height of his individual style and the centre of his work.

There are two books: *Preludes for Memnon* and *Time in the Rock* subtitled respectively *Preludes to Attitude* and *Preludes to Definition*. They were composed separately in 1931 and 1936, though the first of the *Memnon* poems were begun in 1927. As Aiken pointed out in his preface, they were meant to be taken together: 'as *Blue Voyage* [his novel] was my attempt in the guise of fiction to make a statement of my position, or attitude, in mid-career, a filling-out, as it were, of the customs declaration, so this poem and its successor, *Time in the Rock*, which together constitute one unit, were to make a parallel statement in verse.' Others of his poems, he says, had attempted this: 'Psychomachia', 'King Borborigmi', 'Electra', 'Sea Holly', and 'Sound of Breaking', but 'The preludes were planned to be an all-out effort at a probing of the self-in-relation-to-the-world, the formation of a

new *Weltanschaung.*' They were, further, complementary to his autobiographical prose work *Ushant*.

The *Preludes* are generally in pentameters and, as in
music, ideas or themes are introduced, dropped, re-
introduced and developed in conjunction with other
themes. They are 'an exploration of the fragmented ego,
and a celebration of it and of the extraordinary world in
which it *finds* itself, as well.' There are over a hundred
and fifty preludes. Richly attractive, the writing compels
one to read on, but it maintains such a pitch that, eventually, the reader finds it monotonous:

Here are the bickerings of the inconsequential,
The chatterings of the ridiculous, the iterations
Of the meaningless. Memory, like a juggler,
Tosses its colored balls into the light, and again
Receives them into darkness ...

At times, the doctrine of the self intrudes in its complexity so that Aiken mistrusts the poem and becomes directly
didactic, leading us by the hand: 'Come, it is time to
move':

Count the bright minutes; pick a flower and smell it;
Observe the lights and shadows; theorize
Magnificently of life and death; propound
The subtle thesis of pure consciousness ...

He would lead himself, as well as us:

Jesus is not the spokesman of the Lord:
Confucius neither, nor Nietzsche, no, nor Blake;
But you yourself ...

The point is too sharply prosaic. It halts one in the tracks
of discovery. Much better the vagaries, the silences, the
music: 'Music will more nimbly move/than quick wit
can order word'; 'Let us in joy, let us in love,/surrender
speech to music':

But verses can never say these things;
only in music may be heard
the subtle touching of such strings,
never in word.

When Aiken lived in England he struck up a friendship
with John Gould Fletcher, one of the Imagists who had
experimented with 'polyphonic prose'. This 'form' was
to have 'orchestral qualities'. Fletcher's poems too made
forays into the world of what he called 'the emotional
relations that exist between form, colour and sound.' He
too had written verse 'symphonies', though they lacked
the subtleties of Aiken's best tones and key-changes. Both
poets admired Whitman but tempered this admiration
with the strong, controlled tones of Poe, and his insistence
on the power of music and psychology in conjunction.

Aiken, having chosen the United States as his home
and the American tradition as his tradition, became one
of America's most prolific writers. *Earth Triumphant*
(1914) was his first collection of poems, *The Morning
Song of Lord Zero* (1963) his last which, with his *Selected
Poems* (1929) and his *Collected Poems* (1953) include his
major work. He received a number of awards: the Pulitzer Prize, the Shelley Memorial Award, the National
Book Award for Poetry, the Bollingen Prize, and the
Gold Medal for Poetry.

The longer poems are the best, despite the cloying
intensity of rhetoric. The shorter poems are too tidily
drawn together, their conclusions often appear pat. 'The
Sound of Breaking' ends,

> It is a sound
Of everlasting grief, the sound of weeping,
The sound of disaster and misery, the sound
Of passionate heartbreak at the centre of the world.

In the longer poems, the form is flexible, changing subtly
with the themes as they evolve:

No language leaps this chasm like a lightning:
Here is no message of assuagement, blown
From Ecuador to Greenland; here is only

A trumpet blast, that calls dead men to arms;
The granite's pity for the cloud; the whisper
Of time to space.

Archibald MacLeish born 1892

This stranger in my blood, my skin,
can I command him? Will he stand
when I say stand? Come out? Go in?
Do anything?

– 'Tyrant of Syracuse'

Archibald MacLeish's poetry fits into no easy category.
His work ranges from the finely lyrical:

And here face downward in the sun
To feel how swift how secretly
The shadow of the night comes on ...

to the political, sentimental, and philosophical. In each
mode MacLeish writes with authority. A tough-minded
optimism characterizes even his near-nihilistic exercises –
a genuine and uncompromising optimism. Those critics
who suggest the poems are 'shallow' disbelieve the *poet*,
not the poems.

His varied life, rich in incident, is reflected in the
verse, and his wide experience gives his poems the asset
of diversity of form and content, the liability at times of
dissipation of intensity.

He was born at Glencoe, Illinois, a suburb of Chicago,
in 1892. After attending Hotchkiss School he went to
Yale University, graduating at the age of twenty-four.

He entered Harvard Law School. A year later he married and in 1919 graduated from Harvard, having served in France in World War I, first in a hospital unit and then in field artillery. On his return he taught law at Harvard and practised in Boston until 1923 when he decided to live in France.

He had already published *Songs for a Summer's Day* (1915), a cycle of sonnets, and had a prize poem published by Yale University Press. In 1917 his first full collection, *Tower of Ivory*, appeared, and during his period as an expatriate he wrote *The Happy Marriage* (1924), *The Pot of Earth* (1925), *Streets in the Moon* (1926), a verse play called *Nobodaddy* (1926) and *The Hamlet of A. MacLeish* (1928). These books were weakened by un-assimilated influences, notably of Pound, Eliot and the French symbolists. His concern with attitudes to contemporary life and the effect of that life on the creative artist began to develop. However, it does not become sufficiently vital in the poetry to conceal a certain superficiality of technique.

He returned to the United States in time for the Depression, and during the ten years that followed he worked towards a poetic diction closer to the diction of common speech in its various registers.

In 1929 he travelled to Mexico to gather material for his epic poem *Conquistador* (1932), which was awarded the Pulitzer Prize and earned for MacLeish the first of a number of honorary degrees. He worked for the magazine *Fortune* and from 1939 to 1944 was Librarian of Congress. His journalistic work involved wide travel in the United States and he contributed articles on political and social topics to *Fortune*. During the period, he wrote an attack on his contemporaries, *The Irresponsibles* (1940), chastising them for their conscious withdrawal from what he saw as their social responsibilities. This theme he developed further in *Poetry and Experience* (1961), where he advocated a poetry that would serve society.

In his long poem, *Frescoes for Mr Rockefeller's City* (1933), he satirized the excesses of capitalism. Another verse play, *Panic* (1935), followed, and a further collection of poems, *Public Speech* (1936). Distressed at American indifference to the spread of fascism in Europe, he pioneered the radio verse play – in, for example, *The Fall of the City* (1937) – attempting didactically to alert his fellow countrymen. Volumes of verse and plays followed in quick succession, and during the World War II he served as Assistant Secretary of State under F. D. Roosevelt. In 1945 he was a member of the delegation which founded UNESCO. From 1949 to 1962 he was Boylston Professor of Rhetoric and Oratory at Harvard. His own verse began to return from its didactic excesses to a more lyrical vein – the didacticism was concentrated more in his verse plays, notably *J.B.* (1958) in which he develops the Job story in the context of modern American business, God and Satan working out their differences through a capitalist Job called *J.B.* His *Collected Poems 1917–1952* won the Pulitzer Prize, the Bollingen Award and the National Book Award. Later collections have included *Songs for Eve* (1954) and *The Wild Old Wicked Man and Other Poems* (1968).

Dedicated to a life of public service, his poetry was similarly committed. The danger was that his public poetry, rhetorically didactic, often simplified major issues to communicate them, and hence communicated them only partially, emotively. A tendency to simplify undermines the literary impact of his poetry. At his best in the lyrical vein, in poems such as 'You, Andrew Marvell', his public poems – 'Speech to those Who Say Comrade' for instance – are lamed by their rhetoric. He is better as a contemplative. The public poems have lost impact at least in part because the matter has dated.

MacLeish's most famous lines, 'A poem should not mean / But be', occur in his 'Ars Poetica' which itself paradoxically invites us to interpret its meaning. There is a sense in which many of the poems have been arbitrarily cast as poetry – they invite paraphrase, they work up a prose argument:

Even the small spark of pride
That taught the tyrant once is dark
Where gunfire rules the starving street
And justice cheats the dead of horror.

These lines from 'Pole Star for This Year' display the germ of an idea rather than an image: the idea is developed over twelve stanzas. The 'meaning' is detachable from the poetry; poetic directness is forfeited to prosaic clarity of logic.

His most popular poem, 'The End of the World', presents a clear meaning, and yet eludes paraphrase. The metaphor contains the complex emotions as well as the thought behind the poem – it is not decorative. In other words, the meaning is implicit, not explicit. It is a short poem/sonnet. During a circus act the top suddenly blows off the tent:

And there, there overhead, there, there, hung over
Those thousands of white faces, those dazed eyes,
There in the artless dark the poise, the hover,
There with vast wings across the canceled skies,
There in the sudden blackness the black pall
Of nothing, nothing, nothing – nothing at all.

The terror of 'canceled skies' lifts the repetitive rhetoric with it.

Repetition is a mannerism which does not always serve MacLeish well, in other poems producing a retarding effect, apparently due to lack of intensity. In 'How The River Ninfa Runs Through The Ruined Town Beneath The Lime Quarry' we read:

ages ago, ages ago . . .
nobody's shadow now, nobody's shadow . . .
nobody knows anymore now, nobody . . .

and in 'Calypso's Island': 'she will grow grey, grow
older, / Grey and older ...'

But in his return to the lyrical tone in his later volumes,
he achieves something of a rebirth, a style varied and
ample for less pressingly social, more vitally poetic experiences. In 'La Foce' he ponders the fact of being
seventy:

Why grow older in a Tuscan spring
where everything,
follies and flowers, loves and leaves,
grows younger and the loam conceives
and even the slow venerable sun
splashes in the water spills
and hills
invent again the new
first blue?

MacLeish's later, freer lyric style, though its images sometimes seem chosen more for sound than any more pressing
reason, works well until he feels constrained to moralize
or interpret. Then the poems come to mean, not be:

Only one small circling fly
remembers that the world goes by
and we go with it
                he and I.

The moral is, sadly, arbitrarily drawn. But his best
poems, including the recent 'Old Man's Journey', defy
complete interpretation and yet hold a complex *poetic*
clarity to which his public poetry – where we are conscious of the 'stranger' in 'his blood' – does not aspire.

e. e. cummings 1894–1962

i thank You God for most this amazing
day: for the leaping greenly spirits of trees
and a blue true dream of sky; and for everything
which is natural which is infinite which is yes

– 'i thank You God'

There are two complementary impulses in e. e. cummings's poetry: expressions of the joy of 'eternal us' now;
and biting satire, against urban society in particular – the
'busy monster, manunkind' as he calls it:

> of you i
> sing: land of Abraham Lincoln and Lydia E. Pinkham,*
> land above all of Just Add Hot Water And Serve ...

Variations on these themes in an idosyncratic style sustain the numerous collections of poems that have made
Cummings one of the most popular 'modernist' poets.

Edward Estlin Cummings was born in Cambridge,
Massachusetts. His father had begun a career as a teacher
of English at Harvard but later became a Unitarian
minister at the Old South Church in Boston. Edward
himself graduated from Harvard in 1916. The rebel in
him was already developing. His distrust of bureaucracy

---

*A patent medicine to soothe menstrual pain (from 'Poem, or
Beauty Hurts Mr. Vinal').

and its treatment of the individual was confirmed during World War I when he served as a volunteer with the Norton Harjes Ambulance Service in France (1917). A French censor objected to passages in his letters and he found himself, through grotesque misunderstandings, imprisoned in a French detention camp. His autobiographical prose work *The Enormous Room* (1922) records this experience. The book is interesting for its resolute, yet humorous, individualism; and its highly personal idiomatic style prefigures his poetic language: 'I will get upon the soonness of the train and ride into the now of Paris.'

He lived in Paris where he painted, studied art, and wrote poetry, from 1920 to 1924. His first book of poems, *Tulips and Chimneys* (1923), appeared at this time. It is a lyrical and rather sentimental book, more orthodox in style than the later collections. In it there are fewer Chimneys and more Tulips. The poems toy with techniques of the past:

If she a little turn her head
i know that i am wholly dead:
nor ever did on such a throat
the lips of Tristram slowly dote,
La beale Isoud whose leman was.

Cummings never lost sight of the Tudor lyric form which he adapted in his own sensuous style. Even his last book, *73 Poems* (1963) retains the style:

but from this endless end
of briefer each our briefer bliss –
where seeing eyes go blind
(where lips forget to kiss)
where everything's nothing
– arise, my soul; and sing

In the first book experiments with typography – for which Cummings became famous – began:

> ... when over my head a
>
> shooting
> star
> Bur   s
>   (t
>   into a stale shriek
> like an alarm clock)

The poem behind the idiosyncratic typography can – at this stage – still be read aloud as a poem. The gaps, like musical notation, help the reader to pause, to visualize the verb 'burst'. The parenthesis gently severs the final 't' from the word. On the page, the fragmentation implies more. The effect of the gaps and the brackets visually substantiates (though it hardly extends) the meaning. In the later books, the eccentricities are only for the eye. In *No Thanks* (1935), for example, a poem depicts a grasshopper's leap across the page. The insect – as letters in its name – is disorganized after a leap, a landing, and a stretch ready for another leap:

>   r-p-o-p-h-e-s-s-a-g-r
>   who
> a)s w(e loo)k

With effort the insect gathers itself together and begins another leap:

> aThe): l
>   eA
>   !p:

The letters come to earth again, as 'grasshopper', followed by a semicolon since the insect will take a further leap: 'grasshopper;'.

The philosopher-poet T. E. Hulme whose thought and poems lie behind Imagism foresaw this kind of poetry at the turn of the century when he prophesied: 'this new verse resembles sculpture rather than music. It builds

up a plastic image which it hands over to the reader.'
It works best when the visual effect does more than sub-
stantiate the tensions implicit in the language, extends
the meanings. Often, however, the typography in Cummings's poetry replaces in its tensions vital linguistic
tensions.

Cummings became known for his eccentric style. Most
easily recognizable was his suppression of the capital
letter and his use of punctuation to *mean* in itself, rather
than to act merely as a formal adjunct to the language.
He was called 'Mr Lowercase Highbrow' and gave himself the lowercase name e. e. cummings. His many collections played the same game time and again. They include;
& (1925), *is 5* (1926), *Viva* (1931), *No Thanks* (1935), *1 × 1*
(1944), *XAIPE* (1950), *95 Poems* (1958) and the posthumous *73 Poems* (1963).

His work was not confined to poetry. Several one-man
shows of his paintings were held, and he wrote two
allegorical plays, *Him* (1927) and *Santa Claus* (1946) and
a travel book about Russia, *EIMI* (1933). He prepared
a ballet, *Tom* (1935), which satirizes *Uncle Tom's Cabin*.
In 1925 he won the *Dial* Award, and his *Poems 1923–
1954* (1954) earned him a National Book Award Citation
and later the Bollingen Prize. In 1952–3 he delivered the
Charles Eliot Norton lectures at Harvard, calling them
Six Non-Lectures; and *CIOPW* (1931) collects some of
his drawings and paintings in book form. After he returned from Paris he settled in Greenwich Village and
at his New Hampshire farm. He died in 1962.

His *Poems 1923–1954* contains a characteristic introduction in which the two dominant themes of his poems
are expressed in terms of two different kinds of people,
'us' and 'mostpeople'. 'The poems to come are for you
and for me and are not for mostpeople. – it's no use
trying to pretend that mostpeople and ourselves are
alike ... You and I are human beings; mostpeople are
snobs ...' 'Life, for eternal us, is now; ... Life, for most-

people, simply isn't.' For 'eternal us' Cummings wrote
his sonnets, lyrics, and sensuous Catullan lyrics:

O It's Nice To Get Up In, the slipshop mucous kiss
of her riant belly's fooling bore
– When The Sun Begins To (with a phrasing crease
of hot subliminal lips, as if a score
of youngest angels suddenly should stretch neat necks
just to see how always squirms
the skilful mystery of Hell) me suddenly

grips in chuckles of supreme sex.

'Mostpeople' are the butt of his satires, biting and funny.
Using traditional stanzas he lampoons the American
response to the Hungarian Uprising:

so rah-rah-rah democracy
let's all be as thankful as hell
and bury the statue of liberty
(because it begins to smell)

More idiosyncratically, he writes,

LISN bud LISN

       dem
       gud
       am
       lidl yelluh bas
       tuds weer goin

duhSIVILEYzum

Because the witty patterning in spaces and punctuation
has approximation to the accents and inflections of common speech, the satires have at their best a fresh, stinging
quality. The techniques accent the satire, while they
normally fail to disguise the soft centre, the intellectual
thinness and sentimentality, of his all-embracing love
poems, with their often repeated motifs of April, Spring,
flowers and freshness. The critic F. O. Matthieson des-

cribed Cummings in a telling phrase: 'romantic anarch-ist'. He was fully in the New England tradition of individualism, scepticism of authority, and transcenden-talism. Cummings saw the poem as an inspired moment, breaking through the repressive surface. That surface is clear enough – it is never quite as clear what Cummings is escaping *to.*

Hart Crane 1899–1932

> ... knowing us in thrall
> To that deep wonderment, our native clay ...

– The Bridge

Hart Crane's poetry is so attuned to 'that deep wonderment, our native clay' that, although his work is widely read abroad, his style is a clear product of his personal and national affinities. He developed in the Transcendental tradition but was unable to live a retiring life. His mother, an ardent Christian Scientist, influenced him early in life to a belief that the individual spirit should rise above the secondary material world and attempt to attain a primary reality through visionary imagination. His spirit struggled, but physically he remained securely bound to the secondary world. No Walden Pond for him: he was caught in a cruel psychological paradox. With a limited formal education, he found himself at the age of seventeen in a world full of unemployment. His parents had long been separated. He was a homosexual and became an alcoholic. He suffered from fits of optimism followed by fits of abject despair. The paradox was left unresolved with his suicide (1932) when he was thirty-three.

His letters, though they seldom allude to national events, are intensely engaged with literary matters. It is this intense intellectual restlessness that informs his poetry with too many, sometimes conflicting, metaphors. He seems to take life and poetry at the full, desperately, before the next despair.

Hart Crane was born in Garretsville, Ohio, the only child of wealthy parents who separated by the time he was ten. As a child he was given to daydreaming and dressing up; all his life memories of what he called in 'Quaker Hill' 'the curse of sundered parentage' endured. He left school in Cleveland, Ohio, when he was seventeen.

At school he had begun to write poetry. In the earliest preserved poems there is the richness of metaphor and imagery that became both the power and the obscurity of his mature work:

The anxious milk-blood in the veins of the earth,
That strives long and quiet to sever the girth
Of greenery ...

He worked at odd jobs for several years – he was a shop assistant, an advertising copywriter in New York, among other things. Brief bouts of working at unsuitable jobs were interspersed with travel – alone or with his mother – to Europe, Cuba, and elsewhere. In 1919 he was forced by circumstances to accept a job in a store in Akron from his father, with whom he had nothing in common. It did not last long.

He finally settled in New York in 1920 to try to live as a poet, under the patronage of the banker Otto Kahn. He completed his first major long poem, 'For the Marriage of Faustus and Helen', in 1923, and it was included in his first collection, *White Buildings* (1926). Kahn lent him money so that he could write *The Bridge*. He went to the Isle of Pines, off Cuba, where within a few weeks he wrote a number of fine lyrics and the better parts of *The Bridge*. For two desperate years he wrote nothing. He went to Los Angeles, and then to France for another unproductive season. In the autumn of 1929 he returned to the United States and, by strength of will rather than inspiration, completed *The Bridge*. Awarded a Guggenheim Fellowship, in 1931 he travelled to Mexico to plan an epic poem about Montezuma, but his personal disintegration was almost complete. He wrote some short poems which form 'Key West: An Island Sheaf', and 'The Broken Tower':

The bell-rope that gathers God at dawn
Dispatches me as though I dropped down the knell
Of a spent day – to wander the cathedral lawn
From pit to crucifix, feet chill on steps from hell.

His sense of failure was total, in spite of his first full relationship with a woman in 1932. Returning to the United States from Mexico on the SS *Orizaba,* he disappeared overboard on April 27, 1932.

His early poetry attests to his close reading of the rich language of Shakespeare, Webster and Marlowe, who influenced his later brilliant metaphorical style. He was drawn, too, to Jules Laforgue and his use of the ironic tone. He translated Laforgue's 'Locutions des Pierrots', and the influence of the symbolist master is evident in 'Chaplinesque' and 'Black Tambourine'. In 'Chaplinesque' he writes,

We make our meek adjustments,
Contented with such random consolations
As the wind deposits
In slithers and too ample pockets.

But the course he kept was positive: to affirm by means of a Jacobean richness of language all that Eliot had denied to life in *The Waste Land*. In 1923 he wrote in a letter, 'I take Eliot as a point of departure toward an almost complete reverse of direction. His pessimism is amply justified, in his case. But I would apply as much of his erudition and technique as I can absorb and assemble toward a more positive, or (if I must put it so in a sceptical age) ecstatic goal.'

Crane's psychological, rather than stylistic, guide was Whitman:

> Yes, Walt,
> Afoot again, and onward without halt, –
> Not soon, nor suddenly, – No, never to let go
>   My hand
>   in yours,
>   Walt Whitman –
>
>   so –

And Melville suggested to him a rich symbolic use of the sea and sea imagery. He used it powerfully in the 'Voyages' sequence in *White Buildings*:

> – And yet this great wink of eternity,
> Of rimless floods, unfettered leewardings,
> Samite sheeted ...

His approach to the ecstatic goal of transcending the secondary world takes the form of conscious optimism in 'The Marriage of Faustus and Helen'. The three sections of the poem depict in modern terms Faustus, 'the symbol of myself, the poetic or imaginative man of all times' remaining true to Helen, 'the abstract sense of beauty'. It culminates in an emphatic optimism, as it were against the odds:

> Distinctly praise the years, whose volatile
> Blamed bleeding hands extend and thresh the height
> The imagination spans beyond despair,
> Outpacing bargain, vocable and prayer.

Language, structure and imagery are difficult to the point of obscurity. In an essay, 'General Aims and Theories', Crane attempted to explain. His attempt was to build a bridge between classic experience and many 'divergent realities of our seething, confused cosmos of today ... So I found "Helen" sitting in a street car; the Dionysian revels of her court and her seduction were transferred to a Metropolitan roof garden with a jazz orchestra; and the *katharsis* of the fall of Troy I saw approximated in the recent World War.'

He justifies the obscurities of language and metaphor by describing the construction of the poem as 'raised on the organic principle of a "logic of metaphor" '. He implies that the force of metaphor precedes, is more immediate than, logical thought, giving us an experience rather than an idea. Metaphor has its own logic distinct from the logic of ideas. Hence, using an example from the poem, he explains, 'the speed and tense altitude of an aeroplane are much better suggested by the idea of "nimble blue plateaus" – *implying* the aeroplane and its speed against a contrast of stationary elevated earth.' He concludes the essay, 'Language has built towers and bridges, but itself is inevitably as fluid as always.' His explications illuminate but do not resolve the basic difficulty of the clotted imagery; and Crane omits reference to the aural resonance which defies explanation and yet sustains the poem, giving a *sense* of coherence even in the most obscure passages and hinting at the ecstatic goal.

'Voyages' in *White Buildings* is a six-poem sequence moving towards a transcendent conclusion – 'There's/ Nothing like this in the world'. The last section celebrates – the ecstasy must be timeless, not limited to the world of fact but, as it were, metaphysical, transmuted in the realm of imagination:

The imaged Word, it is, that holds
Hushed willows anchored in its glow.
It is the unbetrayable reply
Whose accent no farewell can know.

The importance that *The Bridge* had for Crane is clear from his letters. He compares it in historical and cultural scope to the *Aeneid*: 'It is at least a symphony with an epic theme', and 'as complicated in its structure and inference as *The Waste Land*.' Some critics have regarded it as a romantic folly; but clearly by this work Crane's final stature must be judged. Indeed, he wished it so.

Part of the finale of the poem was written first. To Crane the design was already clear. He thought of it as a 'mystical synthesis of "America"'; 'History and fact, location etc., all have to be transfigured into abstract form that would almost function independently of its subject matter.' Brooklyn Bridge becomes an emblem for hope, the future, America's journey to 'Atlantis'. The journey invokes persons and recalls places in American legend and history. Columbus, Pocahontas, Rip Van Winkle, Whitman, Melville, Poe, and others appear. 'The Tunnel' section expresses disillusion and the traditional epic descent to Hell before emergence into a bright Atlantis. '– One Song, one Bridge of Fire! Is it Cathay ... ?'

In this 'Proem: To Brooklyn Bridge', Crane practises a principle which he developed in his essay 'Modern Poetry': 'Unless poetry can absorb the machine, i.e. *acclimatize* it as naturally as trees' then 'poetry has failed of its full contemporary function.' After the 'Proem', which does indeed attempt to acclimatize the machine, comes the first section, 'Ave Maria'. In it, Columbus, inspired by the ideal of uniting East and West, reaching Cathay by the Western Route, is seen: 'It is morning there –/O where our Indian emperies lie revealed,/Yet lost, all, let this keel one instant yield!' New lands, now, must be discovered, the modern bridge must lead to the unexplored world of the imagination, 'still one shore beyond desire!'

In the second section, 'Powhatan's Daughter', the symbolic 'body of America', the pure Pocahontas, is revealed. The five sub-sections develop the image of a journey from New York's impoverishing materialism to the ideal West, from the present to the past (and implicit future). In the process, the protagonist identifies with Pocahontas's lover. Through his own sacrifice at the stake he is reborn for the spiritual journey: 'Wrapped in that fire, I saw more escorts wake/– Flickering, sprint up the hill groins like a tide.'

'Cutty Sark', the third section, evokes the nineteenth-century clipper ships sailing to Cathay, 'scarfed of foam, their bellies veered green esplanades,/locked in wind-humors, ran their eastings down.' The fourth section features the airman as the successor of the seaman, 'Through sparkling visibility, outspread, unsleeping,/ Wings clip the last peripheries of light.'

In the fifth section there are 'Three Songs' with the theme of woman, 'the body of America'. The sixth section, 'Quaker Hill', with autobiographical material, laments the decay of the integrity of New England values: 'This was the Promised Land.'

The descent into Hell in 'The Tunnel' is portrayed symbolically as a descent into the New York underground. 'Whose head is swinging from the swollen strap?/Whose body smokes along the bitten rails?' The tortured souls are no less damned for being fellow-citizens, experiencing the daily indignity of the routine. The section ends – echoing Eliot:

Kiss of our agony Thou gatherest,
            O Hand of Fire
                 gatherest –

The poem gropes outward for the open air, and in the last section, 'Atlantis', the bridge is completed:

O Thou steeled Cognizance whose leap commits
The agile precincts of the lark's return;
Within whose lariat sweep encinctured sing
In single chrysalis the many twain ...

Striving for epic effect, *The Bridge* remains one of the most difficult poems in the language. Flawed, particularly in those passages written with great effort after an unproductive period – 'Indiana', 'Cape Hatteras', and

'Quaker Hill' – its idealism and the ecstasy of its optimism, at times forced, but often compelling, are hardly rivalled in American poetry. It is a flawed masterpiece. The epic and the romantic impulses seem at variance. Only a thousand lines in length, the flaws are serious: obscurity, labouredness, and a degree of dishonesty, perhaps, in the forced optimism. But read aloud it carries in its rhythms the tension of its idealistic ambitions and a strong conviction in the importance of the attempt:

– One Song, one Bridge of Fire! Is it Cathay,
Now pity steeps the grass and rainbows ring
The serpent with the eagle in the leaves ... ?
Whispers antiphonal in azure swing.

Crane produced little further verse in his last two years. He was burned out with the effort of *The Bridge*. But 'The Broken Tower' raises a poignant question:

My word I poured. But was it cognate, scored
Of that tribunal monarch of the air
Whose thigh embronzes earth, strokes crystal Word
In wounds pledged once to hope – cleft to despair?

Allen Tate 1899–1979

> ... tasseling corn,
> Fat beans, grapes sweeter than muscadine
> Rot on the vine: in that land were we born.
>
> – 'The Mediterranean'

Tate's poetry often expresses the stagnation of a potentially rich life, fragmentation due to industrialism and
mechanization. If we could return to past rural tradition,
live closer to nature, those 'grapes sweeter than musca-
dine' would not rot on the vine. But in 'Aeneas in
Washington' he writes,

> There was a time when the young eyes were slow,
> Their flame steady beyond the firstling fire,
> I stood in the rain, far from home at nightfall
> By the Potomac, the great Dome lit the water,
> The city my blood had built I knew no more
> While the screech owl whistled his new delight
> Consecutively dark.

This attitude, natural in a man of Tate's sensibility and
upbringing, was fully articulated in his essay for the
1930 critical anthology *I'll Take My Stand: The South
and the Agrarian Tradition*. It urged Southerners to
spurn industrialization and its values, to return to the
agrarian tradition and the ordered religious environment

that went with it. The need for *belief* was Tate's other major theme.

Allen Tate was borne in Winchester, Kentucky, in 1899, educated at schools in Nashville and Louisville before his single year at Georgetown University Preparatory School. He went on to Vanderbilt University. As his graduation approached, he retreated to a mountain resort in North Carolina to recover from alarming symptoms of tuberculosis. He graduated in 1923. In his sophomore year at Vanderbilt he enrolled as a student in an Advanced Composition Class run by the thirty-one-year-old Professor of English, a man who became a close and influential friend of Tate: John Crowe Ransom. Tate excelled. He was the first undergraduate invited to join the Fugitives, a group of poets and critics whose work appeared in the magazine *The Fugitive*. Robert Penn Warren, with whom Tate shared a room, joined them later.

At this time Tate was writing many poems. Forty were published in *The Fugitive*. Of these, he retained six in his 1960 volume, *Poems*. One of them, 'Homily', appeared in 1925. It possesses many of the qualities of the later work. There is the strict, intense formality and the dry exactitude that give the poems a keen intellectual edge. But even in the young poet there is no sense of burning inspiration. Tate was as wary of that as Ransom. This must be regarded as a positive virtue. The poetry, though not emotive in the romantic manner, is compelling rather for its clarity. Robert Lowell said he learned from Tate that, 'A good poem had nothing to do with exalted feelings of being moved by the spirit', that it was 'a piece of craftsmanship'. 'Homily' evokes an offending head:

Why, cut it off, piece after piece,
And throw the tough cortex away,
And when you've marvelled on the wars
That wove their interior smoke its way,

Tear out the close vermiculate crease
Where death crawled angrily at bay.

'And I think', Lowell said, 'Tate and I felt that we wanted our formal pattern to seem a hardship and something that we couldn't rattle off easily.' There is no psychological or passionate stress in the syntax in his early poems, no arresting focal image, but a developed metaphor. Already the hammering of the craftsman can be felt.

Early in his career Tate met another friend important to him: Hart Crane. Both had contributed to the magazine *The Double-Dealer*, and in 1922 Crane wrote to Tate to introduce himself. Eliot's *The Waste Land* appeared the same year and divided the Fugitives into two critical camps. Only Tate and Warren liked the work, almost as Crane had – as a challenge. Tate went so far as to write a poem in a Laforgue-Eliot style – 'Nuptials':

The whistle blows for five o'clock.
He rubs an eye, pulls on a sock,
Observes his bride still in bed,
Wonders: Now is she in bed dead?

After Vanderbilt, Tate taught briefly, then moved to New York where Crane introduced him to some of the literati. There he met the writer Caroline Gordon. They were married, and Crane and the Tates moved to Paterson, New Jersey, to write. They were virtually penniless. It was on his return to Greenwich Village in 1926 that Tate began what is generally regarded as his finest poem, 'Ode to the Confederate Dead'. It was not completed to Tate's satisfaction until 1936. A letter from Hart Crane in 1927 offers an interesting criticism of an early draft. The letter concludes, 'The intensity of this "meditation" gives the lie, of course, to all previous factual statements regarding the impermanency of your grief ... But you are, of course, speaking throughout less from a personal angle than a social viewpoint. Or are you? Both, of course ... I think the sarcasm is over-bitter, marring the beauty of the poem as a whole. The fierce resignation at the last is beautiful, the irony *will* sell, if you get what I mean.' The final version was a difficult and often an obscure poem. However it is one that, by sheer intensity of feeling (an intensity rare in Tate) expressed, generally, in ironic terms, manages to rise above its intellectual conception.

Tate describes the theme as 'the failure of the human personality to function properly in nature and society,' the theme of many of Tate's poems. The 'Ode' seems to draw on Elizabethan models for its extended ironies:

> Now that the salt of their blood
> Stiffens the saltier oblivion of the sea,
> Seals the malignant purity of the flood,
> What shall we who count our days and bow
> Our heads with a commemorial woe
> In the ribboned coats of grim felicity,
> What shall we say of the bones, unclean,
> Whose verdurous anonymity will grow?

At this time, Tate was moved to a strong defence of the South. The Agrarian Movement began in 1925. The South was being ridiculed for its retardedness. For example, a law in Tennessee forbade the teaching of the theory of evolution in state schools. The Fugitive writers counter-attacked, at the same time raising Southern literature to unprecedented achievement. *I'll Take My Stand* included essays exploring a possible agrarianism for the South, opposed to the values of the industrial North. Tate set about further studies of the history of the South. The result was a biography of Stonewall Jackson (1928) and of Jefferson Davies (1929).

Tate won a Guggenheim Fellowship, largely on the strength of Ford Madox Ford's support, and went to

Paris to live for a time among the expatriates. He returned to teach at Southwestern University at Memphis in 1934 and later at Princeton and New York. Since 1951 he has taught in Minnesota.

His only novel, *The Fathers* (1938), explores the history of two Virginia families in the nineteenth century, the tension between old and young, between traditionalism and pragmatism. Some critics regard this as his finest work. From 1944 to 1946 he edited the *Sewanee Review*. As his many volumes of essays show (the best were collected in *The Man of Letters in the Modern World: Selected Essays 1928–1955*), he is a formidable critic. Three of his best studies are of Hart Crane, Emily Dickinson, and Edgar Allan Poe. Perhaps his most influential general essay is 'Tension in Poetry'. Most of his prose writings bring a disciplined ironic understatement to bear on his chosen subject. He is true to his master, Ransom, the founder of the New Criticism, in arguing the serious purpose of poetry and its demanding responsibilities. He applies the same rigour and seriousness to his own poetry that he applies to others' in his essays.

In 1950 Tate became a Roman Catholic. His autobiographical poem-in-progress 'The Buried Lake', added to a reprint of his 1960 *Poems*, illuminates his conversion. Written in difficult *terza-rima*, the poem emerges haltingly from the dark tunnel of his biography into a possible enduring affirmation – the affirmation of faith:

Light choir upon my shoulder, speaking Dove
  The dream is over and the dark expired.
  I knew that I had known enduring love.

In spite of the rigidity of the form, a relaxed and sometimes almost conversational voice speaks in this poem – a voice new in his work.

The rigours of strict formalism, obscure syntax and vocabulary, normally create a tension in Tate's work that gives a harsh quality to the complexities. The Sonnets, for example, are impressive, but fail to achieve that necessary *feeling* of completion; some of the poems remain coldly intellectual. Perhaps, apart from 'Ode for the Confederate Dead' and 'The Swimmers', magnificent but obscure poems, Tate may be most readily approached through some of the lesser works, still fine in their formalism but less ambitious and therefore less contorted and difficult. 'Death of Little Boys' for example with its fine ending is immediate in its appeal:

The bleak sunshine shrieks its chipped music then
Out to the milkweed amid the fields of wheat.
There is a calm for you where men and women
Unroll the chill precision of moving feet.

Tate has received various awards: The Bollingen Prize (1956), the Brandeis Award (1961), the Gold Medal of the Dante Society of Florence (1962) and the Award of the Academy of American Poets (1963). His work, deeply rooted in a social and cultural milieu – that of the South – does not surrender its meanings easily to British readers. But, with Ransom, Tate is one of the best Southern poets and an exacting model for the poets of the next generation – Lowell and Jarrell in particular, who learned important lessons at his feet.

Yvor Winters 1900–1968

The young are quick of speech.
Grown middle-aged, I teach
Corrosion and distrust.

– 'On Teaching the Young'

Known in Britain primarily as a critic and teacher, Yvor
Winters was a considerable poet whose critical predilections were lucidly reflected in his own creative writing.
His choice of a poem by Hardy for an anthology on the
grounds of its 'quiet skill' and his praise for the English
syllabic poet Elizabeth Daryush, 'one of the few distinguished poets of our century', confirm the abiding
criteria by which he would have us judge him: rigorously disciplined form, containing rationally controlled
reflections on experiences of moral significance. He consistently chastised poetry of romantic vagueness and
'immorality' and favoured the logical and logically
spoken poem – but a logic so refined, so resolutely puri-
fied beyond prose logic, as to be final. He sharply criticizes
any 'pseudo-reference' which reflects what he calls the
'fallacy of imitative form'. Unfocused or effusive subjective writing is anathema to him; hence even Eliot has
drawn adverse criticism from him, in spite of the intellectual content and generally objective standpoint of
Eliot's work.

Winters admires a symmetry and balance that may sometimes border on the mechanical. Teaching at Stanford University, he impressed these predispositions on his students. He also argued against the blind following of literary trends, referring the reader and writer to past models as touchstones for achievement.

Born in Chicago in 1900, he went with his family to California in 1904. He returned to study at the University of Chicago but had to withdraw after a year because of tuberculosis. Eventually he earned his MA at the University of Colorado. In 1926 he married the American novelist Janet Lewis and they moved to Stanford, California, where he was first a graduate student and later Professor of English. He received his PhD in 1934 and remained at Stanford teaching until his death in 1968.

His principal volume of criticism is *In Defense of Reason* (1947), a collected edition of his most important books: *Primitivism and Decadence* (1937), *Maule's Curse* (1938) and *Anatomy of Nonsense* (1943). *The Function of Criticism* (1957) and *Forms of Discovery* (1968) followed. He prepared an extended study of Edwin Arlington Robinson in 1946. In 1960 he was awarded the Bollingen Prize for his poetry, included in *The Immobile Wind* (1921), *The Magpie's Shadow* (1922), *The Bare Hills* (1927), and *The Giant Weapon* (1943). His *Collected Poems* came out in 1952 and 1960; and in 1978 a *Collected Poems* appeared in Britain which included all the early poems as well.

Winters's early poems reflect the new styles of the period – notably the Imagist experiments of Pound, Carlos Williams, and occasionally Marianne Moore. In 'The Upper Meadows', he wrote with poise,

Apricots,
The clustered
Fur of bees
Above the gray rocks of the uplands.

He was attracted to the impersonality of Imagism. But he soon found that it lacked intellectual backbone and convincing structure for him; he was drawn to traditional forms through which he could comment lucidly and concisely on experience. His critical writings helped to free him from romantic and experimental hankerings. He came to concentrate on a more classical technique, admirable for its thematic and textural clarity. He was able in the verse to perform at once as poet, scholar, critic and teacher in finely argued lines of pure precision and 'quiet skill'.

Frequently there are long, complex – but not wilfully complicated – syntactical cadences that supply a music without recent precedent in English. Even if we take a poem in mid-sentence, we hear the modulations of the controlled voice satisfyingly at work:

... Grew and contracted down through infinite
And sub-atomic roar of Time on Time
Toward meaning that its changing cannot find;
So, stripped of color of an earth, and lit
With motion only of some inner rime,
The naked passion of the human mind.

The final line of this passage from 'The Invaders' is given prominence by the balanced placing of phrases and the confirming rhyme. Even where Winters expresses an emotion, there is a *willed* control of that emotion, for example in 'To Emily Dickinson', where the 'If' is all-important:

If I could make some tortured pilgrimage
Through words or Time or the blank pain of Doom
And kneel before you as you found your tomb,
Then I might rise to face my heritage ...

The lines recall words Winters wrote early in his critical career in 'Notes on Contemporary Criticism' (1929): 'The basis of Evil is an emotion: Good rests in the power of rational selection in action, as a preliminary to which the emotion in any situation must be as far as possible eliminated, and, in so far as it cannot be eliminated, understood.'

In this context, Winters is epitomized in the word 'understood'. Understanding is the essential quest for him. Of poems by J. V. Cunningham he wrote, 'they offer no solace unless clear understanding be solace.' His own search for understanding meant that he had to leave behind his early *vers libre* which did not provide him with the exacting austerity his intellect demanded. Metrical severity was the only adequate discipline: by means of it he could not only *find* but *present* certitude. It was his quarrel with Eliot's poetry that, although Eliot was for him 'one of the finest minds extant', his thoughts moved and slid 'as the feeling alone demands', and he achieved no more coherence than Pound achieved while wandering through history in some of the less successful Cantos.

Winters's attraction was to the short poem which prohibited 'the fine indignant sprawl':

Write little; do it well.
Your knowledge will be such,
At last, as to dispel
What moves you overmuch.

In a fine poem 'To the Holy Spirit', he meets Him in a deserted graveyard. All feeling is dispensed with:

Yet when I go from sense
And trace thee down in thought,
I meet thee, then, intense,
And know thee as I ought.

And, more important:

But thou art mind alone,
And I, alas, am bound

Pure mind to flesh and bone,
And flesh and bone to ground.

He can find only one certainty:

Only one certainty
Beside thine unfleshed eye,
Beside the spectral tree,
Can I discern: these die.

This certainty offers no solace unless clear understanding be solace. And in Winters's poetry it is. Consistent and persistent in his beliefs and practice, he is one of the seminal poetic minds of the century, willing literature and his own poetry into a formalism that gives it not only the resonance, but the power of certitude. One of his last poems gives 'small' the sense of 'concise':

I had grown away from youth,
Shedding error where I could;
I was now essential wood,
Concentrating into truth;
What I did was small but good.

Laura (Riding) Jackson
born 1901

We must learn better
What we are and are not.

– 'The Why of the Wind'

Laura Riding's passionate search for what she calls 'an ultimate of perfect truth' is admirable. Also admirable are the extremes to which she has gone in prose to express not only the details of that search but also the reasons for her renunciation of poetry as an inadequate medium. She made her fullest statement when she published with her *Selected Poems* (1970) an extensive disclaimer, asserting that the poetic currency she was handing over to us – as it were against her wishes – was counterfeit.

She was born Laura Reichenthal in New York City in 1901, the daughter of an Austrian-born tailor, a naturalized American. She attended Cornell University and there married a history tutor, Louis Gottschalk. She published her first poems in periodicals as Laura Riding Gottschalk. Until she contributed to *The Fugitive*, she remained virtually unknown. But when the Fugitives – including Ransom, Penn Warren and Tate – took her work up, they awarded her a prize and made her an honorary member of the group.

Her first marriage broke up in 1925 and she dropped the Gottschalk from her name, writing as Laura Riding.

In 1926 she became associated with Robert Graves and went to live in Mallorca, there establishing the Seizin Press in Deyá in 1927. With Graves she edited the literary magazine *Epilogue* (1935–8). After the publication of her *Collected Poems* in 1938 she rejected poetry and returned to the United States. In 1941 she married Schuyler Jackson and has signed her few published prose works since as Laura (Riding) Jackson. She and her second husband collaborated on a work of linguistics, still unfinished at his death in 1968, which was to provide 'a single terminology of truth'. She has completed the vast undertaking on her own. It was intended to be 'a work that would help to dissipate the confusion existing in the knowledge of word-meanings – where, I believed, all probity of word must start.'

Her volumes of poetry include *The Close Chaplet* (1926), *Poems: A Joking Word* (1930), *Poet: A Lying Word* (1933), *Collected Poems* (1938) and *Selected Poems: in Five Sets* (1970); and a definitive *Collected Poems* published in Britain in 1980. With Robert Graves she wrote a novel (using the name Barbara Riche) called *No Decency Left* (1932), *A Survey of Modernist Poetry* (1927) and *Contemporaries and Snobs* (1928). Two further novels written by her alone were *A Trojan Ending* (1937) and *Lives of Wives* (1939). In the magazine *Chelsea* (1962 and 1964) she has given her reasons for renouncing poetry, and in issues 20/21 (1967) she published *The Telling* (published in Britain in 1972), a prose work in which she declares, 'My subject is all ourselves, the human reality. And my subject is All, and One, the reality of All, of which we are exponents.'

She made several statements of her original commitment to poetry, too; and the foreword to her *Collected Poems* (1938) – an interesting corrective to the introduction to the *Selected* – tells us, 'A poem is an uncovering of truth of so fundamental and general a kind that no other name besides poetry is adequate except truth.' That

poetry should tell the truth: this belief ultimately led
her to reject it, for she came to feel that it could not do
so. It fails because it has in it no provision 'for ultimate
practical attainment of that rightness of word that *is*
truth, but led on ever only to a temporizing less-than-
truth (that lack eked out with illusions of truth produced
by physical word-effects).' For her, then, metaphorical
language, even the use of imagery, does not illuminate
the object or idea in question but simply avoids the issue
by blurring it into poeticism. The poems she included,
after more than thirty years' silence, in her *Selected Poems*
indicate that even when she was fully committed to poetry
this concern was very much in her mind:

With the face goes a mirror
As with the mind a world.
Likeness tells the doubting eye
That strangeness is not strange.
At an early hour and knowledge
Identity not yet familiar
Looks back upon itself from later,
And seems itself.

She fitted well into the company of the Fugitives: the
discipline is there, and a mannered irony of which they
would have approved. And when she writes in 'The Time
Beneath':

When beauty rises from the blackened queens
And the lachrymatory vessels sparkle
With tears from unbound eyes
That grieve sincerely how they lay
Long closed ...

they would have applauded the verbal poise. She lacks,
however, their verbal variety and dexterity – qualities
she might argue contribute to the untruth of their work.
Nor does she follow their forms, nor use their rhyme

schemes and regular metres. Still, she cannot be said to write 'free verse', since the feeling of a constricting form is constantly present in the tensions she creates in striving for clarity and purity of diction.

Taken on the Fugitives' terms, hers are fine poems. But taken on Laura Riding's more recent terms, they are not. In the introduction to her *Selected Poems* she calls the poem 'The Mask' a 'terrible early poem of mine'. Still, she includes it in the selection with a prefatory gloss, 'the "taint" referred to in the poem is eternal only if the poetry is eternal'.

Is there no pure then?
The eternal taint wears beauty like a mask.
But a mask eternal.

We cannot doubt the sincerity of her rejection of poetry as humanly inadequate. But it is now difficult to read even her best poems without seeing at each turn points at which she might sense a failure of 'truth'. She has done less than justice to our enjoyment of the poems she has allowed to be reprinted. And yet 'enjoyment' is not the end she is after.

In the introduction to the *Selected*, with characteristic aplomb, she tells us, 'I have initiated enough poets into the idea of linguistic discipline for truth's sake, in the past, to know how verbally insensitive to considerations of truth poets can be, though behaving as persons born privy to it.' To be conscious of a limited idea is one thing: to use that idea of linguistic discipline to the exclusion of other poetic qualities is quite another. Some of her poems reveal the tension between resonance – of rhythm and suggestion – and linguistic discipline almost as examples of the conflict in her. We are undecided whether she is attempting to tell a truth or expressing the fact that, through her chosen medium, it is impossible to tell the truth:

Pain is impossible to describe
Pain is the impossibility of describing
Describing what is impossible to describe
Which must be a thing beyond description
Beyond description not to be known
Beyond knowing but not mystery
Not mystery but pain not plain but pain
But pain beyond but here beyond!

When at the height of her creative activity, her influence
was positive and not inconsiderable, notably on W. H.
Auden. But since then, her silence, followed by the
prose writings so intellectually rigorous, her explications
which themselves require a gloss, have argued against her
real achievement as a poet. For the poems find a truth
that is unlike the truth she is – in prose – delving to find:

This is not exactly what I mean
Any more than the sun is the sun.
But how to mean more closely
If the sun shines but approximately?
What a world of awkwardness!

Langston Hughes 1902–1967

I, too, sing America.
I am the darker brother.

– 'I, too'

Langston Hughes identified himself so closely with his
race and the decades through which the Blacks struggled
for basic rights in the United States that his writings
provide a clear reflection of Black achievements, frustrations and values in mid-century America. He not only
helped to clarify what Black culture was but helped to
extend it, with his ear for Black rhythms and his own
public ebullience and humour. The poems suggest the
wealth of that *different* American culture – though
Hughes' models were Whitman, Vachel Lindsay, and
Sandburg. From that different culture he elicits in his
verse cadences and a vocabulary that define a new register
in literary language. The poems suggest, on one level,
the elemental identity of Black culture. In 'The Negro
Speaks of Rivers', for instance, Hughes writes:

I've known rivers:
Ancient dusky rivers.
My soul has grown deep like the rivers.

In 'Fire' he evokes the spiritual nature of his culture:

Fire,
Fire, Lord!
Fire gonna burn ma soul!

I ain't been good,
I ain't been clean –
I been stinkin', low-down, mean.

In 'Down and Out' he reflects its self-pity:

If you love me, baby,
Help me when I'm down and out,
I'm a po' gal
Nobody gives a damn about.

Most powerfully he expresses its pride, especially in 'I,
too':

Besides,
They'll see how beautiful I am
And be ashamed –

I, too, am America.

Whether the language is the rhetoric of a revivalist meeting, the rhythm of jazz lyrics, or a more studied literary
language, Hughes retains a strong thread of irony, a
critical distance and perspective, projecting some of his
poems through personae, distancing others with characteristically understated humour.

Hughes was born in Joplin, Missouri. After attending
Columbia for a year, he graduated from Lincoln University in 1929. He led a restless early life, teaching in
Mexico, living in the Soviet Union, farming in Staten
Island, cooking in a Montmartre night club, and acting
as a bus-boy in a Washington hotel. He recalls in his
autobiographies, *The Big Sea* (1940) and *I Wonder as I
Wander* (1956), how at the Washington hotel he persuaded Vachel Lindsay to read his poems at a recital.

Hughes also worked as a seaman on voyages to Africa and Europe.

The Weary Blues (1926), his first book of poems, celebrates Harlem in the full swing of the New Negro Movement. 'The people of Harlem,' he wrote in his autobiography, 'seem not very different from others, except in language. I love the colour of their language: and being a Harlemite myself, their problems and interests are my problems and interests.' The poems develop jazz rhythms, reflecting the Harlem of the cabarets of the period. But behind the strong rhythms, implicit indeed in the 'Blues' tradition, is a current of resigned weariness:

The singer stopped playing and went to bed
While the Weary Blues echoed through his head.

The last poem in the book, 'Disillusionment', moves beyond resignation. 'I would be simple again,/Simple and clean ...'

Oh, great dark city.
Let me forget.
I will not come
To you again.

For Hughes, Harlem had failed: its exoticism gave and reflected little but the ephemeral elations of night-club life.

After his first book, he became increasingly prolific, producing more than fifty volumes of poetry, plays and novels. *The Weary Blues* was followed by another collection, *Fine Clothes to the Jew* (1927), and he captured the bitter mood of the thirties in his play, *Mulatto* (1935). The Depression of 1929 struck Harlem hard and by the end of the 1935 riots it had lost its attraction and was on its way to becoming a drab ghetto. Hughes's collection *Shakespeare in Harlem* itemizes the depressing futilities: 'Lawd, I wish I could die –/But who would miss me if I left?'

It is self-consciously tired verse, but ready for change. Another collection, *Fields of Wonder*, followed in 1947. Some of the poems express yearning wonder for things unattainable: 'Reach up your hand, dark boy, and take a star.' But it is a social unrest rather than a desire to escape that advances the poetry in *One Way Ticket* (1949) and *Montage of a Dream Deferred* (1951). *One Way Ticket* includes the spirited and provocative 'Ballad of Margie Polite' who caused a riot and the shooting of a Black soldier who sided with her. The tensions latent in Hughes' earlier style burst to the surface.

Perhaps *Montage of a Dream Deferred* is his finest book. It includes over ninety poems which together form a jazz festival of variations on Harlem themes and rhythms. In a preface Hughes explains his techniques: 'In terms of current Afro-American popular music ... this poem on contemporary Harlem, like be-bob, is marked by conflicting changes, sudden nuances, sharp and impudent interjections, broken rhythms, and passages sometimes in the manner of the jam session, sometimes the popular song, punctuated by the rifts, runs, breaks, and distortions of the music of a community in transition.' He explains the structure in musical terms, and the title suggests an analogy with painting. The poems represent a confluence of many voices, ideas and rhythms. The sense of unrest and frustration is evoked in its rhythmic variations. The persistent recurrence of the themes accentuates the tragedy of Harlem, and highlights the hopes of its people. There is humour and bathos as well. The poetry is written for an audience, for a people. Harlem is both a setting and a symbol for Hughes.

Ask Your Mama (1961) and *The Panther and the Lash* (1967) were further collections of verse. But Hughes' creative activity was not confined to verse. He wrote on music in *The First Book of Jazz* (1955) and on Black culture in *The Book of Negro Folklore* (1958). *Fight for*

Freedom (1962) examined the origins and objectives of racial protest.

Jesse B. Simple is Hughes' most engaging creation – a comic character whose adventures, originally satirical sketches for a Black newspaper, were collected into books; *Simple Speaks his Mind* (1950), *Simple Stakes his Claim* (1957), *The Best of Simple* (1961) and *Simple's Uncle Sam* (1965).

Hughes is too much of a realist to harbour ideal visions. When he writes, 'I, too, sing America./I am the darker brother', his American-ness is at once clear and passionate. His poems, however, portray rather than project. They rise out of experience, commitment, conviction; they do not admit escapist idealism. One of his characteristic effects is anti-climax:

I put my nickel
In the raffle of the night.
Somehow that raffle
Didn't turn out right ...

Or, in another poem,

I could just as well've
Stayed home inside:
My bread wasn't buttered
On neither side.

But, because of the irony and understatement, the poems are the more resonant:

Dance! Whirl! Whirl!
Till the quick day is done.
Rest at pale evening ...
A tall, slim tree ...
Night coming tenderly
    Black like me.

Louis Zukofsky 1904–1978

The test of poetry is the range of pleasure it affords as sight, sound, and intellection. This is its purpose as art ...'

– Zukofsky's preface to *A Test of Poetry*: 1948

Louis Zukofsky, in 'A Statement for Poetry' (1950), wrote, 'The best way to find out about poetry is to read the poems.' This principle hardly applies to his own work. Some introduction is needed – and not of the kind supplied by him or by his passionate advocates. Together they have intellectualized his poetry almost out of existence. There is a world of difference between explication and intellectualization. Zukofsky's critical prose style is indigestible: '... How much what is sounded by words has to do with what is seen by them, and how much what is at once sounded and seen by them crosscuts an interplay among themselves – will naturally sustain the scientific definition of poetry we are looking for. To endure it would be compelled to integrate these functions: time, and what is seen in time (as held by a song), and an action whose words are actors or, if you will, mimes composing steps as of a dance that at proper instants calls in the vocal cords to transfer it into plain speech ...' (from 'Poetry *A*'). The implications become clear, but the expression is almost wilfully confusing. The poetry, too, is difficult:

(mouth?) –
exult
tally,
wiggle
exult
tally –
(one:
three)
sun
eye

This is the last stanza of '*A* 14 *beginning An*'. Could the word 'month' be substituted for 'mouth'? The answer should be 'no'; a poet of Zukofsky's experimental integrity should deserve our trust. The poem proves to be a love poem, and the words refer back to an experience.

Zukofsky is the natural successor to William Carlos Williams, having taken Williams's theories a step further into committed experimentation. And his poetry has become a starting point for several contemporary poets – Robert Duncan, Robert Creeley and Gary Snyder, for instance – all of whom have diverted poetry from the tradition represented by Frost and Aiken and made Williams and Zukofsky their models. Creeley described an attraction: 'It is a peculiar virtue of Zukofsky's work that it offers an extraordinary handbook for the writing of poems.'

Louis Zukofsky was born in Manhattan in 1904 and lived in New York for most of his life. He was educated at Columbia University, taking his MA in 1924. He taught English at the University of Wisconsin (1930–31) and travelled in Europe, returning eventually to settle in Brooklyn Heights. He taught at Colgate University in 1947 and at the Polytechnic Institute of Brooklyn from 1947 to 1966. He was at San Francisco State College, as poet in residence, in 1958. He married the composer Celia Thaew in 1939. Their son Paul is a distinguished violinist.

His work first attracted notice in February 1931, when he edited a special 'objectivist' issue of the magazine *Poetry* in which, among others, he included poems by Williams and Charles Reznikoff which conformed to his idea of an 'objectivist poem'. Williams describes 'The Objectivist theory' in his autobiography: 'We had had "Imagism" ... which ran quickly out. That, though it had been useful in ridding the field of verbiage, had no formal necessity implicit in it. It had already dribbled off into so called "free verse" which, as we saw, was a misnomer. There is no such thing as free verse! Verse is a measure of some sort ... But we argued, the poem, like every other form of art, is an object, an object that in itself formally presents its case and its meaning by the very form it assumes. Therefore, being an object, it should be so treated and controlled – but not as in the past. For past objects have about them past necessities – like the sonnet – which have conditioned them and from which, as a form itself, they cannot be freed. The poem being an object (like a symphony or a cubist painting) it must be the purpose of the poet to make of his words a new form: to invent, that is, an object consonant with his day. This was what we wished to imply by Objectivism, an antidote, in a sense, to the bare image haphazardly presented in loose verse.'

A press was founded, financed by the poet George Oppen, and in 1932 under the name of 'To' Publishers, it brought out *An 'Objectivists' Anthology*, edited by Zukofsky, with poems by Basil Bunting, Oppen, Carl Rakosi, Kenneth Rexroth, Reznikoff and Williams. Pound was represented by 'Yittischer Charleston' and Eliot by 'Marina'. 'To', under the general editorship of Zukofsky, Williams and Pound became the Objectivist Press. Zukofsky, in the original Objectivist issue of *Poetry*, specifies as required reading Pound's *XXX Cantos*, Williams's *Spring and All*, Eliot's *The Waste Land* and 'Marina', Marianne Moore's *Observations*, e.e. cummings's *Is 5* and Wallace Stevens's *Harmonium*, among others. Helpful to an understanding of Zukofsky's own poetry is his comment, 'In contemporary writing the poems of Ezra Pound alone possess objectivication to a most constant degree; *his objects are musical shapes*' (my italics). The words: 'objects', 'musical', and 'shapes' provide a key to Zukofsky's poetry.

In his *Five Statements for Poetry* (1958) Zukofsky spoke of his work as moving towards a 'process of active literary omission', a conscious rejection of crude metaphor and symbolism and an exploitation of typography to demonstrate 'how the voice should sound'. His work thus consciously subordinates meaning to sound – in this he recalls Gertrude Stein – for, having admitted the objectiveness of the poem and applied the principle to the *word*, treating it too as an object, its sound and look become, perhaps, more important than its meaning. The *poem* becomes a *score*. As he abandons metaphor, symbol, and connotation in language, meaning takes a subordinate place. The clearest example of this approach is in his *Catullus* (1969), prepared in collaboration with his wife. His 'translations' of Catullus are into a language that attempts in his words to 'breathe the "literal" meaning with him'. In the Latin, Catullus's poem CXII reads:

Multus homo es, Naso, neque tecum multus homost qui
   descendit: Naso, multus es et pathicus.

Swanson's translation reads:

You're a made man, Naso, nor is he who lays you made:
   you're a made man, Naso, and a – maid.

Zukofsky's version is:

Mool 'tis homos' 'Naso, 'n' queer take 'im mool 'tis ho most *he*
   descended: Naso, mool 'tis – is it pathic, cuss.

Which is nearer the Latin? But that begs the question: what *is* Latin? What do we mean by 'being nearer'? The larger question Zukofsky has spent a lifetime probing is, what is language?

The point is that Zukofsky – along with Bunting – recognized that the order and movement of *sound* in a poem might itself create a cohesion of the emotions underlying the literal meaning of the words. This is no new discovery. We need only think of certain lines in Shakespeare to see the truth of it. In *Richard III* Lady Anne kneels before the corpse of Henry VI and begins her lamentation, 'Poor key-cold figure of a holy king'. The stiffness of 'key-cold', the warm devotion of 'holy king', are sufficient in themselves to convey the emotion, complex though it is; but Shakespeare is generous, allowing the line to accommodate visual imagery and metaphor as well. This is the danger in Zukofsky's approach: that by stressing the sound at the expense of meaning he is limiting his poetry, indeed sterilizing it.

But he is persistent and courageous. We do best to concentrate on his difficult work, where his integrity is most clear. Anthologies have naturally tended to serve up his shorter, more accessible poems. They sometimes resemble Imagist verse, as parts of 'All of December Toward New Year' shows:

Not the branches
half in shadow

But the length
of each branch

Half in shadow

As if it had snowed
on each upper half

But it is his main poem, *A*, that deserves close attention. There is no compromise in that evolving work, though there are passages with literal meanings:

An
  hinny
by
  stallion
out of
  she-ass

He neigh halie low h'who y'he gall mood
So roar cruel hire
Lo to achieve an eye leer rot off
Mass th'lo low o loam echo –
How deal me many coeval yammer
Naked on face of white rock-sea.

The poem is a continuous day-book of Zukofsky's marriage and life:

An
orange
our
sun
fire
pulp

whets
us
(everyday)
for
us
eat
it
its
fire's
unconsumed

In one section the music (notation) takes over. A masque
by Celia Zukofsky is introduced, to music by Handel to
be played (and danced) as words taken from Zukofsky's
writings. 'The speed at which each voice speaks is cor-

related to the time-space factor of the music,' writes Celia Zukofsky. 'The words are NEVER SUNG to the music.' This is central to Zukofsky's work: the words carry their own music, it must not be imposed on them by a singing voice.

And yet there is no centre to *A*, nor could there be, since a continuous, open-ended work of this nature remains a reaction rather than a comment. As such, the commonplace takes equal weight with the exultant, the good with the bad; it is life – for Zukofsky, 'the words are my life'. It shares something with Williams's *Paterson*. '*A*' *1–21* has appeared in two volumes (1959, 1969); and '*A*' *22 & 23* was published in Britain in 1977. Zukofsky's other poetic works include *Some Time* (1956), *I's* (*pronounced eyes*) (1963), *After I's* (1964) and *Found Objects 1926–1962* (1964). *All: The Collected Shorter Poems 1923–1958* (1965) and *All: The Collected Poems 1956–1964* appeared in 1967. His main prose work is *Bottom: On Shakespeare* (1963) in two volumes. The first is a study of Shakespeare, the second a musical setting of *Pericles* by Celia Zukofsky. *Prepositions* (1967) is a collection of his critical essays and *Ferdinand* (published with *It Was* in 1968) is fiction.

Ezra Pound dedicated his *Guide to Kulchur* (1938) to Zukofsky and Bunting: 'To/LOUIS ZUKOFSKY/and/ BASIL BUNTING/strugglers/in the/desert'. It is a tribute to the early ambitions of these experimental writers. Courageous though Zukofsky has been in developing one area of the poetic voice, striving for a fine musical purity, the limitations he has imposed on his writing may be helping to perpetuate that 'desert', or create a new one.

Robert Penn Warren born 1905

We live in time so little time
And we learn all so painfully
That we may spare this hour's term
To practise for eternity.

– 'Bearded Oaks'

Robert Penn Warren's preoccupation with human existence in time, while nature in its patterns of recurrence
seems able to transcend time, has been central to his
poetry. He has developed the theme with clarity, almost
with dryness of tone, and a rigorous control:

This small owl calls from the moat now,
And across all the years and miles that
Are the only Truth I have learned,
That other owl answers him ...

Persistent attention to time, nature, and human life
marks his earliest work. He was the youngest of the
Fugitives, with them supporting Agrarianism in the
South and opposing the industrial materialism of the
North.

Born and raised in Todd County, Kentucky, he went
to Vanderbilt University in 1921. There he was strongly
influenced by John Crowe Ransom and Allen Tate who –
with Donald Davidson – founded *The Fugitive*, a magazine with close affinities to Southern Agrarianism. It
published Warren's student poems. Warren's view of

Agrarianism was romantic. Ransom and Davidson saw the policy in an historical perspective and Tate saw it as an impossible but desirable idea. For Warren it was an unattainable poetic ideal which – with its promise of community and closeness to nature – highlighted the actual isolation of the individual in modern society. It seemed that, with Agrarianism, the solitary agonies man suffers would be alleviated in a social existence and in proximity to the soil. Warren's characters live lives of tragic loneliness within time, untouched by the timeless nature of the seasons, rebirth and decay. He is conscious primarily of the reminders of mortality:

The days draw in:
Southward, the red suns trim
Daily, and tim, and spin
Their bleakening paradigm.
Summer has been.

Warren went from Vanderbilt to the University of California (1925–7), then to Yale (1928–9) and to Oxford as a Rhodes Scholar (1929–30). While at Oxford he contributed to the anthology of essays *I'll Take My Stand: The South and the Agrarian Tradition* (1930). The twelve contributors urged a return to nature, to the fields, and to the ordered religious life, spurning modern industrialism.

His subsequent career has consisted primarily of University teaching and the writing of poems, novels and criticism. His university posts have included Vanderbilt (1931–4), Louisiana State (1934–42), Minnesota (1942–50), and Yale (since 1950). From 1935 to 1942 he co-edited the influential *Southern Review*, and with Cleanth Brooks compiled anthologies and three important books of criticism, *Understanding Poetry* (1938), *Understanding Fiction* (1943), and *Fundamentals of Good Writing* (1950). These expounded the theory and practice of the New Criticism. For Ransom and his followers, it meant consideration of a poem's 'structure' and 'texture', elements which give the poem its *own* integrity, rather than a consideration of the poem's place in a social and historical context. Warren's *Selected Essays* (1958) includes studies of Conrad and Coleridge. His eight novels deal with Southern problems as expressions of universal conflicts. His non-literary essays deal with the South: indeed, his first book was a study of *John Brown, The Making of a Martyr* (1929). Later he wrote *Who Speaks for the Negro?* (1965). As a young man he had espoused racial segregation, but in later life he changed his mind and added an eloquent voice to the integrationist lobbies. He explained that, as a young man, away from the South, he saw the issue in traditional Southern terms, but on his return to live in the South, the issue became humanly real.

Warren's poetry embraces the small complex lyrics included in *Selected Poems 1923–1943* and the long 'tale in verse and voices', *Brother to Dragons* (1953), the story of the nineteenth-century murder of a Negro by Jefferson's nephew. His large poetic *oeuvre* includes *Promises, Poems 1954–6* (1957), and *Incarnations* (1968).

Some of Warren's themes have an element of Transcendentalism, particularly those that stress the importance of the natural world and its implicit symbolism. But his poems continually return to the theme of man constrained by time. The possibility of transcending those constraints is a secondary theme. In 'The Ballad of Billie Potts', nature progresses – in the image of the salmon – by yearly recurrences, while the protagonist makes his way home not implicated in that pattern:

The salmon heaves at the falls, and wanderer, you
Heave at the great fall of Time, and gorgeous, gleam
In the powerful arc, and anger and outrage like dew,
In your plunge, fling, and plunge to the thunderous stream:
Back to the silence, back to the pool, back
To the high pool, motionless, and the unmurmuring dream.

Nature has its laws. But there is a pervasive pessimism in his vision of man.

History, in 'What Day Is', has its patterns, but apparently no law answering to natural law:

In Pliny, *Phoenice*, Phoenicians,
Of course. Before that, Celts.
Rome, in the end, as always:
A handful of coins, a late emperor.
Hewn stone, footings for what?

And the pessimism takes a more arresting form:

All day, cicadas,
At the foot of infinity, like
A tree, saw. The sawdust
Of that incessant effort,
Like filings of brass, sun-brilliant,
Heaps up at the tree-foot. That
Is what day is ...

Nature supplies the force of light:

When you
Split the fig, you will see
Lifting from the coarse and purple seed, its
Flesh like flame, purer
Than blood.
It fills
The darkening room with light.

But that light can be harrowing:

Do not
Look too long at the sea, for
That brightness will rinse out your eyeballs.

The sincerity recommends Warren's poems – not any startling use of language or imagery. And if his poems do not stand up to many re-readings, they nonetheless have an immediacy which is engaging. The sense of the 'real'

lived experience makes his writing at times powerful.
With a clear sense of the human predicament he wrote:

... Our feet once wrought the hollow street
With echo when the lamps were dead
At windows, once our headlight glare
Disturbed the doe that, leaping, fled.

I do not love you less that now
The caged heart makes iron stroke,
Or less that all that light once gave
The graduate dark should now revoke.

We live in time so little time
And we learn all so painfully,
That we may spare this hour's term
To practise for eternity.

Theodore Roethke 1908–1963

Tell me:
Which is the way I take;
Out of what door do I go,
Where and to whom?

– 'The Lost Son'

Roethke's poetry attempted to answer this question –
searching not so much *for* experience as *through* it. 'To
go forward (as a spiritual man),' he wrote in a letter in
1948, 'it is necessary first to go back.' The return led him
to moments as disparate and yet *equally* honest as:

And all the waters
Of all the streams
Sang in my veins
That summer day.

and the more measured and tentative,

In a dark time, the eye begins to see,
I meet my shadow in the deepening shade;
I hear my echo in the echoing wood –
A lord of nature weeping to a tree.

His attempt to articulate his whole self might seem to
imply either narcissism or an obsession with psychology.
But 'I've read almost no psychology,' he wrote, and the

frequent, unresolved tension, the moments when he touches the point of breakdown or foresees his own death, reveal not narcissism but integrity of spirit. The struggle for self-knowledge was to enable the poet to understand and perhaps eventually to accept, rather than to confront himself with the self discovered. 'I have tried,' he wrote, 'to transmute and purify my "life", the sense of being defiled by it.' Understanding might be sufficient to *cause* the purification or transmutation of the self. His attempt to purify through knowledge of his defilement creates the necessary tension to sustain his superior kind of self-revelation. The series of mental breakdowns he suffered were part of the process.

It was partly his early love for the work of Emerson and Thoreau that encouraged him to persevere and find find acceptance. 'A wretch needs his wretchedness,' he wrote in his last major poems, 'North American Sequence':

In the long journey out of self
There are many detours, washed-out interrupted raw places
Where the shale slides dangerously ...

But he knows, too, 'Beautiful my desire, and the place of my desire.' On his own terms he finds it, 'I have come to a still, but not a deep center, / A point outside the glittering current ...' He went a long way before he reached that acceptance, that 'Silence of water above a sunken tree: / The pure serene of memory in one man ...'

Significantly, a period in Roethke's childhood provided him with experiences that were uniquely his and yet sufficiently removed in time to enable him to objectify them and produce a body of poems in his second volume, *The Lost Son* (1948) – the so-called 'greenhouse poems' – that were at once a 'personal history and a history of the race itself', as Roethke commented in a letter.

He was born the son of the owner of one of the largest floral businesses in the state of Michigan. His parents were German immigrants who had settled in Saginaw, and Roethke spent the crucial years of his childhood near the greenhouses, where orchids,

> ... lean over the path,
> Adder-mouthed,
> Swaying close to the face ...

and,

> Under the concrete branches,
> Hacking at black, hairy roots, –
> ...
> Me down in the fetor of weeds,
> Crawling on all fours,
> Alive, in a slippery grave.

He was educated at Michigan State University and then at Harvard and professed to have hated both, though he received consistently high grades. It took him ten years to write his first 'little book' of poems, *Open House* (1941), remarkably controlled verses of considerable power, closely associated with the landscape and life of the North West:

> I remember the crossing-tender's geranium border
> That blossomed in soot; a black cat licking its paw;
> The bronze wheat arranged in strict and formal order;
> And the precision that for you was ultimate law ...

But it was in his second book, *The Lost Son and Other Poems* (1948), that his poetry matured.

Open House received excellent reviews from exacting critics – Auden and Winters among them – and Roethke was encouraged. It had been achieved after considerable difficulty. He had spent the Depression years teaching and coaching tennis at Lafayette College. Just as he had begun his first and only term teaching at Michigan State University he suffered his first nervous breakdown (1935). Insecurity about his own achievement and a persistent and deeply rooted need for recognition – traits that remained with him throughout his life – contributed to his collapse.

He taught at Pennsylvania State University (1936–43) and then moved to Bennington College (1943–6). In 1947 he took a post at the University of Washington, where he remained until his sudden death in 1963. In 1953 he married and travelled in Europe, lecturing as a Fulbright Scholar in Italy. He won the Pulitzer Prize for his book *The Waking* (1953), the Bollingen Prize for *Words for the Wind* (1958). *I Am! Says the Lamb* (1961) was followed by a children's book, *Party at the Zoo* (1963) and *Sequence, Sometimes Metaphysical* (1963), more poems. A year after his death, *The Far Field* (1964) was published and received the National Book Award. His *Collected Poems* appeared in 1966.

The Lost Son and Other Poems is his best book. It includes a long sequence of open-form poems, mainly autobiographical, which he declared are not only a personal spiritual history but the history of all 'haunted and harried men'. They trace the painful development of self-awareness in terms that are effective not only because the varied style is skilfully controlled but because he achieves objectivity despite his use of the first person.

The 'greenhouse poems' form the early part of the sequence which is carried on into the later books, *Praise to the End* (1951) and *The Waking* (1953). Of these, Roethke wrote, 'In this kind of poem, to be most true to himself and to that which is universal in him, the poet should not rely on allusion.' He adds, 'In this kind of poem, the poet should not "comment", or use many judgement words: instead he should render the experience, however condensed or elliptical that experience may be.' In 'Child on Top of a Greenhouse' he writes,

The wind billowing out the seat of my britches,
My feet crackling splinters of glass and dried putty,
The half-grown chrysanthemums staring up like accusers ...

And in 'Frau Bauman, Frau Schmidt, and Frau Schwartz', he recalls, 'I remember how they picked me up, a spindly kid,/Pinching and poking my thin ribs ...' It is not only incidents but people, the people who acted upon him and shaped his early life, that his poems evoke, not assessing them but defining them, clarifying areas of the past, reconstructing the experience. In 'My Papa's Waltz' he writes,

You beat time on my head
With a palm caked hard by dirt,
Then waltzed me off to bed
Still clinging to your shirt.

The experiences were vitally real to Roethke, so strong that they could provide the link between his present and his past, between that past and 'nature' in its broadest sense, tending to the archetypal:

... one tulip on top,
One swaggering head
Over the dying, the newly dead.

And out of early dreams the images emerge, renewed:

Over the gulfs of dream
Flew a tremendous bird
Further and further away
Into a moonless black,
Deep in the brain, far back.

The birds take on a symbolic power for Roethke. They bring into the day a restless freedom.

The sun glittered on a small rapids.
Some morning thing came, beating its wings.
The great elm filled with birds.

Roethke's dependence on other poets for style and structure has been widely chronicled by critics. Yeats's influence is perhaps dominant. Roethke passionately attacked such critics in his essay, 'How To Write like Somebody Else'. But his negations are not convincing. For Roethke was competitive. He adapted a style to appropriate it, to compete against the originator of that style. His individual voice never disappears, but the echoes of his models can be strong and distracting. His originality lies primarily in the way he develops an experience, not in his rhythms. In 'Four for Sir John Davies' he confesses – and at once withdraws the confession: 'I take this cadence from a man named Yeats;/I take it, and I give it back again'. The sequence is redolent of Yeats – but Roethke, developing his own themes, makes the cadence his own. The echo subsides.

Roethke wrote, 'Form is regarded not as a neat mould to be filled, but rather as a sieve to catch certain kinds of material.' In his later poems, as well as the accomplished formal pieces, we find a longer, easier line in some of the poems that begins to encompass a calm, meditative sense of repose:

I long for the imperishable quiet at the heart of form;
I would be a stream, winding between great striated rocks in
    late summer;
A leaf, I would love the leaves, delighting in the redolent
    disorder of this mortal life ...

Searching still, the anguished uncertainty of the earlier work is replaced by a sense of goal. The poetry toys with resignation, but advances in the end resolutely towards acceptance:

I am renewed by death, thought of my death,
The dry scent of a dying garden in September,
The wind fanning the ash of a low fire.
What I love is near at hand,
Always, in earth and air.

Charles Olson 1910–1970

> I have this sense,
> that I am one
> with my skin.
>
> Plus this – plus this:
> that forever the geography
> leans in
> on me ...

– 'Letter 27', *The Maximus Poem*

In the preface to the 1855 edition of *Leaves of Grass* Whitman wrote, 'The rhyme and uniformity of perfect poems show the free growth of metrical laws and bud from them as unerringly and loosely as lilacs or roses on a bush, and take shapes as compact as the shapes of chestnuts and oranges and melons and pears, and shed the perfume impalpable to form.' In 1913 the Imagists proclaimed that the poet should 'compose in sequence of the musical phrase, not in sequence of a metronome.' This 'natural' and implicitly 'organic' notion of the growth of poetry recalls Emerson and the Transcendentalists and provided a starting point for both William Carlos Williams's theory of 'the variable foot' (1954), in which he describes lines written according to the length of a 'musical pace' (a single beat is counted to each line); and for Charles Olson's theory of Projective Verse, developed in 1950. PROJECTIVE VERSE teaches ... that that verse will only do in which a poet manages to register both the acquisitions of his ear *and* the pressures of his breath.' 'Breath' is the source and measure of individual lines, the individual breath patterns of the poet at the moment that he writes. Lines which do not come from 'breath' are unnatural. Olson criticizes T. S. Eliot: 'it is because [he] has stayed inside the non-projective that he fails as a dramatist – that his root is the mind alone, and a scholastic mind at that (no high *intelletto* despite his apparent clarities) – and that, in his listenings he has stayed there where the ear and the mind are, has only gone from his fine ear outward rather than, as I say a projective poet will, down through the workings of his own throat to that place where breath comes from, where breath has its beginnings, where drama has to come from, where, the coincidence is, all act springs.' But this unmitigated subjectivity only begs questions, and does not produce positive criticism. Does drama *have* to come from where breath has its beginnings? Olson asserts without demonstrating. Having articulated his theory to his own satisfaction, he applies it to verse regardless.

But Projective Verse is more than breath. He describes form: 'OPEN, or what can else be called COMPOSITION BY FIELD, as opposed to inherited line, stanza, over-all form'. The poem 'is energy transferred from where the poet got it ... by way of the poem itself to, all the way over to, the reader. Okay. Then the poem itself must, at all points, be a high energy construct and, at all points, an energy-discharge.' The poet must meet this energy with equal energy to ensure that the reader encounters the same energy. This energy can be dissipated by description and simile. Thus they are to be avoided: 'ONE PER-CEPTION MUST IMMEDIATELY AND DIRECTLY LEAD TO A FURTHER PERCEPTION ... USE USE USE the process at all points, in any given poem always,

always one perception must must must MOVE, IN-
STANTER, ON ANOTHER!'

This pressing energy means that there is no necessary
need for conventional syntax, punctuation, or traditional
poetic form. 'FORM IS NEVER MORE THAN AN
EXTENSION OF CONTENT,' Olson tells us. The
theory was adopted, with adjustments, by various poets,
some of them students of Olson, others imitators. Robert
Creeley, Robert Duncan, Denise Levertov, and many less
original poets took up the new faith.

Olson's poetry is better than his theories. He understands verse better than his rhetorical prose. An extract
from a letter to Elaine Feinstein, attempting to drive his
definitions further, displays his lack of clarity in prose
where his subject is *instinctive*, unparaphrasable, subjective knowledge. He projects meanings on to words,
regardless of the common meanings. He writes of the
image: '"the Image" (wow, that you capitalize it makes
sense: it is *all* we had (post-circum *The Two Noble
Kinsmen*), as we had a sterile grammar (an insufficient
"sentence") we had analogy only: images, no matter how
learned or how simple: even Burns say, allowing etc. and
including Frost! Comparison. Thus representation was
never off the dead-spot of description. Nothing was *happening* as of the poem itself – ding and zing or something.
It was referential to reality. And that a p. poor crawling
actuarial "real" ...' What is puzzling is the archaisms
that litter the 'new' style, and the apparent rejection of all
English poetry. Olson's mission would seem to be that of
New Broom.

It is wrong, perhaps, to search through Projectivist
verse for sudden, inspired – perhaps accidental – lyrical
passages. Rather, one should attend to the speech
rhythms, the breath lines, the 'feel' of the verse:

   I have this sense
that I am one
with my skin

It is essentially a physiological poetry, clarified by intellect but not enhanced by exact language or the tensions of traditional forms. And yet – having rejected traditional forms – the Projectivist Olson does not suggest any viable new form. His longer poems become sadly diffuse and dull. The breathing theory is arbitrary, subjective to the point of solipsism. Nonetheless, Olson is the best exponent of his theory.

Born in 1910 in Worcester, Massachusetts, Charles Olson was, in his own words, 'uneducated' at Wesleyan, Yale and Harvard. He taught at Clark, Harvard (1936–39) and at Black Mountain College, where he was instructor and rector (1951–6). Black Mountain College, which closed in 1956, was important in the history of American education and art. It was founded during the Depression as an experiment in community education (1933). It became a Mecca for those dissatisfied with traditional academic methods and focused its attention on creative activity, art-as-object. Distinguished writers, artists and musicians were associated with it, among them John Andrew Rice, the founder; the philosopher John Dewey; the artists De Kooning, Kline and Rauschenberg; the writers Robert Duncan, Robert Creeley, and Jonathan Williams; and among the musicians, John Cage. Two magazines, Cid Corman's *Origin* (1951–6) and Creeley's *Black Mountain Review* – were published from the College and included work by, among others, Paul Blackburn, Denise Levertov, Allen Ginsberg, Olson, Zukofsky, Williams, Jack Kerouac, Ed Dorn, Gary Snyder, and Michael McClure.

Olson's first important publication was the essay 'Lear and Moby Dick' in *Twice a Year* (1938) and his first published poem appeared in 1945. In 1947 his finest prose work, *Call Me Ishmael*, was published. It explores the meaning of Melville's *Moby Dick* in a vitally original spoken style not yet reduced to mannerism. In 1952 he travelled to Mexico to study Mayan hieroglyphics in

Yucatan and wrote his *Mayan Letters* (1953) to Robert
Creeley. Olson was an archaeologist and anthropologist.
These interests underlie much of his writing. In his
longer works, the rise and fall of civilizations are an
implicit intellectual rhythm and often an explicit pattern
of allusions. Historical material recurs frequently in
quotations and impressions, generating the larger themes,
as in 'a Plantation a beginning' from *The Maximus
Poems*:

I sit here on a Sunday
with grey water, the winter
staring me in the face

'the Snow lyes indeed
about a foot thicke
for ten weekes' John White

warns any prospective
planter

'The Kingfishers', one of his finest poems, includes the
theme:

... if I have any taste
it is because I have interested myself
in what was slain in the sun

I pose you your question:

shall you uncover honey/where maggots are?

I hunt among stones.

His concern with history and time, and their novel expression in his verse, have probably contributed more to
contemporary poetry than his Projective theories. He sees
Time, not in parallel plains of world cultures as Pound
did, nor as a continuity with which the poet could forge
intellectual links as Eliot did, but rather archaeologically.
Looking down he at once sees, as if through strata, all that

has happened or been in a certain place, throughout time, as though he had excavated it. What occurred or was remains active in the place it occurred or was. In 'Letter, May 2, 1959' from *The Maximus Poems* he writes,

                From
then to now nothing
new, in the meaning
that that wall walked
today, happened a bull-
dozer discloses
Meeting House Hill
was a sanddune under
what was valued for
still the sun makes
a west here as on
each Gloucester hill

Olson settled in Gloucester, Massachusetts. Rooted in one place, his imagination could take its particular soundings. His devotion to Melville, too, whose library he recovered, complemented his poetic exploration of the history and geography of the seaport town.

As early as 1948 Olson was writing in open forms. In one poem, 'La Preface', he attacks the closed parenthesis as a symbol of 'closed form'. His annoyance against closed form had its counterpart in his open hostility to traditional academe. In 1951 the Melville Society held a party to celebrate the hundredth birthday of *Moby Dick*. This party inspired Olson's 'Letter for Melville 1951', an acrimonious attack on academic careerism, *'written to be read* AWAY FROM *the Melville Society's "One Hundredth Birthday Party" for* Moby Dick *at Williams College, Labor Day Weekend, Sept. 2-4, 1951'* – 'that I find anywhere in my being any excuses for this abomination, for the false & dirty thing which it is – nothing more than a bunch of commercial travellers from the several colleges?' He continues,

Please to carry my damnations to each of them
as they sit upon their arse-bones variously
however differently padded ...

Olson's early poetry was included in *Y & X* (1948),
Letter for Melville (1951), and *This* (1952). Then followed
the first ten sections of his major work, *The Maximus
Poems* (1953). Other sections came in 1956 and 1960, and
in 1961 a single poem, *Maximus, from Dogtown – I*. In
1968 *Maximus IV, V, VI* was published. In these poems
the poet is the protagonist and Gloucester his stamping
ground. A number of the poems are called 'Letters' and
are addressed to the citizens of Gloucester, admonishing
them and attacking, on their behalf, apparently worthy,
but in fact superficial, contemporary values:

They whine to my people, these entertainers, sellers

they play upon their bigotries (upon their fears

these   they have the nerve
to speak of that lovely hour
the Waiting Station, 5 o'clock, the Magnolia bus, Al Levy
on duty (the difference ...

He cries to the citizens,

o tansy city, root city
let them not make you
as the nation is

The poem is diffuse. Though it is a misreading, in Olson's
terms, to do so, we do well to locate the splendid fragments of verse that stand out, and work into the poem
from them. 'History is the Memory of Time' begins:

1622 to 1626 was the fish rush   (with Pilgrims the Mormons
                                 on the side like side bets
10 boats New England waters
the year before, then BANG:

37 vessels (mostly Damariscove?) 1622,
45 Piscataqua and Cape Anne, 1623
50, 1624 – & WAR, with Spain

After troubles and fighting, it ends quietly with the common citizen:

They should raise a monument
to a fisherman crouched down
behind a hogshead, protecting
his dried fish

Olson's other major book of poems is *Distances* (1960) which contains most of the later work not connected with *Maximus* – in particular what is perhaps his best poem, 'The Kingfishers'. This of all Olson's work most nearly approximates Pound's technique and feeling. The poem, roughly two hundred lines, is divided into three main sections, the first of which is subdivided into four. Like Pound (and unlike the Olson of *The Maximus Poems*) he suggests parallel cultures – in this case American and ancient Cambodian, with recurrent motifs: an ancient symbol 'E', a quotation from Mao Tse-tung, and the kingfisher:

I thought of the E in the stone, and of what Mao said
la lumiere"
            but the kingfisher
de l'aurore"
            but the kingfisher flew west
est devant nous!
            he got the color of his breast
            from the heat of the setting sun!

The lines in French are from Mao's 1948 report to his party. There is more tension in this briefer poem than in the sprawling *Maximus* poems. 'The Kingfishers' is aware of a loss:

'The kingfishers!
who cares
for their feathers
now?'

But the feathers were only a symbol of wealth:

The legends are
legends. Dead, hung up indoors, the kingfisher
will not indicate a favoring wind,
or avert the thunderbolt ...

Olson follows this with a contemplation of change:

And all now is war
where so lately there was peace,
and the sweet brotherhood, the use
of tilled fields.

The poet is troubled by 'change'. The poem begins with the statement,

What does not change/is the will to change

The kingfisher comes to represent the continuance of the best qualities in civilization. Our immediate society is of 'maggots':

Shall you uncover honey/where maggots are?
    I hunt among stones

The poem is brief enough so that Olson's style does not become monotonous, long enough to create effective tensions.

His prose books, which include *Human Universe and Other Essays* (1965) and *Letters for Origin 1950-1956* (1969) do not live up to his early study of Melville, *Call Me Ishmael*. In their casual, epistolary form – a form Olson has used extensively in verse and prose – they tend to be wilfully confusing.

His influence both as a poet and a teacher was considerable, but his followers haven't his natural ear, or vision, or a clear understanding of the subjectivity of his 'breath' principles. The almost inevitable flaccidity of verse written in pursuance of his Projective theories or in imitation of his idiosyncratic practice has meant that his influence – as yet – has not been to the good. But his theories and his poems raise various basic questions about the nature of poetic form and language. When time has provided an adequate perspective on his work, when imitation and apology give way to critical understanding, his poems will begin to provide a positive example, a vital text.

Elizabeth Bishop born 1911

Oh, must we dream our dreams
and have them, too?

– 'Questions of Travel'

The dream-like sharpness of Elizabeth Bishop's poetry is
immediately engaging because it lacks the vagaries of
wilful poetic dreaminess; it looks at objects in the world
of waking, imparting to them almost a surreal quality, the
product of uncanny exactitude, not distortion. The more
her poems focus on an object, a creature, a landscape, the
more they become – arrested in time – unreal. As they
become unreal in the world of waking, they become meaningful to the eye that observes them, passing into the subjective 'dream' world, even if only momentarily. 'The
Man-Moth' veers towards nightmare:

> Here, above,
> cracks in the buildings are filled with battered moonlight.
> The whole shadow of Man is only as big as his hat.
> It lies at his feet like a circle for a doll to stand on,
> and he makes an inverted pin, the point magnetized to the
> moon.

In a less overtly allegorical poem, 'The Fish', she writes,

> Here and there
> his brown skin hung in strips

like ancient wallpaper,
and its pattern of darker brown
was like wallpaper:
shapes like full-blown roses
stained and lost through age.
He was speckled with barnacles,
fine rosettes of lime,
and infested
with tiny white sea-lice ...

Her respect for the objects in her poems recalls the care
and accuracy of the better surrealist painters; but her
writing is not layered with Freudian allusions, not finally
obscure, but lucid. Her wit, charity, and the undistracting
but unerring skill of her art makes hers an affirmative
poetry, even when the themes are potentially tragic. In
'At the Fishhouses' she watches the scene, and it watches
her: experience and dream are completely fused:

> One seal particularly
I have seen here evening after evening.
He was curious about me. He was interested in music;
like me a believer in total immersion,
so I used to sing him Baptist hymns.
I also sang 'A Mighty Fortress Is Our God'.
He stood up in the water and regarded me
steadily, moving his head a little.
Then he would disappear, then suddenly emerge
almost in the same spot, with a sort of shrug
as if it were against his better judgement.

A creature from that other element, the sea, 'bearable to
no mortal', is in all its supposed immortality contacted by
a creature from this. They communicate. The currents of
religious imagery, baptism, temptation are implicitly developed, not laboured. The sea pervades the poem:

If you should dip your hand in,
your wrist would ache immediately,

your bones would begin to ache and your hand would burn
as if the water were a transmutation of fire
that feeds on stones and burns with a dark grey flame.
If you tasted it ...

The sea is another element, another geography, full of
concealed mysteries.

Exploration and discovery occasionally lead to apparently universal insights, even if they originate in
ordinary matters. In 'Filling Station' the poet's eye roams
the garage, picking out details. She questions: why the
extraneous plant, the taboret, the doily? And she concludes:

Somebody embroidered the doily.
Somebody waters the plant,
or oils it, maybe. Somebody
arranges the rows of cans
so that they softly say:
ESSO-SO-SO-SO
to high-strung automobiles.
Somebody loves us all.

It is an ambiguous discovery; for the joy, always ironically in check, that pervades her poetry is tinged, despite
her objective approach, with a human sadness: the sadness of isolation, rootlessness, final incomprehension. She
keeps at a distance herself, detached for further exploration. Her attempt is to breach the isolation, something
she achieves in a few triumphant poems where an *action*
rather than an idea momentarily permits the individual
to step beyond itself.

Elizabeth Bishop was born in Worcester, Massachusetts,
in 1911 – the year her father died and her mother was
committed to a mental institution. She was raised by her
maternal grandparents in Nova Scotia, Canada, and by an
aunt in Boston. Educated at Vassar College, she graduated in 1934. Much of her life since has been spent in

travel. In 1952 she settled in Brazil. In recent years she has returned to Massachusetts to live in Cambridge and teach at Harvard.

Her book *North and South* (1946) brought her recognition, and *Poems* (1955) which combined *North and South* and a new book, *A Cold Spring*, was awarded the Pulitzer Prize. *Questions of Travel* (1966) and *Complete Poems* (1969) have established her firmly as one of the outstanding poets of her generation. The *Complete Poems* won the National Book Award. A further book, *Geography III*, was published in Britain in 1977.

Her poetry – especially the early poems – has affinities with the work of her friend, Marianne Moore, but Elizabeth Bishop is not, in her mature work, as experimental or idiosyncratic as the older poet, and she relies on a strongly musical rhythm. Her complex vision, finally more generous than Marianne Moore's, hovers like hers between real and surreal, the surrealism of uncanny precision. Her aim was to provide 'glimpses of the always-more-successful surrealism of everyday life', she wrote. That is her achievement. Randall Jarrell said, 'all her poems have written underneath, *I have seen it.*'

She is fascinated by geography rather than history – geography and travel, experiences in the present. When she portrays the early explorers of Brazil, she evokes their wonder before a new continent. A map can provide her with a total imaginative experience. In 'The Map' she writes, 'Topography displays no favorites; North's as near as West.' Under her fingers the map becomes a place for imaginative exploration:

... We can stroke these lovely bays,
under a glass as if they were expected to blossom,
or as if to provide a clean cage for invisible fish ...

By quiet artifice she achieves the natural spoken tone of her poems. Her meticulousness is second-nature. For example, she contributed a very brief essay to a book of essays in memory of Randall Jarrell. In less than a page she attempts to evoke the man as *she* had known and seen him: 'I like to think of him as I saw him once after we had gone swimming together on Cape Cod; wearing only bathing trunks and a very queer straw cap with a big visor, seated on the crest of a high sand dune, writing in a notebook. It was a bright and dazzling day. Randall looked small and rather delicate, but bright and dazzling too ...' She turns the image over in her hands as though it were an object, viewing it from various angles. And yet her vision is in no sense 'objectivist'. Strict, unobtrusive formal structure and a tendency to draw meanings from, or suggest meanings through, her images indicates that.

Within her forms the length of line varies. The rhymes are either taken for granted or startlingly unexpected: in other words, rhyme becomes part of the *poem*, not simply part of the form. The tone, sometimes calculatedly impersonal, is in its quest for precision frequently idiosyncratic – her own voice slips in, as it were, through the back door. She cannot help but reclaim the poem with her voice, freeing it from cold objectivity so that it can penetrate into the dream. A bus (in 'Cape Breton'):

... stops, and a man carrying a baby gets off,
climbs over a stile, and goes down through a small steep
    meadow,
which establishes its poverty in a snowfall of daisies,
to his invisible house beside the water.

The birds keep on singing, a calf bawls, the bus starts.
The thin mist follows
the white mutations of its dream;
an ancient chill is rippling the dark brooks.

In the celebrated fish poem, having caught and examined the creature, she releases it:

where oil had spread a rainbow
around the rusted engine
to the bailer rusted orange,
the sun-cracked thwarts,

the oarlocks on their strings,
the gunnels – until everything
was rainbow, rainbow, rainbow!
And I let the fish go.

It is reported that Elizabeth Bishop works slowly, pinning manuscripts of her poems to the wall, filling in words, phrases and lines when they come clear. Robert Lowell alluded to this in his poems for her in *Notebook*:

> Do
> you still hang words in air, ten years imperfect,
> joke-letters, glued to cardboard posters, with gaps
> and empties for the unimagined phrase,
> unerring Muse who scorns less casual friendships?

Her patient unwillingness to err found the perfect phrases in her love poem, 'The Shampoo':

> The still explosions on the rocks,
> the lichens, grow
> by spreading, gray, concentric shocks ...

With the same care she develops the line of wit in her travel poems, moving by standing still: 'Should we have stayed at home and thought of here?' Packing her memory's valise, she wonders, 'And have we room/for one more folded sunset, still quite warm?' For her, travel *is* home. Rootless, isolated – in a recent long poem Crusoe is the protagonist – she explores. The map is the symbol of the potential journey, stilled, promising or not:

> and then a sudden golden silence
> in which the traveller takes a notebook, writes:

> '*Is it lack of imagination that makes us come*
> *to imagined places, not just stay at home?*
> *Or could Pascal have been not entirely right*
> *about just sitting quietly in one's room?*

Continent, city, country, society:
the choice is never wide and never free.
And here, or there ... No. Should we have stayed at home,
wherever that may be?'

Delmore Schwartz 1913–1966

The past, a giant shadow like the twilight,
The moving street on which the autos slide,
The buildings' heights, like broken teeth,
Repeat necessity on every side,
The age requires death and is not denied,
He has come as a young man to be hanged once more!

– 'Someone is Harshly Coughing as Before'

Delmore Schwartz had the sharp intellect of a trained
philosopher; and a persistent, nagging conscience. His
poems reflect the tension between these qualities. In the
early poems, responsible and eloquent, Schwartz works
from particular experiences towards lucid generalizations.
In the later poems, less controlled, he struggles to find an
alternative to his early, lucid style, having found that
logic and the understanding it seemed to bring were inadequate against his developing mental illness. Though
he knew its source and its manifestations, when it settled
on him he could not by act of will recover.

The intellect, unassisted by imagery, sometimes dictates a stanza of excessive abstraction, formulating what
the poet could better have said in prose. In 'The Kingdom of Poetry' (a later poem), the lines are undistinguished as verse and as thought:

For reality is various and rich, powerful and vivid, but it is
not enough

Because it is disorderly and stupid or only at times, and
erratically, intelligent:
For without poetry, reality is speechless or incoherent ...

One need only contrast this with the vividly achieved
lines from 'The Sin of Hamlet':

And when it comes, escape is small; the dooi
Creaks; the worms of fear spread veins; the furtive
Fugitive, looking backward, sees his
Ghost in the mirror, his shameful eyes, his mouth diseased.

Schwartz was born in Brooklyn, New York, in 1913,
the elder of two sons. His best-known short story, 'In
Dreams Begin Responsibilities', portrays the incompati-
bility of his parents and the estrangement it occasioned
in him. His father's ambition was to become rich, and he
succeeded in the years before the Depression, during
which he died. Delmore grew up to sudden poverty.
Characters of many of his short stories and the themes of
poems and fiction were taken from this period. Financial
failures, victims of the Depression recur; hatred for his
mother, to whom he was emotionally bound by his
parents' divorce and his father's death, tensions created
by a disturbed family background, being Jewish, being
insecure: these were central themes.

In 1931 he went to the University of Wisconsin and the
following year transferred to New York University. He
graduated in philosophy in 1935. As a graduate student,
he attended Harvard and did well, though he left before
taking a further degree. Some of his fiction, verse and
criticism had begun to appear in periodicals. In 1938 he
married and his first collection of poems and stories, *In
Dreams Begin Responsibilities*, was published. After his
translation of Rimbaud's *Saison en Enfer* appeared, he
took up residence at Harvard where he taught advanced
composition (1940–47) and became associated with the
publishing house New Directions, at that time situated
in Cambridge, Massachusetts.

His books at this period included a verse play, *Shenandoah* (1941); a collection of essays, *The Imitation of Life* (1941); and a long autobiographical poem about the development of a Jewish boy in New York, *Genesis, Book I* (1943). In 1943 Schwartz became an editor of *Partisan Review*, a post he held until 1955, and in 1944 – the year of his divorce – he was appointed Assistant Professor of English Composition at Harvard. He resigned in 1947.

His best collection of short stories, *The World is a Wedding*, appeared in 1948. He married again in 1949 and was separated from his second wife in 1957. Much in demand as a visiting lecturer, he went to many universities during this period, speaking mainly on T. S. Eliot and Yeats. In 1950 another collection of poems and stories appeared, *Vaudeville for a Princess. Summer Knowledge: New and Selected Poems 1938–1958* appeared nine years later. Part of the cause for his later disintegration was his major early success. He was the youngest poet ever to win the Bollingen Prize and the Shelley Memorial Award. He craved further major successes, but they did not come to him. For two years he was poetry editor of the *New Republic* (1955–7), and his last book, *Successful Love and Other Poems*, appeared in 1961.

There are as yet few known details about Schwartz's life from 1957 until his death in 1966. He taught for a time at Syracuse University, New York, then lived in Greenwich Village and was committed to hospital several times suffering from persecution mania. He tried to stave it off by drugs and drink, but they accentuated his paranoia. His last year was spent largely in the isolation of hotel rooms in New York. He died of a heart attack alone in a drab hotel room in Manhattan. A desk clerk at the hotel reported that Schwartz 'spent most of the time in his room typing, and he used to order food from a nearby delicatessen'. No one claimed the body or possessions and his manuscripts disappeared.

In an article published in *The Southern Review*, 'Poetry and Belief in Thomas Hardy' (1940), Schwartz wrote, 'The subject of poetry is experience, not truth, even when the poet is writing about ideas. When the poet can get the whole experience of his sensibility into his poem, then there will be an adequate relationship between the details of his poem and the beliefs he asserts, whether they are true or not.' This statement applies to Schwartz's own poetry. His experiences of family tension, of being Jewish, an artist in an unresponsive society, and so on, were the experiences out of which the poems came, while his study of philosophy had taught him a higher discipline. Experience eventually taught him the bounds of philosophy, which at times hardly related to reality, and was unable to alleviate the acute guilt he came to suffer.

In an early dialogue poem, 'Father and Son', the father says, 'Your guilt is nameless, because its name is time,/ Because its name is death ...' He adds, 'You must meet your death face to face.' The son attempts to evade the issue but the father insists: 'You must, like one in an old play,/Decide, once and for all, your heart's place.' The son's quest is to find that place, to make that crucial decision. The father's final words touch the quick of Schwartz's work: 'Be guilty of yourself in the full looking-glass.'

As Schwartz points out in another poem, 'The Ballad of the Children of the Czar', the irony is that 'The past is inevitable' and the sins of the fathers live obscurely but ineradicably in the sons. Schwartz identifies with the children of the Czar, soon to be murdered: 'I am my father's father,/You are your children's guilt.'

In the poem 'Parlez-Vous Français?' the implicit guilt proves alienating; the artist, wishing to tell the truth, to express meaning, is not understood. In a barber's shop, Caesar (Hitler?) is heard speaking over the radio. 'Caesar proposes, Caesar promises/Pride, justice, and the sun ...'

And now who enters quietly? Who is this one
Shy, pale, and quite abstracted? Who is he?
It is the writer merely ...

The writer speaks only French. 'He stands there speaking
and they laugh to hear/Rage and excitement from the
foreigner.' Part of the irony is that the people in the shop
do not understand the writer's language: 'Ecoutez! La
plupart des hommes/Vivent des vies de désespoir silen-
cieux', a translation of Thoreau's words, 'Most men live
lives of quiet desperation.' A further aspect of the irony
is that the writer cannot act, cannot communicate. It is
an intense alienation.

Schwartz is driven to contemplate the self and its
milieu, to formulate his relationship with the mass. He
tests Marxism, psychology, measuring as nearly as he can
their possible effects, their validity. But it is the self that
is at the centre of his quest, looking for the 'heart's place'.
In 'By Circumstances Fed' he writes.

So, once in the drugstore,
Amid all the poppy, salve and ointment,
I suddenly saw, estranged there,
Beyond all disappointment,
My own face in the mirror.

In 'The Sin of Hamlet' it is guilt that corners the self.

In most of the early poems, among the best he wrote,
Schwartz is the engaged observer. He sees the banalities,
the ugliness of life symbolized in the city and its futile
patterns, clear in the sonnet 'O City, City':

Being amid six million souls, their breath
An empty song suppressed on every side,
Where the sliding auto's catastrophe
Is a gust past the curb, where numb and high
The office building rises to its tyranny,
Is our anguished diminution until we die.

Even on the holiday beach, the futility is present, expressed in 'Far Rockaway': 'Time unheard moves and the heart of man is eaten/Consummately at leisure.' With Eliot, Schwartz sees the crucial human delusion in the subjugation of individuality to the mass – not to the community with its forms and values, but to the manipulable *demos*:

See the evasions which so many don,
To flee the guilt of time they become one,
That is, the one number among masses,
The one anonymous in the audience,
The one expressionless in the subway,
In the subway evening among so many faces ...

The alternative symbols for Schwartz are the blue, perfect sky, the whiteness of snow, or simply the colour white. In *Genesis* he writes,

Everything happens in the mind of God?
– This news is thrilling and I hope it true!
It is like looking at the sky's round blue,
Blue within blue and endlessly
And does the angel Gabriel know it too?

'O City, City' suggests those symbols powerfully by contrast with the urban world:

Whence, if ever shall come the actuality
Of a voice speaking the mind's knowing,
The sunlight bright on the green windowshade,
And the self articulate, affectionate, and flowing,
Ease, warmth, light, the utter showing,
When in the white bed all things are made.

Schwartz is at his best when he lets his intellect engage some image from the 'real' world, sometimes banalities. He sees and is able to transform their ordinariness into an abstraction or generality. 'Transform' is the operative word – the transformations Schwartz achieves are often brilliant. In the poem 'Someone is Harshly Coughing as Before' he hears someone coughing on the floor above. The unknown man becomes Christ, Keats, 'longing for Eden, afraid of the coming war'. He becomes the figure of the victim throughout history: 'He has come as a young man to be hanged once more! / Another mystery to be crucified ...' The world outside the house is everything that opposes the ideal of Eden.

In Schwartz's later poetry the transformations are less frequent and less effective. His style changed from predominantly iambic short lines to long, rambling lines, attempting to assimilate prose rather than speech rhythms, as though he were attempting to formulate a language that could combine prose and verse. Only one poem, 'Seurat's Sunday Afternoon along the Seine', decisively succeeds in Schwartz's later style. He responds to Seurat's intellectual approach to light in his *pointilliste* technique, its dots enabling light to suffuse the painting. For Schwartz it is as though the figures in the painting are participating *as a group* in a form of communion with light:

The sunlight, the soaring trees and the Seine
Are as a great net in which Seurat seeks to seize and hold
All living being in a parade and promenade of mild calm
   happiness...

But Berryman is right when he laments, 'I'd bleed to say his lovely work improved / But it is not so.' His finest work has earned its place among the best poems in his generation. He produced a handful of haunting lyrics, as well, unlike any others in American poetry:

What is to be given,
Is spirit, yet animal,
Colored, like heaven,
Blue, yellow, beautiful.

The blood is checkered by
So many stains and wishes,
Between it and the sky
You could not choose, for riches.

Yet let me now be careful
Not to give too much
To one so shy and fearful
For like a gun is touch.

Randall Jarrell 1914–1965

Here I am.
        But it's not *right*.
If just living can do this,
Living is more dangerous than anything:

It is terrible to be alive.

– 'The Face'

Randell Jarrell knew that, although 'Behind everything there is always/The unknown unwanted life', it was the known and wanted life that was blighted or unattainable. He had tried to live 'By trading another's sorrow' for his own but eventually he became 'an object among dreams' himself. During the composition of his best collection, *The Lost World*, he stepped in front of a truck and was killed. He was fifty-one.

Compassion for those who could not cope with everyday psychological hazards – loneliness in particular – dominates his work. Various critics have dismissed him as sentimental, but his contemporary Robert Lowell knew him better, describing him as 'the most heartbreaking English poet of his generation'.

He was born in Nashville, Tennessee in 1914 and spent much of his childhood in California. A memory that haunted him in particular was the year he spent in Hollywood with his paternal grandparents at the time of his parents' divorce. He evokes the memory at length in 'The Lost World'.

A brilliant student, he left school during the Depression and worked for his uncle, studying shorthand at a secretarial college. He went to Vanderbilt University (1935), the centre of the Fugitive group. He was drawn into the group by Ransom and Warren, and there met Tate as well. Though Jarrell was not fully committed to the Fugitives' Agrarian programme, the tight elliptical style of their verse influenced his early poems.

Jarrell followed Ransom to Kenyon College (1938), but moved on shortly to the University of Texas. In 1940 his poetry was first published in book format in the anthology *Five Young American Poets* followed in 1942 by his first full collection, *Blood for a Stranger*. In 1942 he joined the Army Air Force – an experience which produced some of his best work and, for many, the best American poetry to come out of World War II, though he did not see active service. In 'Losses' he wrote,

In bombers named for girls, we burned
The cities we had learned about in school –
Till our lives wore out; our bodies lay among
The people we had killed and never seen.

Several volumes of poetry appeared during this period: *Little Friend, Little Friend* (1945), *Losses* (1948) and, still on the war theme, *The Seven-League Crutches* (1951). His *Selected Poems* (1955) included the best poems from these early volumes.

Robert Lowell remembers Jarrell saying, 'If I were a rich man, I would pay money for the privilege of being able to teach.' He followed that vocation after the war. He taught briefly at Sarah Lawrence College, New York, then settled for almost twenty years at the Women's College of the University of North Carolina at Greensboro, where he taught English and Imaginative Writing. Only two more books of his poetry were published: *The*

Woman at the Washington Zoo (1960) and, in the year of his death, *The Lost World* (1965). His *Complete Poems* (1969) included a number of poems and translations omitted from his earlier volumes.

He was a brilliant critic as well as a poet. Lowell says, 'He had a deadly hand for killing what he despised.' But his genius is better revealed in his general essays and his positive reviews – for he was an eloquent and lucid advocate. His critical writings were collected in three volumes: *Poetry and the Age* (1953), *A Sad Heart at the Supermarket* (1962), and *The Third Book of Criticism* (1969). He also wrote a telling satirical novel, *Pictures from an Institution* (1954), the story of life on a minor American campus.

From the beginning, Jarrell was preoccupied with innocence and the loss of innocence. Many of his poems include in their titles the words 'loss', 'lost' and 'child'. The suffering and recognition that follow the loss of innocence lured him into nostalgia. In the *Complete Poems*, seventeen begin, 'When ...'. The recollection of innocence (usually in the form of childhood) can transform and redeem a present solitude:

Each evening, as the sun sank, didn't I grieve
To leave *my* tree house for reality?
There was nothing there for me to disbelieve.

The nostalgia sometimes borders on the sentimental or whimsical, but Jarrell is constantly aware of the present reality. Nostalgia, far from being an escape, heightens the present situation.

It's so: I have pictures,
Not such old ones; people behaved
Differently then ... When they meet me they say:
You haven't changed.
I want to say: You haven't looked.

There is no misuse of imagination here, no blurring

towards sentimentality, but uncompromising awareness of the withered inner life of the speaker of the poem.

The war was for Jarrell a powerful symbol of loss, innocence violated, and conscience implicated. He becomes one of the 'other people' in his war poems, acting and responding with them. His most anthologized poem, 'The Death of the Ball Turret Gunner' equates the innocence of the unborn with the colder innocence of the gunner, hunched in the belly of the ball turret beneath the plane: 'From my mother's sleep I fell into the State,/ And I hunched in its belly till my wet fur froze.' The death of the gunner is expressed in terms of a terrible birth: 'When I died they washed me out of the turret with a hose.'

In many of his poems the fairy tale had become a metaphor for lived experience. Here the lived experience becomes the metaphor: the image – complex and ambiguous – has a stronger reality than what it is intended to illuminate. But experience still remains something beyond rational understanding. There is no rational answer in Jarrell's poems. Their open-endedness, formal and thematic, their questioning, gives them their poignant integrity. The wounded man, in 'A Field Hospital', may find some comfort:

His arm stings; then, alone,
He neither knows, remembers – but instead
Sleeps, comforted.

But he will wake up. The poem 'Siegfried' enacts the waking. It begins 'In the turret's great glass dome, the apparition, death ...' But,

      in the gunner's skull,
It is a dream: and he, the watcher, guiltily
Watches the him, the actor, who is innocent.
It happens as it does because it does.
It is unnecessary to understand ...

But he does understand, and the poem modulates in tone:
from understanding dreams and wishes, he comes to
understand (though not rationally) the real:

> You look at the people who look back at you, at home,
> And it is different – you have understood
> Your world at last: you have tasted your own blood.

The tonal changes recall two of Jarrell's favourite poets,
Rilke and Wordsworth, whose visions of childhood his
own resembles to a degree, and whose vision of innocence
is, like his, embodied in the child and its instinctive understanding.

Dreams are a recurrent image in Jarrell: the transition
of images, and tones of voice, the movement between past
and present, are facilitated by the dream mechanism, best
exploited in poems such as 'In the Ward: The Sacred
Wood'. The fluidity of the dream convention makes it
possible for Jarrell at once to suggest and question his
suggestions about the actual world: 'All this I dreamed
in my great ragged bed .../Or so I dreamed,' he declares
in 'The Island'. The poems raise questions, but seldom
answer them.

Jarrell's taut early style evolves to the use of richly
varied iambic pentameter. The openness of form and
theme carries through into Jarrell's last books. There he
turns to children and ageing women as his living metaphors. Many of the poems are dramatic monologues. The
controlled voices that speak through the whole range of
human emotions are developed with Jarrell's unerring
ear for tonal nuance, emotional ambiguity. The verse
becomes freer, line length is varied with the changes of
tone. The title poem of *The Woman at the Washington
Zoo* exemplifies his monologue style:

> The saris go by me from the embassies.
>
> Cloth from the moon. Cloth from another planet.
> They look back at the leopard like the leopard.

And I...
>
> this print of mine, that has kept its color
Alive through so many cleanings ...

The woman is like her own dress, kept alive through so
many cleanings. The animals she sees are caged, but she
too is caged: 'Oh, bars of my own body, open, open!'
But the animals at least attract attention. She can only
evolve her fantasies:

> Vulture,
When you come for the white rat that the foxes left,
Take off the red helmet of your head, the black
Wings that have shadowed me, and step to me as man:
The wild brother at whose feet the white wolves fawn,
To whose hand of power the great lioness
Stalks, purring ...
> You know what I was,
You see what I am: change me, change me!

The sexual frustration is perfectly expressed in terms of
the things about her. She knows that fantasy cannot
change her.

In his last book, *The Lost World*, the themes are fully
developed, here in the first person as well as through the
dramatic monologue. In 'Next Day', a woman at the
supermarket, like the woman at the zoo, wishes to be
noticed:

> Now that I'm old, my wish
Is womanish:
That the boy putting groceries in my car
>
> See me.

Her final inability to understand her life is poignant:

No one has anything, I'm anybody,
I stand beside my grave
Confused with my life, that is commonplace and solitary.

A few critics have complained of a lack of depth in Jarrell's language. It is his sense of dramatic rightness that supplies the 'flat' word when it is needed. His speakers have real doubts. Jarrell's compassion in the poems does not take the form of cleverness at the expense of his subject matter. His poetic skill is in the manipulation of ordinary words to highlight authentic emotions. 'What can be more tedious,' he asks, 'than a man whose every sentence is a balanced epigram without wit, profundity, or taste?'

Delmore Schwartz, reviewing *Little Friend, Little Friend* in 1945, identified the qualities central in Jarrell's work: 'the motives of honesty, courage, and inconsolable love of life are here submitted to the conditions of poetry and fulfilled in them. If, as one poem declares, this life is a dream from which no one wakes, the dreamer has refused to deceive himself, to let himself go, and to forget what he believes and loves.'

John Berryman 1914–1972

Henry rested, possessed of many pills
& gin & whiskey. He put up his feet
& switched on Schubert.
His tranquillity lasted five minutes
for (1) all that undone all the heavy weeks
and (2) images shook him alert.

– 'no. 256', *His Toy, His Dream, His Rest*

Despite the various guides that critics have provided to his work, Berryman remains an enigma. At times his idiosyncratic mature style is a natural mode of expression, at others it is wilful, mannered, constricted by its forms. Critics have described his work as convoluted, obscure, archaic, distorted, pretentious, artificial, offensive. Yet many agree with Robert Lowell: 'I think *Dream Songs*, now completed, is one of the glories of the age, the single most heroic work in English poetry since the War ... Berryman handles the language, as if he made it.'

The key words are 'handles the language, as if he made it'. What compels the reader to return to Berryman's poems is fascination with his sometimes brilliant idiom. His eccentricities are *like* a voice (though not an actual voice), while his more traditional poems tend to be dull, laboured. A worrying question is, how much of the attraction of Berryman's mature work is the attraction of *technique*, mere surface effects?

John Berryman was born in McAlester, Oklahoma, of
Roman Catholic parents. His father was a banker, his
mother a school-teacher. The family moved to Florida,
and there, when Berryman was twelve, his father committed suicide in front of the boy's window. The image
haunted Berryman for the rest of his life. His father's
death was in part the cause for Berryman's compulsive
need for human contact, firm faith, certainty. His
attempts to explore and assimilate the experience in
verse, and to escape it – by drink, promiscuity, and experiment – in life, led on to his suicide. In a 'Dream
Song' (235) in memory of Hemingway, he cries:

Mercy! my father; do not pull the trigger
or all my life I will suffer from your anger
killing what you began.

In 'Freshman Blues' the irony masks an acutely real
anguish:

Thought much I then of perforated daddy,
daddy boxed in & let down with strong straps,
when I my friends' homes visited, with fathers
universal & intact ...

The family moved to Gloucester, Massachusetts and
on to New York, where they settled. Berryman went to
Columbia. He was awarded a travelling scholarship to
Clare College, Cambridge, for two years. He returned to
New York and then taught at Harvard for three years,
at Princeton on and off for ten years, and finally at the
University of Minnesota, where he stayed. On a winter
morning in Minneapolis he jumped from a bridge, fell
on to the frozen Mississippi and died. He left no note
to explain the suicide, but several poems broach the
subject: 'Reflexions on suicide, & on my father, possess
me,' he begins a poem entitled 'Of Suicide'. Randall
Jarrell's suicide haunts him more than once in the *Dream
Songs*: 'He saw in the forest something coming, grim, /

but did not change his purpose.' In his autobiographical poems, he remembers his suicidal games at prep-school – in 'Drunks', for example. The poems do not so much explore the theme as allude to it fascinatedly.

Berryman's early ambition was to be a writer, but he did not imagine he would be a poet until he reviewed *A Winter Diary* by Mark Van Doren. That decided him. After what he calls 'work in verse-making', he came under the overwhelming influence of Yeats. 'I didn't so much wish to resemble [Yeats] as to *be*, and for several fumbling years I wrote in what it's convenient to call "period style", the Anglo-American style of the 1930s, with no voice of my own, learning chiefly from middle and later Yeats and from the brilliant young Englishman W. H. Auden. Yeats somehow saved me from the then crushing influence of Ezra Pound and T. S. Eliot ... but he could not teach me to sound like myself.'

The first intimations of that 'self' came in the poem 'Winter Landscape', which derives its individuality, he declares, 'from a peculiar steadiness of sombre tone ... and from its peculiar relation to its materials – drawn, of course, from Brueghel's famous painting.'

The three men coming down the winter hill
In brown, with tall poles and a pack of hounds
At heel, through the arrangement of the trees
Past the five figures at the burning straw,
Returning cold and silent to their town ...

Measured, slow, extremely literary, the strong influence we may feel here is Auden's. The poem taught Berryman that – because he could pretend ignorance of the title of the picture, 'Hunters in the Snow' – he could call their spears 'poles' and create a tone of stubborn incredulity as the world prepared itself for war again in 1938–9. He explains, 'This is not the subject of Brueghel's painting at all, and the interpretation of *the event of the poem* proves that the picture has merely provided necessary material, from a tranquil world, for what is necessary to be said – but which the poet refuses to say – about a violent world.'

His next crucial discovery was that 'a commitment of identity can be "reserved", so to speak, with an ambiguous pronoun. The poet himself is both left out and put in; the boy (in "The Ball Poem") does and does not become him, and we are confronted with a process which is at once a process of life and a process of art.' Berryman places such importance on this discovery that he declares, without it 'I could not have written either of the two long poems that constitute the bulk of my work so far,' namely: *Homage to Mistress Bradstreet,* in which the 'I' is sometimes Anne Bradstreet, sometimes Berryman; and the *Dream Songs,* in which a character called Henry and some of his friends take over the first person. The poet sometimes becomes a third person 'he' to Henry, sometimes 'you'.

Berryman's early poems work towards the style that matured in his major works. Dudley Fitts said that the early stanzas had 'an aura of academic contrivancy'. Even the later poems retain some of this quality, despite their freer forms. Berryman first appeared in book form in *Five American Poets* (1940), and his own collections *Poems* (1942) and *The Dispossessed* (1948) followed. At this time he was writing the sonnets which finally appeared as *Berryman's Sonnets* (1968), a sequence of 115 love sonnets written to an unspecified woman. They were virtually unaltered by Berryman in the twenty years between their composition and publication. They are strict in form and thematically modish, giving a preview of the adulterous, hard-drinking poet of the later work, but here still bound by fashionable models, particularly Auden, Hopkins, and Donne. In the twenty-third sonnet he writes, 'I want a verse fresh as a bubble breaks,' and ends the poem, 'Trapped in my rib-cage something throes and aches!'

The fresh style came in *Homage to Mistress Bradstreet* (1956). When he first woke to the fact that he was involved in a long poem, he exclaimed, 'Narrative! let's have narrative, and at least one dominant personality, and no fragmentation! – in short, let us have something spectacularly NOT *The Waste Land* ...' He composed the first stanza and the first three lines of the second, and progressed no further for almost five years. But already he had determined the form and subject. 'The eight-line stanza I invented here after a lifetime's study, especially of Yeats and in particular the one he adapted from Abraham Cowley for his elegy "In Memory of Major Robert Gregory".' For subject Berryman took, or was – he reports – chosen by, the 17th Century poet Anne Bradstreet, whose work he did not enjoy but whose life he found engaging. After four and a half years accumulating the material, he presented it in a poem in three sections and a total of fifty-seven stanzas.

The Puritan Anne Bradstreet is represented, rebelling against her new environment on landing, against her marriage, and finally against her prolonged old age and illness. Her voice speaks much of the poem, but Berryman occasionally comments in the first person and at times they converse. They become lovers. The stanza Berryman 'invented' proves flexible enough to cope with shifts of tone and narrative. It can be appreciated best *in extenso* in the childbirth passages. Something of the variety can be appreciated in stanza ten:

vellum I palm, and dream. Their forest dies
to greensward, privets, elms & towers, whence
a nightingale is throbbing.
Women sleep sound. I was happy once ...
(Something keeps on not happening; I shrink?)
These minutes all their passions & powers sink
and I am not one chance
for an unknown cry or a flicker of unknown eyes.

The dialogue achieves a dramatic intensity:

> Often now,
> I am afraid of you.
> I am a sobersides; I know.
> I *want* to take you for my lover. – Do.
> – I hear a madness. Harmless I to you
> am not, not I? – No.
> – I cannot but be. Sing a concord of our thought.

A far more resourceful poem came in the *Dream Songs*. A first batch of 77 *Dream Songs* (1964) was followed by a sequence of 308, *His Toy, His Dream, His Rest* (1968). He gives the subject of the first sequence as 'Turbulence: the modern world, and memory, and wants.' The form is, '18-line sections, three six-line stanzas, each normally (for feet) 5-5-3-5-5-3, variously rhymed and not but mostly rhymed with great strictness.' The character of Henry – Mr Bones – is often identified with Berryman himself, but Berryman protested, '... I am not Henry, You know, I pay income tax; Henry pays no income tax.'

Henry is something of an outcast, a victim, a white negro, and 'nigger-minstrel' cross-talk plays its part in the general mêlée of styles. The poet acknowledges his debt to the minstrel shows with their 'Mr Interlocutor', to the language of the Blues:

> Wishin I was dyin but I gotta make
> it all this way to that bed on these feet
> where peoples said to meet.
> Maybe but even if I see my son
> forever never, get back on the take,
> free, black & forty-one.

Henry dies part way through the poem and a series of 'Op Posth' follows:

> The cold is ultimating. The cold is cold.
> I am – I should be held together by –
> but I am breaking up

and Henry now has come to a full stop –
vanisht his vision, if there was, & fold
him over himself quietly.

The poem continues after Henry's death. 'I miss him.
When I get back to camp/I'll dig him up ...' Henry digs
himself out of the grave. He is a vulnerable creature, but
tenacious, coming up to be knocked back, tender, cynical,
ridiculous, not quite heroic. When Henry is gone for
good, Berryman contemplates deaths – the deaths of other
poets and of his father, of people known and unknown.
The 'Dream Song' form rings its elegiac changes.

Within the context of so long a poem the moments of
self-indulgence can be moving; but they spoil his later,
shorter works. The drama is in the way the emotions
develop, from celebration sliding into elegy and into
mad depression, slowly freeing himself and working up
again, cyclically. Like Henry, the poem remains open:

Is there more to say? Surely I've said enough,
my mind has been laid open
for thirty years, as when I spoke of love
& either could not get it or had too much of it,
impenetrable Henry, goatish, reserved,
whose heart is broken.

The paradox is that the objectively impenetrable is subjectively vulnerable. Henry, alive to things around him,
prays nonetheless, 'In sleep, of a heart attack, let Henry
go.' Eccentricities of style, mere patter, mere nonsense,
the cruelly forced syntax, the self-pity and humour are
accommodated, and a wide range of themes. There cannot be indifference, which is part of Henry's and Berryman's tragedy:

I spit upon this dreadful banker's grave
who shot his heart out in a Florida dawn
O ho alas alas
When will indifference come ...

In his form he had learned from Tudor lyrics, lessons of syntax from Emily Dickinson, thematic lessons perhaps from Stephen Crane. For all its colloquial variety and crude drama, the whole 'Dream Song' experiment is resolutely literary. But, literary or not, it was his ideal vehicle. 77 *Dream Songs* was awarded the Pulitzer Prize, *His Toy, His Dream, His Rest* won the National Book Award, and the Bollingen Prize.

The later books are less impressive: *Love and Fame* (1971) and *Delusions, etc* (1972) – in proof before his death and another posthumous volume, *Henry's Fate and Other Poems* (1978), contains a group of uncollected Dream Songs. *Love and Fame* in particular is over-full of confessional exhibitionism without the linguistic panache of the *Dream Songs*. Where the *Dream Songs* are generous in their personal themes, *Love and Fame* is more a private chronicle revealing a man intensely alone, self-preoccupied and finally self-pitying. His treatment of the women in the poems is casual, often crude. The book ends with a passionate attempt to reassert his relationship with God and celebrates his return to Catholicism. 'Eleven Addresses to the Lord' is the strongest section of the book. *Delusions, etc* develops the religious themes further, opening with a prayer sequence, 'Opus Dei'. 'Problem. I cannot come among Your saints,/it's not in me – "Velle" eh? – I will, and fail.' He can't bring himself to treat God familiarly – and yet the formal language he uses to address him is inadequate. Berryman is certainly not indifferent in the face of faith or death – but the tone is forced, the faith seems just another gesture at unattainable union with some force external to himself. He is more at home with Anne Bradstreet or with Henry, in the pubs, with the girls, with the joys, guilts, and fears of the *Dream Songs*. He needs the other voices to help his self-elucidation.

Robert Lowell 1917–1977

one life, one writing! But the downward glide
and bias of existing wrings us dry –

– 'Night Sweat'

Robert Lowell is *par excellence* the poet of the 'downward glide and bias of existing' that impoverishes us. He
sees the symptoms variously: in the destruction of the
hearts of cities, the tragic loss of political leaders, and
perhaps most terrifyingly in the personal decline and
fragmentation – as in 'Skunk Hour':

I watched for love-cars. Lights turned down,
they lay together, hull to hull,
where the graveyard shelves on the town ...
My mind's not right.

A car radio bleats,
'Love, O careless Love ...' I hear
my ill-spirit sob in each blood cell,
as if my hand were at its throat ...
I myself am hell,
nobody's here ...

The 'wringing dry' affects the poet, too. This forthright
and muscular writer spent much of his later verse fumbling, reforming earlier poems, making amends for poems
that ought not to have been printed in the first place by

improving and reprinting them. His last four books include substantial rewriting of material from *Notebook 1967–68* and from earlier collections.

He was born in Boston, Massachusetts, in 1917 into a distinguished New England family that traced its ancestry back through the Lowell, Winslow and Stark lines. He went to St Mark's School and then to Harvard. After a year there, he transferred to Kenyon College to study with John Crowe Ransom, through whom he met Allen Tate. Together, these Fugitive writers had an important formative effect on the young Lowell, who reported, 'I became converted to formalism and changed my style from brilliant free verse, all in two months.' He adds, 'And everything was in rhyme, and it still wasn't any good. But that was a great incentive. I poured out poems and went to writers' conferences.' He graduated in classics from Kenyon in 1940 and in the same year became a Roman Catholic, partly in protest against his background, partly in response to a craving for strict forms and an exacting faith. In 1943, also as a protest, this time against Allied bombing of civilian centres, he refused to report for military service and was sentenced to a year's imprisonment.

His first two books of poems were *Land of Unlikeness* (1944) and the Pulitzer Prize winning book *Lord Weary's Castle* (1946). The influence of the Fugitives is clear. There is, too, an abundance of Roman Catholic themes and imagery, contributing to his eloquent despair at the destruction of values. Lowell, preoccupied with traditions, presented his poetry in an ornamented formalism meant at once to preserve and commemorate. There is a tension between the elegaic strain (for personal and communal losses) and an informed anger. It is tough poetry, sometimes syntactically and prosodically musclebound. In 'Colloquy in Black Rock' – Black Rock is where he was detained as a conscientious objector – he writes:

Here the jack-hammer jabs into the ocean;
My heart, you race and stagger and demand
More blood-gangs for your nigger-brass percussions,
Till I, the stunned machine of your devotion,
Clanging upon this cymbal of a hand,
Am rattled screw and footloose ...

The rhythmic fist bangs home the rhymes and alliterations. But the worked up intensity becomes a speaking voice in a few lines from the same poem:

> ... and the mud
> Flies from his hunching wings and beak – my heart,
> The blue kingfisher dives on you in fire.

Lowell wrote better poems later, but never again a verse with such strong emphases.

The outstanding poem from this early period is 'The Quaker Graveyard in Nantucket', an elegy to Warren Winslow, Lowell's cousin, lost at sea in World War II. Much of the material derives from family history. It is not only a technical *tour de force* but a moving document as well, working on the moral plane, exploring man and his relationship to man and God. The poem is in seven sections, the first describing the corpse of a sailor dragged up from the sea, weighted, and thrown back. The formal lines are strong, but the rhythmic power is in Lowell's disruption of the basic regularity, his controlled modulation of the tone:

A brackish reach of shoal off Madaket, –
The sea was still breaking violently and night
Had steamed into our North Atlantic Fleet,
When the drowned sailor clutched the drag-net. Light
Flashed from his matted head and marble feet ...

The authority of the lines transports the poem (punctuated with references to Ahab from *Moby Dick*) beyond particular elegy. Other deaths, and major issues –

personal and social – are involved in the loss of Warren Winslow. The length of line varies with the tone and the development of imagery, mimetically:

The corpse was bloodless, a botch of reds and whites,
Its open, staring eyes
Were lustreless dead-lights
Or cabin-windows on a stranded hulk
Heavy with sand. We weight the body, close
Its eyes and heave it seaward whence it came ...

Sections II–V of the poem centre on the Quaker grave-yard, while section VI evokes the shrine of Our Lady of Walsingham. Water, a destructive element in the earlier sections, here becomes life-giving. Yet there is a sense in which Lowell imposes meanings on his images. The neutral images are religious. The face of Our Lady, 'Expressionless, expresses God ...' In the last section the poem moves back to the graveyard and to a helpless acceptance and celebration:

... the Lord God formed man from the sea's slime
And breathed into his face the breath of life,
The blue-lung'd combers lumbered to the kill.
The Lord survives the rainbow of His will.

Lowell was less successful with many poems of this period. Often they do not admit discovery. The taut language and syntax, the forms, exclude more than they include, become compelling baroque surfaces of language. Material and form are forced, too much self-conscious seeking, too little found. But at times they prefigure the work to come. In 'Between the Porch and the Altar', for instance, a relaxed familiar tone retains sufficient authority to ring its various changes, but it accommodates the 'I' more comfortably.

The Mills of the Kavanaughs (1951) was Lowell's third book. The Catholic symbolism has been overlaid with classical myth. Iambic pentameters are still the rhythmic base and the title poem – a twenty-page psychological novelette – is in rhymed iambic pentameter couplets grouped in sixteen-line stanzas. The 'downward glide' of life is still the central theme: death and madness are recurrent images. But Lowell's religion was wearing thin, and his next book, *Life Studies* (1959) has let much of the symbolism and the emphatic tone go, along with the prescriptive formalism. It is a significant abandonment, a liberation from his accomplished apprentice work. His return to the *self* for evaluation of experience was the beginning of what is loosely termed 'confessional poetry'. Lowell said of this change, 'By the time I came to *Life Studies* I'd been writing my autobiography and also writing poems that broke metre. I'd been doing a lot of reading aloud. I went on a trip to the West Coast and read at least once a day and sometimes twice for fourteen days, and more and more I found that I was simplifying my poems. If I had a Latin quotation I'd translate it into English. If adding a couple of syllables in a line made it clearer I'd add them, and I'd make little changes just impromptu as I read. That seemed to improve the reading.' His discovery begs the question: did it improve the *poems*? The answer in Lowell's case is a qualified 'yes' – yes because Lowell remained in control. But he has necessarily forfeited some of the power of language. Were the poems not finished, that they could be altered 'impromptu'? Is this why Lowell restlessly revised his work latterly? Is all his work 'work in progress', and does he not aspire to the finished poem? And could the older poet hope to rewrite his earlier work without betraying the earlier poet? There is another problem: in making the 'self' central to his poetry, he did not adequately distinguish between self-exploration and self-dramatization, a problem which weakened at least a few of his later poems.

Happily in *Life Studies* there is a centre other than the self: 'The morality seems much the same,' Lowell remarked, 'But the symbolism is gone: you couldn't possibly say what creed I believed in.' The writing, too, is more limber, more inclusive. It readily accommodates the 'ordinary', whether conversation or description. Details of autobiography and family history are naturally included:

'I won't go with you. I want to stay with Grandpa!'
That's how I threw cold water
on my Mother's and Father's
watery martini pipe dreams at Sunday dinner.

In 'Skunk Hour', the last poem in the book, and certainly one of the best, he observes skunks. In his strained mental condition they come to resemble the inhabitants of the small Maine resort:

I stand on top
of our back steps and breathe the rich air –
a mother skunk with her column of kittens swills the garbage
    pail.
She jabs her wedge-head in a cup
of sour cream, drops her ostrich tail,
and will not scare.

The poem retains, despite its freedom, rhymes in a variable rhythm.

Life Studies includes an autobiographical prose piece, '91 Revere Street', poems on Hart Crane, George Santayana and Ford Madox Ford, poems about mental hospital and prison.

In his *Poems 1938–1949*, a generous selection from his earlier books, there are a number of pieces subtitled 'after Rimbaud', 'after Valéry', 'after Rilke', etc. Lowell's next book was *Imitations* (1961), a work which together with his free translation of Racine's *Phèdre* (1961) contains some of his best verse. The 'imitations' are re-conceptions of poems by Sappho, Villon, Leopardi, Rimbaud, Rilke, Montale, Pasternak and others. They are more than

translations – and less. Lowell takes the original text as a
starting point, working through it, as it were trying to
find an English poem which, in his terms, recreates the
original in a new language, does not merely reflect it. As
we might expect, the 'imitation' tells us more about
Lowell than about his original, but the poems he achieves
are often outstanding.

For the Union Dead (1964) reveals the full individuality of Lowell's mature style. His concern with the vul-
nerability of values, relationships, and traditions, his
controlled anger at the gradual destruction of things
important to him – and by extension, to us – is compelling. Lowell incorporates historical, political and
autobiographical material. The tone is that of the speaking voice, but subtle rhymes and resonant vocabulary and
imagery add sinew. If *Life Studies* was a release from the
muscle-bound early style, in this volume Lowell begins to
flex different muscles.

In the title poem, Lowell uses as epigraph the inscrip-
tion on the Boston memorial honouring Col Robert
Shaw who commanded the first Negro regiment from the
free states to serve in the Civil War. Shaw and many of
his men were killed. Lowell puts the epigraph into the
plural: 'Relinquunt Omnia Servare Rem Publicam' –
'they give up everything to serve the Republic'. Opposite
the statue there used to be an Aquarium. Lowell visits
the site. A car park is being built: 'The ditch is nearer',
he writes:

on Boyleston Street, a commercial photographer
Shows Hiroshima boiling
over a Mosler Safe, the 'Rock of Ages'
that survived the blast. Space is nearer ...

Disgust is too weak a word. The photograph of Hiroshima, a symbol of ineffable inhumanity – is used to
advertise a safe – a symbol of the materialist religion.
The image is reported without Lowell's earlier rhetoric:

it is set down, unmoralized, but the more eloquent for that. The book is more than a social lament. It is a personal lament as well:

No longer to lie reading *Tess of the d'Urbervilles*,
while the high, mysterious squirrels
rain small green branches on our sleep!

The volume encompasses the whole range of Lowell's experience. If he confesses, his confession is placed in a context of wider relevance. It is not solipsistic. His self-mythologizing here, and in many of his later poems, is an act of immense social responsibility, none the less effective for its – sometimes excessive – candidness.

In 1965 Lowell published a three part play, *The Old Glory*, dramatizing stories of Hawthorne and Melville. Again there is the anger, society is arraigned. The crowd cry, 'Don't tread on me! Don't tread on me!' There is less tension, however, in his dramatic writing, and less tension in his next collection of poems, *Near the Ocean* (1967). Characteristic themes are developed, but not with the same immediacy. In *Life Studies* and *For the Union Dead* Lowell achieved an authentic impersonality *through* personality, but the poems in *Near the Ocean* suffer a dissipation of emotion and structure that later weakened the *Notebook*. *Notebook 1967–8* marked the beginning of Lowell's insecure rewriting and revising. *Notebook* (1970) *History* (1973), *For Lizzie and Harriet* (1973) and some of *The Dolphin* (1973) are reworkings of a large group of fourteen-line poems, loose sonnets in irregular iambic pentameters. As an 'Afterthought' to *Notebook* Lowell wrote, 'as my title intends, the poems in this book' (there are over two hundred and fifty) 'are written as one poem ... it is less an almanac than the story of my life ... My plot rolls with the seasons ... Accident threw up subjects and the plot swallowed them ...' In *History*, which includes revisions of eighty or so of the earlier poems, Lowell confesses, 'My old title, *Notebook*, was more accurate than I wished, ie the composition was jumbled. I hope this jumble or jungle is cleared – that I have cut the waste marble from the figure.' What he did was to compartmentalize the poems: historical poems in one book, recording a very personal reading of history; the report on the breakdown of one marriage in another book, and the celebration of a new marriage in the third. The earlier *Notebook* was more complete and in a sense more honest in its integration and interpenetration of themes, for many of the historical poems are only nominally historical. Segregated into their various books, part of the completeness of the 'jumbled' experience has been lost to an arbitrary design.

Yet the arbitrary design is an extension of an arbitrary form. The fourteen-line poem is a verse straitjacket in many cases. The poems where too much material asks admittance are clotted. The poems where there is an insufficient impulse are hammered thin. We glimpse into Lowell's private life, into his thoughts on Vietnam, on the American Presidential election, historical figures, his to-ing and fro-ing between the United States and England, his trips to Mexico, and so forth. There is not sufficient continuity, except in a few outstanding sequences – the one about Mexico, for instance – where the fourteen-line form becomes a stanza form rather than anecdotal sonnet form. In some of the weaker pieces, Lowell has the habit of dissolving his effects in an apparent ambiguity which, if we study it, is either impenetrable or meaningless, a rhetorical sleight of hand.

Lowell may have developed his conception of the original *Notebook* at least partly in emulation of Berryman's *Dream Songs* which he admired. His poem is as long as Berryman's and rather wider in scope. It may, in fact, be more substantial. For Berryman's sequence has all the baffling charm of his idiosyncratic dialect. It is hard to tell which passages are stylistically amiss, which poems are merely mechanical. But Lowell's style is at once more accessible and more vulnerable. Because the critics have identified the flaws more easily, they have tended to be dismissive about the whole. Lowell has not chosen stylistic camouflage; he has been denied the kid-glove treatment Berryman has commanded.

Lowell in a poem at the end of *History* quotes one of his critics:

surviving to dissipate *Lord Weary's Castle*
and nine subsequent useful poems
in the seedy grandiloquence of *Notebook*.

One half agrees. The form has led him by the nose. And yet there are poems, particularly in *The Dolphin*, which suggest that the Lowell genius, temporarily dissipated, is nonetheless intact, reforming. The posthumous volume, *Day by Day*, published in Britain in 1978, and the later poetry in periodicals has confirmed this suggestion. He has broken out of the fourteen-line form, coming back with his old power, and something new as well. In 'To Mother', for example, he writes:

The bent brisk sidewalks at Harvard
bump me brusquely,
as if allowed the licence of age;
persons who could hardly walk or swallow
when I was a student, angrily grate like old squirrels
with bandages of white hair about their ears.

Robert Duncan born 1919

I am beside myself with this
     thought of the One in the World-Egg,
enclosed,   in a shell of murmurings ...

– 'Passages 1'

Robert Duncan is one of the better exponents of Projectivist poetry. But he has acknowledged a number of
contemporary influences besides that of Olson. He cites
Stein, Lawrence, Pound, H.D. (Hilda Doolittle), Williams, Moore, Stevens, and Edith Sitwell, adding, 'They
are all problematic aren't they? And the two *sure* things
– Frost and Eliot – are not there.'

Duncan was born in Oakland, California, in 1919. His
mother died at his birth and he was adopted and brought
up under the name of Symmes. He tells us that he
learned from his high school teacher to see poetry as a
'vital process of the spirit' rather than a 'cultural com-
modity'. His studies under Ernst Kantorowitcz at the
University of California extended this view. Kantorowitcz's absorbing interest in Medieval history and art
brought to Duncan 'a new vision of the creative spirit
and the world of forms in which that spirit is manifest.'
In a characteristically portentous statement, he tells us
that he became aware that 'a metaphor is not a literary
device but an actual meaning arising from, operating in,

and leading us to realize the co-inherence of being in being, that we perceive forms because there are correspondences.' This sense of what he calls 'a metaphorical ground in life' – recalling thinly Emerson's Transcendentalism – has led to a poetry with, at times, mystical ambitions. The poem becomes for him 'a ritual referring to divine orders':

Glad Christ! of whom partaking I
am – as a universe is crucified in me –
Christ-crossed upon the body of my world.

In the 1940s he was co-editor of *The Experimental Review* and a leading poet in a San Francisco group that included Jack Spicer and Kenneth Rexroth. His early collections included *Heavenly City, Earthly City* (1947) and *Selected Poems 1948–49* (1949). 'The Venice Poem' (1948) he regards as a turning point in which he moved from 'the concept of a dramatic form to a concept of musical form in poetry'. In the early 1950s he experimented with imitations of Gertrude Stein, attempting to dislocate the syllable units of words to force a new sense of interrupted movement.

He taught at Black Mountain College in 1956 and became closely associated with Olson and Robert Creeley. His verse was released into 'open forms'; in other words, the content of the poem shaped the form as the poem developed. He has described his attempt to express 'a wholeness of what we are that we will never know'. Attempting to define his meaning a little more closely, he continues, 'we are always, as the line or the phrase or the word is, the moment of that wholeness – an event; but it, the wholeness of what we are, goes back into an obscurity and extends to and into an obscurity. The obscurity is part too of the work, of the form, if it be whole.' We do not have to look far for that obscurity in Duncan's work.

Since he made that statement in 1959, his many books in many modes have developed the idea. Collections of poems include *The Opening of the Field* (1960), *Roots and Branches* (1964), and *Bending the Bow* (1968). Poems have been supplemented by plays – *Medea at Kolchis* (1965) and *Adam's Way: A Play upon Theosophical Themes* (1966) – and prose books – *The Sweetness and Greatness of Dante's Divine Comedy* (1965), *As Testimony* (1965), and *The H. D. Book, Part 1: Beginnings* (1971).

Though his poems 'Passages' in *Bending the Bow* and in *Tribunals: Passages 31–35* (1970) carry political criticism of the monopoly system in the United States, most of his poetry flows from a subjective impulse, often undisciplined and indulgent. 'Poetry is the very life of the soul,' he informs us, adding, 'the body's discovery that it can dream.'

The sun is the everlasting centre of what we know,
a steady radiance.

The changes of light in which we dwell,
colors among colors that come and go,
are in the earth's turning.

And we are, in his words, 'all the many expressions of living matter, grandchildren of Gaia, Earth, and Uranus, the Heavens.' We must not, however, let the rhythms of Gaia monopolize our speech, or 'there is a monotonous rapture of persistent regular stresses and waves of lines breaking rime after rime.'

Not only heart and brain but 'all the internal organs' – as Olson suggested – are engaged in the creative act. The organization of the words 'bears the imprint of the physical man'. Intuition too plays a part, 'for in our common human suffering, in loss and longing, an intuition of poetic truth may arise.'

He admires Pound's *Pisan Cantos*, for with them, and Williams's *Paterson*, and 'the *Symphony in Three Movements* of Stravinsky, I began to be aware of the possibility that the locus of form might be in the immediate minim of the work, and that one might concentrate upon the sound and meaning present where one was and derive melody and story from impulse not from plan. I was not alone, for other poets – Louis Zukofsky, Charles Olson, Denise Levertov, Robert Creeley, following seriously the work of Pound and Williams, became aware, as I was, that what they had mastered opened out upon a new art where they were first ones working. In music John Cage, Pierre Boulez, or Karlheinz Stockhausen seem in the same way to realize that Stravinsky, Schönberg and Webern stand like doors, mastering what music was, opening out upon what music must be.' The actual poems that Duncan has written hardly add up to the ambitions he has for them.

He is particularly sensitive to the occasion of his poetry and is able instinctively to subdue his personality to the theme, at his best avoiding the pitfall of rambling, self-satisfied patter and the resolute facility prevalent among lesser Projectivists. Thus, in 'After Reading H.D.'s *Hermetic Definition*' he is able subtly to echo her style without direct imitation:

I do not remember
bees working over the garden on such a day.
But in the full sunlight
the warmth of its fire

hums;
and, covered with pollens,
the honey gatherers
go to the heart of things ...

He can acknowledge other poets in quotation, too, not extending or changing the meaning of his original as Eliot does when he transplants a quote into a new context, but rather commenting on the quote or taking it as a point of departure. Pound's *Canto XXXIX* includes the sound of Circe's loom. Odysseus compares it to the sound of a cat, and Duncan quotes it (in italics):

>   A cat's purr
> in the hwirr thkk   *'thgk, thkk'*
>   of Kirke's loom in Pound's Cantos
>   *'I heard a song of that kind ...'*
>
> my mind a shuttle among
>   set strings of music
> lets a weft of dream grow in the day time,
>   an increment of associations ...

Duncan's mind similarly shuttles among associations. Describing his poem, 'A Poem Beginning with a Line of Pindar' in a Voice of America Forum Lecture, he explains that 'the germ of the poem quickened as I was reading one evening the *Pythian Odes* ... I have an affinity with Pindar, but here it was my inability to understand that began the work or it was the work beginning that proposed the words I was reading in such a way that they no longer belonged to Pindar's *Pythian 1.*' The poem comes from a reciprocity between Duncan and his original:

> *The light foot hears you and the brightness begins,*
> god-step at the margins of thought,
>   quick adulterous tread at the heart.
> Who is it that goes there?
>   Where I see your quick face
> notes of an old music pace the air,
> torso-reverberations of a Grecian lyre.

Duncan's themes are large. Attempts have been made to summarize them under three vague headings: 'cosmic consciousness of love', 'poetry', and 'the imagination'. He is at his best, no doubt, when he is probing the mystery of what he calls 'a wholeness of what we are that we will never know', and discovers, in 'Apprehensions',

> It is the earth turning
> that lifts our shores from the dark
> into the cold light of morning ...

and when he senses that, in 'A New Poem for Jack Spicer',

What we call Poetry is the lake itself,
the bewildering circling water way –
having our power in what we know nothing of ...

He is at his least engaging when he expatiates – in prose or verse – about his work, and draws his smaller genius, by comparison, into the orbit of his less self-congratulatory and intellectually more rigorous mentors.

Richard Wilbur born 1921

It takes a sky-blue juggler with five red balls
To shake our gravity up ...
For him we batter our hands
Who has won for once over the world's weight.

– 'Juggler'

Richard Wilbur chose the exacting craft of traditional
forms because, as he puts it, 'The strength of the genie
comes of his being confined in a bottle.' In a Voice of
America Forum Lecture he provided a valuable comment
on his method of writing. 'Every poem of mine is autonomous, or feels so to me in the writing, and consists of
an effort to exhaust my personal sense of the subject. It
is for this reason that a poem sometimes takes me years to
finish.' More importantly, he adds, 'No poem of mine
is ever undertaken as a technical experiment; the form
which it takes, whether conventional or innovating, develops naturally as the poem develops, as a part of the
utterance.' He does not force the genie into the bottle:
it must rest comfortably inside.

Richard Wilbur was born in New York in 1921. He
graduated from Amherst College in 1942, served in the
Infantry in Italy in World War II, and returned to the
United States, taking a further degree at Harvard in
1947. It was during this period (1943–7) that he wrote

the forty-two poems included in *The Beautiful Changes* (1947). 'My first poems,' he says, 'were written in answer to the inner and outer disorders of the Second World War, and they helped me, as poems should, to take hold of raw events and convert them, provisionally, into experience.' The words 'take hold' and 'convert' are particularly relevant to Wilbur's poetry. Events become experience only in context, and Wilbur's forms supply the context, his steady voice balances disparate elements, relates them, draws them into a structure.

In the early poems, however, a conscious and at times obtrusive wittiness and word-play mar the work: awkwardness, as in the over-elaborate 'Lightness': a bird's nest falls:

> ... The chalice now bobbing above,
> Of interlaid daintiest timber, began the chute
>   Down forty fell feet towards stone and root
>   With a drift and a sampan spin, and gripped
> Loosely its fineshelled life ...

Words such as 'fell' and 'fineshelled' call attention to their niceness. Were the passage more than an intricate description, the effects might contribute a further dimension. The poem recovers, as many of the early poems do, in the balanced gentle irony, used with authority, at the end:

> Seeing her there in the garden, in her gay shroud
>   As vague and as self-possessed as a cloud,
>   Requiring nothing of them any more,
> And one hand lightly laid on a fatal door,
> Thought of the health of the sick, and, what mocked their sighing,
>   Of the strange intactness of the gladly dying.

Many of the poems express complex joy, and only six are concerned *directly* with war subjects. Wilbur's strong forms often lift an apparently banal thought or image, rendering it new and memorable. A sonnet, 'Praise in Summer', imagines the world upside-down, sparrows burrowing like moles in the sky:

Does sense so stale that it must needs derange
The world to know it? To a praiseful eye
Should it not be enough of fresh and strange
That trees grow green, and moles can course in clay,
And sparrows sweep the ceiling of our day?

A celebration of actuality recurs in his work:

... the beautiful changes
In such kind ways,
Wishing ever to sunder
Things and things' selves for a second finding, to lose
For a moment all that it touches back to wonder.

But Wilbur is not self-deceived in a world of wonders. He calls upon the dodo to 'Sit vastly on the branches of our trees,/And chant us grandly all improbabilities'; but he knows the 'unreturning leaves' and reminds himself of a loss he suffered as a child of ten, when his dog died:

In my kind world the dead were out of range
And I could not forgive the sad or strange
In beast or man.

The dog returns in a dream, 'clothed in a hymn of flies/And death was breeding in his lively eyes.' In rhythms that recall Frost, he says,

... I dreamt the past was never past redeeming:
But whether this was false or honest dreaming
I beg death's pardon now. And mourn the dead.

The fact that Wilbur wrote no 'war poems' in the manner of his contemporaries indicates what could have been a fault in a lesser poet: a bland evasiveness of extreme content. But his meditative argument and counter-argument, his attempt to turn raw events into experience, ensure a balance more complete and resonant than the rhetoric of poets more interested in effect and sensation than full apprehension. Extremity enters the poems only when an experience has changed him: the poem records the change *and* the experience.

When later his poetry became more dramatic, the style became plainer and the language less prone to preciousness. He retains the artifice and his subject matter in fine balance with his sharp wit. 'In the Smoking Car' is an example of his controlled but natural style:

The eyelids meet. He'll catch a little nap.
The grizzled, crew-cut head drops to his chest.
It shakes above the briefcase on his lap.
Close-voices breathe, 'Poor sweet, he did his best.'

'Poor sweet, poor sweet,' the bird-hushed glades repeat,
Through which in quiet pomp his litter goes . . .

Wilbur's skills have been well applied in his miraculously successful translations of Molière's *The Misanthrope* and *Tartuffe*. The precision and flexibility of his own formal structures, with his lightness of touch, admirably bring Molière alive in English. This also explains his success with Voltaire and the light musical *Candide*, in which he wrote lyrics for Bernstein's music.

In Wilbur's own poems, characteristic themes return, didactically perhaps, but he instructs himself as well as us. In 'Juggler' he writes,

A ball will bounce, but less and less. It's not
A light-hearted thing, resents its own resilience.
Falling is what it loves, and the earth falls
So in our hearts from brilliance,
Settles and is forgot . . .

Often in Wilbur's considerations of things, ideas, and their relationships, he comes to no firm conclusion but portrays – in form and imagery – the relationship. His poems originate in the object world, and it is to that world, clarifying it, that they return. In 'Love Calls us to the Things of This World' angels are articles of clothing on a line.

> The eyes open to a cry of pulleys,
> And spirited from sleep, the astounded soul
> Hangs for a moment bodiless and simple
> As false dawn.
> > Outside the open window
> The morning air is all awash with angels.

The wit of the early poems is still there, in the words 'spirited' and 'bodiless', in the initial suggestion that the eyes are pulled open by pulleys, in the suggestion, however fleeting, of Herbert's poem 'The Pulley'. But the wit is entirely functional, deepening rather than merely decorating the idea, enhancing and pointing rather than distracting from the meaning. He distrusts abstraction. His faith, aroused, returns to the materiality of the world. This theme recurs in all his books: *Ceremony and Other Poems* (1950), *Advice to a Prophet* (1961), and *Walking to Sleep* (1969). This last volume includes more translations, this time from Borges, Akhmatova, Voznesensky, Charles d'Orléans and Villon. In the long title poem he advises us:

> Try to remember this: what you project
> Is what you will perceive; what you perceive
> With any passion, be it love or terror,
> May take on whims and powers of its own.
> Therefore a numb and grudging circumspection
> Will serve you best ...

In Wilbur's finished poems there are no overwhelming passions, none of the gestures at raw experience which characterize the work of some of his contemporaries, nor does he support his poems with elaborate explications and apologetics which mask a deficient technique. His poems balance contradictory impulses and emotions, they are contexts in which emotion is not merely expressed but related and realized.

Most engaging is Wilbur's communicated sense of wonder and his formal skill. Grace and precision are not academic virtues in his poetry: the academic poet teases out meanings, while Wilbur's task is to discover forms. His is a warm art. He has made his position as a poet clear: poetry 'should include every resource which can be made to work ... I share (Aristostle's) feeling that an art should contain as much as it can and still be itself. As a poet, my relationship to the (poetic) revolution of which we've been speaking is that I am the grateful inheritor of all that my talent can employ, but that I will not accept any limitations or prohibitions, or exclude anything in the name of purity. So far as possible, I try to play the whole instrument.'

James Dickey born 1923

While the world fades, it is *becoming*.
As the trees shut away all seeing,
In my mouth I mix it with sunlight.
Here, in the dark, it is *being*.

– 'On the Coosawattee'

James Dickey is one of the most widely read modern American poets – hardly surprising, since some of his poems, including 'On the Coosawattee', 'The Lifeguard' and 'Falling', are compelling reading. The dramatic story-line beguiles, even if the quality of the verse does not. The emphatic clarity of diction, the baldness of the symbols and the expansive prosiness of the style contribute to his popularity. But compelling as they are, Dickey's narrative poems are flawed. He has provided details of his poetic progress and his aims. We can judge his approach from them.

He was born in Atlanta, Georgia and educated at Clemson College and Vanderbilt University. After serving in the Air Force in World War II and in Korea, and after a year in France, he began in 1955 a successful career in advertising. But after his poetry drew recognition, he abandoned his other career in 1961 to concentrate on writing.

He spent a year (1962–3) in Italy on a Guggenheim

Fellowship, and the following year he spent as Poet in Residence at Reed College and later he taught at the University of Florida. He was consultant in poetry at the Library of Congress and in 1966 received the National Book Award for his volume *Buckdancer's Choice*. Other volumes included *Into the Stone and Other Poems* (1960), *Drowning with Others* (1962), *Helmets* (1964), and *Poems 1947–67* (1967), a selection from previous books with a new section called 'Falling'. His collection *The Eyebeaters, Blood, Victory, Madness, Buckhead and Mercy* came out in 1970, the same year as his novel *Deliverance*, which was made into a film. A collection of critical essays, *The Suspect in Poetry* (1964), was republished in an enlarged form as *Babel to Byzantium* (1968). *Self-Interviews* (1970) is a further prose work based on taped interviews.

James Dickey began writing verse when he was twenty-four. By that time he was aware of the power of language, and that the most concentrated language, revealing the right correlation between words and experience, was the mark of great poetry. From the outset he distrusted rhyming poems and fought shy of 'artificiality'. It took some time for him to sort out the difference between craft and artifice. But rhythm was important to him: 'I have always liked strongly cadenced language, and the sound of words in a line of verse is to me a very important part of its appeal.' Dickey's predisposition is sometimes unfortunate, for the rhythm of his poems often falls into monotonous anapaests. The later poems are more varied rhythmically, but many of them achieve a slackness of cadence which hardly adds to the poems' power.

Dickey has told us, '... I was working toward ... a very stripped kind of simplicity in verse; what I really wanted to be able to do was to make effective *statements*.' Even in his meditative work, the nature poems for instance, he takes experience and *makes a statement* about it. He draws analogies and on them draws conclusions. It is a parable of nature that attracts him. The poems, therefore, do not go beyond their statements. In 'On the Coosawattee' for example, he sets down the statement at the outset. The first section, subtitled 'By Canoe through the Fir Forest', begins:

Into the slain tons of needles,
On something like time and dark knowledge
That cannot be told, we are riding
Over white stones forward through fir trees,
To follow whatever the river
Through the clasping of roots follows deeply.

The river *means* 'something like time and dark knowledge'. What follows begs interpretation in that light. In 'Awaiting the Swimmer' the meaning is asserted before the poetry has worked upon us. A man stands on the bank of a river anxiously awaiting the swimmer: 'Shall she fail, and go down to the sea?/Shall she call, as she changes to water?' The evocation is struck dead by the *statement*: 'The way to move upon water/Is to work lying down, as in love'. The arbitrary analogy is taken up when 'she' is safely on land and in the house, 'The bed like the river is shining'. We draw the obvious meaning.

The experience does not *generate* a meaning – it decorates it. The preconceived statement tethers the poem. The same problem arises for different reasons in Dickey's best-known poem, 'Falling'. An air hostess falls to her death through the emergency door of a plane. The poem traces her thoughts and feelings as she falls, undressing, to earth. Some of the imagery is skilfully handled. The poem is dramatic in its pace:

She is hung high up in the overwhelming middle of things in her
Self in low body-whistling wrapped intensely in all her dark dance-weight

Coming down from a marvellous leap   with the delaying,
        dumbfounding ease
Of a dream of being drawn   like endless moonlight to the
        harvest soil
Of a central state of one's country . . .

Here the poem is constrained by its detailed over-writing.
The poem is descriptive, prosaic, rather than evocative.
The form, however, is interesting. Dickey has explained
the gaps in the lines. His attempt was to find an 'open'
poem which could involve the reader: 'I experimented
with short lines some more, and eventually with putting
several of these lines together on the same physical plane
to make up what I called the "split line", in which spaces
between the word-groups would take the place of punctuation . . .'

His first poem in the 'split line' style was 'The Fire-
bombing'. The 'split line' is used to evoke the sensations
of a pilot over Japan. Dickey hasn't quite taken the
measure of the technique here: the pilot, somewhat out
of breath, gasps the experiment:

                Enemy rivers and trees
Sliding off me like snakeskin,
Strips of vapor spooled from the wingtips
Going   invisible   passing   over   on
Over   bridges   roads for nightwalkers
Sunday night in the enemy's country   absolute
Calm   the moon's face   coming   slowly
About
        the inland sea

It is significant that he should have sensed the monotony
of rhythm in his earlier poems, more significant that he
sensed the limitations he was imposing on his writing:
'Of late my interest has been mainly in the conclusionless
poem, the open or ungeneralizing poem, the un-wellmade
poem. I hope in the future to get the reader more and

more into the actions and happenings of the lines, and
require him less and less to stand off and draw judge-
ments.'

In *The Eye-Beaters* his new ambition is to a degree
realized. In 'Madness', for instance, a domestic dog is
bitten by a rabid fox, runs mad, and is hunted down
and beheaded. The lines are centred on the page:

Through the weather of love running wild and the horses full
Of strangers coming after Fence wire fell and rose
Flaming with messages as the spirit ran
Ran with house-hair
Burr-picking madly and after came

Men   horses   spirits
Of households leaping crazily beyond
Their limits, dragging their bodies by the foaming throat/
through grass
And beggar-lice and by the red dust
Road where men blazed and roared ...

It is a compelling poem suited to Dickey's penchant for
dramatic narrative. The new freedom of line and breathing works, though the effect is clotted and hysterical.
But virtually all the poems in the book are developed in
the same style. The insistency of image and rhetoric only
work in the dramatic context; otherwise, a new monotony
has replaced the old, the product of mechanical artifice,
not craft. Yet the variety of his themes which he para-
phrases – perhaps too well – need not produce monotony:
'the continuity of the human family, the necessity of
both caused and causeless joy, and the permanent interest
of what the painter John Marin called "the big basic
forms" – rivers, mountains, woods, clouds, oceans and
the creatures that live naturally among them. The forfeited animal grace of human beings, occasionally re-
deemed by athletes, interests me also, and the hunter's
sense of understanding with the hunted animal.'

Allen Ginsberg born 1926

Everything is holy! everybody's holy! everywhere is holy!
everyday is in eternity! Everyman's an angel!

– 'Footnote to Howl'

When William Carlos Williams wrote in his introduction
to *Howl and Other Poems* by Allen Ginsberg, 'Hold back
the edges of your gowns, Ladies, we are going through
hell', he had perhaps been infected – not surprisingly –
by Ginsberg's flair for hyperbole. In Ginsberg, both Hell
and Holiness are at work. That other Beat Poet, Gregory
Corso, said 'I am the substance of my poetry'. So is
Ginsberg: substance not merely of the written word, but
of the performance. Many of his poems lie dead on the
page, heavily asleep in the clotted rhetoric from which
his performances raise them. The Hell and Holiness are
Ginsberg's, expressed in such a way that we can share
them. 'He avoids nothing,' says Williams, 'but experiences
it to the hilt.' He adds, 'We are blind and live our blind
lives out in blindness. Poets are damned but they are not
blind, they see with the eyes of angels.' Ginsberg himself
advises us, 'my poetry is Angelical Ravings'. Corso's words
apply to Ginsberg even at his most extreme:

4 Sniffs & I'm High,
Underwear in bed,
    white cotton in left hand,
  archetype degenerate ...

In 'Kaddish I' he wrote after his mother's death,

Strange now to think of you, gone without corsets and eyes,
    while I walk on the sunny pavement of Greenwich Village
downtown Manhattan, clear winter noon, and I've been up all
    night, talking, talking, reading the Kaddish aloud, listening
    to Ray Charles blues shout blind on the phonograph
the rhythm the rhythm – and your memory in my head three
    years after – And read Adonais' last triumphant stanzas
    aloud – wept, realizing how we suffer – ...

Allen Ginsberg was born in Paterson, New Jersey, son
of the poet and teacher Louis Ginsberg and Naomi Ginsberg, a Russian *émigrée*. He studied at Columbia University, but broke off his university career for a year to
travel and work at odd jobs. After university, wandering
became a vocation. He worked as a dish-washer, night
porter, welder, seaman, and book reviewer for *Newsweek*.
The high spot of his wandering was perhaps in Czecho-
slovakia where, in 1965, he was elected King of the May
by students and immediately expelled from the country,
an episode he celebrated in 'Kral Majales' ('King of the
May'):

And *tho* I am the King of May, the Marxists have beat me
    upon the street, kept me up all night in Police Station,
    followed me thru Springtime Prague, detained me in secret
    and deported me from our kingdom by airplane.

He emerged from his earlier travels as the guru of the
'Beat Generation' in the fifties, particularly with his first
book, *Howl and Other Poems* (1956). His early work,
influenced by the ideas of Williams, possesses little of
Williams's poised objectivity. A romantic softness exploits
the borrowed form, sentimentalizing it:

The warm bodies
        shine together
in the darkness,
        the hand moves

to the centre
of the flesh,
the skin trembles
in happiness
and the soul comes
joyful to the eye ...

It was with *Howl* that he became king of the 'Beats', a loosely knit group which included Lawrence Ferlinghetti, Gregory Corso, and Jack Kerouac – better known as a novelist. Kerouac invented the term 'beat generation' to describe his friends. Some critics believe the word derives from the musical term and alludes to the jazz beat. Others say it means 'beaten' – the drop-out who rejects society before it rejects him. There is, too, a suggested connection with 'beatitude'. Certainly there are spiritual and pseudo-spiritual elements in 'beat'. The Beats, rejecting conformity, have generally sought to release their authentic selves. Their attempts have lead to experiments with drugs and a naïve interest in Eastern religion. They drew a large following, performing in coffee-houses and other, then,/unorthodox places. There are facile elements in their rejection of conformity. Their non-conformity conformed to new patterns. Their verse includes sick humour, obscenity, easy knocks at politics, and a sad intolerance of general 'inhibited' social behaviour.

It is the least inhibited of the Beats who attracted the crown of the 'guru'. In 'America' Ginsberg writes,

I smoke marijuana every chance I get.
I sit in my house for days on end and stare at the roses in the closet.
When I go to Chinatown I get drunk and never get laid.

These, then, are his qualifications.

Before Ginsberg wrote *Howl* he was writing poems 'adapted from prose seeds, journals, scratchings, arranged by phrasing or breath groups into little short-line patterns according to ideas of measure of American speech I'd picked up from W. C. Williams's imagist preoccupations.' Suddenly he allowed his romantic inspiration find its own forms and began to write with his 'Hebraic-Melvillian bardic breath'. The debt to Whitman's long line is effusively acknowledged: 'I saw you, Walt Whitman, childless, lonely old grubber, poking among the meats in the refrigerator and eyeing the grocery boys,' one line reads. The control of the long lines relies much on Olson's 'breath' theories, its sound relies on the model of Kerouac's prose, 'taking off from his own inspired prose line,' remarks Ginsberg.

The title poem from *Howl and Other Poems* is a Beat gospel, expressing lament at the fate of the 'best minds of my generation', loose satire against the system – characterized in 'Part II' as Moloch. In the third part Ginsberg identifies himself with a fellow beat – Carl Solomon – undergoing shock treatment in a mental hospital. He promises Solomon, and all of us, a facile freedom. 'O starry-spangled shock of mercy,' he cries. The shock is a rain of angelic bombs from 'our souls' airoplanes'. 'O victory forget your underwear we're free ...' The poem begins characteristically in full flood:

I saw the best minds of my generation destroyed by madness,
    starving hysterical naked,
dragging themselves through the negro streets at dawn look-
    ing for an angry fix,
angelheaded hipsters burning for the ancient heavenly connec-
    tion
    to the starry dynamo in the machinery of night ...

A long list of those 'best minds' follows, with a ritual, psalmodic beat on the word 'who' in each line:

who burned cigarette holes in their arms protesting the
    narcotic tobacco haze of Capitalism
who distributed Supercommunist pamphlets in Union Square
    weeping and undressing ...

Ginsberg tells us the poem started off light-heartedly but 'got serious'. 'I went on to what my imagination believed true to Eternity (for I'd had a beatific illumination years before during which I'd heard Blake's ancient voice & saw the universe unfold in my brain), & what my memory could reconstitute of the data of celestial experience.'

The inspiration for the second part was equally ghostly. He 'got high on Peyote, & saw an image of the robot skullface of Moloch in the upper stories of a big hotel glaring into my window; got high weeks later again, the Visage was still there ...' And the poem rants against Moloch, who assumes the form of all that the Beats hate. In the third section, however, Carl Solomon, in verse if not in life, is beatified. Ginsberg admits that, 'A lot of these forms developed out of an extreme rhapsodic wail I once heard in a madhouse.'

'The Sunflower Sutra' – not surprisingly – he wrote in twenty minutes, 'me at desk scribbling, Kerouac at cottage door waiting for me to finish so we could go off somewhere party ...' A grimy dying sunflower is discovered by a railway track in the poem: 'How many flies buzzed round you innocent of your grime, while you cursed the heavens of the railroad and your flower soul?' He asserts that the flower is a flower and the locomotive is a locomotive. The 'sermon to my soul' is: '– We're not our skin of grime, we're not our dread bleak dusty imageless locomotive, we're all beautiful golden sunflowers inside ...' Ginsberg's hell, for all its mannered devils, is more palatable than his platitudinous heaven. Often he goes through a harrowing experience only to emerge into a gilt platitude. There is body to his ravings, but the Angelical is sentimental. The universe, he says, is a 'new flower' – a frail antidote to Hell. He admits in 'Transcription of Organ Music':

I want people to bow as they see me and say he is gifted with poetry, he has seen the presence of the Creator.

And the Creator gave me a shot of his presence to gratify my wish, so as not to cheat me of my yearning for him.

The humour is pale.

His second book, *Kaddish and Other Poems* (1960) is better balanced. The title poem is a long lament in Hebrew form for his mother who died of a stroke in a mental hospital. The anguish is truly expressed: 'In the world, given, flower maddened, made no Utopia, shut under pine, almed in Earth, balmed in Lone, Jehovah, accept ...' The poem is in five parts and ends with an evocation of crows winging over the cemetery where his mother is buried.

The rest of the book consists primarily of poems about mind-expanding drugs and their effects. Other collections followed: *Empty Mirror: Early Poems* (1960) and *Reality Sandwiches* (1963), a diary sequence in which he searches for illumination in Peru, Mexico, San Francisco, and so on.

In 1963, he tells us, on the Kyoto Tokyo express, he 'had a very strange ecstatic experience' which opened him out to write 'The Change'. Restraining his slack long lines, he returns to a more measured pace. After his return to the United States in 1965 he composed his 'Wichita Vortex Sutra', published in 1966 in *Planet News*. This is a long poem with more realistic political commitments than his earlier vague anarchism. The poem is partly based on transcriptions of verbal recordings and impressions from his travels. A more steady control of language gives the poem an authority Ginsberg's outcries never possess:

> Hawks swooping thru the newspapers
>   talons visible
> wings outspread in the giant updraft of hot air
> loosing their dry screech in the skies
>   over the Capitol

Napalm and black clouds emerging in newsprint
    Flesh soft as a Kansas girl's
        ripped open by metal explosion –

His positive anger, his more varied rhetoric, has some sinew:

The war is over now –
    Except for the souls
        held prisoner in Niggertown
    still pining for love of your tender white bodies O children
                of Wichita!

The style is further developed in *Ankor Wat* (1968) and *Airplane Dreams* (1968); and *Mind Breaths* (1978) collects the poems written between 1972 and 1977.

A. R. Ammons born 1926

I look for the way
things will turn
out spiralling from a center,
the shape
things will take to come forth in ...

– 'Poetics'

Emerson, Whitman, Frost, Pound, Stevens, Williams:
this is the line of descent critics trace to A. R. Ammons,
placing him in the central 'tradition' of American poetry.
The line includes the stylistic divide at Frost and
Williams. The critics suggest a complex ancestry. But
Ammons's originality is individual. He has not written
well experimentally – his *Tape for the Turn of the Year*
is a failure. His skill is in displaying the multiplicity of
the natural world by means of frugal understatement.
His joy at the profusion is expressed not in the tidal
catalogues of Whitman or Ginsberg, but rather in poems
of austere concentration and brevity.

Ammons's books are numerous: *Ommateum* (1955),
Expressions of Sea Level (1964), *Corson's Inlet* (1965),
Tape for the Turning of the Year (1965), *Northfield
Poems* (1966), *Selected Poems* (1968), *Uplands* (1970),
Briefings (1971) and *Collected Poems 1951–1971*, which
received the National Book Award in 1973.

A. R. Ammons was born in Whiteville, North Carolina. He studied at Wake Forest College (1949) and at the University of California at Berkeley (1950–52). For nine years he worked at Frederich Dommock, Inc, in Atlantic City, New Jersey, where he became executive vice-president. Since 1964 he has been a teacher of creative writing at Cornell University in Ithaca, New York.

Few human beings appear in his poems apart from the ever-present 'I'. In the *Collected Poems*, sixty-nine begin, 'I ...' The 'I' prefers to talk to trees and rocks rather than other people:

I went out on
a rustling day
and
lectured the willow:
it nodded profoundly
and held
out many arms ...

The nicety of 'profoundly', the willow's 'arms', are characteristic. For Ammons, despite the unpeopled quality of his poems, is hardly misanthropic, nor is his natural vision whimsical. He asks simply,

Dispossess me of belief:
between life and me obtrude
no symbolic forms:

grant me no missions: let my
mystical talents be beasts
in dark trees ...

His poetry is profoundly humane and – in a real sense – self-effacing, even impersonal, even when he says in 'Come Prima': 'I am perfect: /the wind is perfect', for he adds 'ditchwater, running, is perfect'. That is as far as his list extends. He is a resolute modernist to the extent that he stays close to *things*, clarifies himself in his relationship to things or in perceiving the relationship between them.

He is conscious of what he calls 'amness' – his existing – and is holy in that 'as stars or/paperclips'. The holiness is in the existence, not in what that existence signifies or symbolizes. But his vision isn't all wind in the trees, bluejays and squirrels. He sings 'delphiniums/seasonless, seedless/out of debris' – not in an easy full-summer garden:

> how many
> times must I be broken and reassembled! anguish of becoming,
>   pain of moulting,
> descent! before the unending moment of vision:
>
> how much disorder must I learn to tolerate
>   to find material
>   for the new house of my sight!

Ammons is committed to the 'organic form' his subjects dictate. They 'turn/out spiralling from the center.' The poem finds its measure in the experience: no prescriptive metre or rhythm, no personal rhetoric forces the lines, where Ammons's ambition is to accommodate the subject matter. Apart from a few instances, the subject of the experience can be encompassed in a short poem, and Ammons's austere submission allows the poems to suggest a wide reference for the experience.

One of the exceptions to this rule is his experimental *Tape for the Turning of the Year*, another is his 'Essay on Poetics'. The *Tape* begins with an explanation:

6 Dec:
today I
decided to write
a long
   thin
   poem ...

It is in fact a journal, from December 6, 1963, to January 10, 1964, written on what to the reader must seem a very long roll of adding-machine tape. It ends:

the roll has lifted
from the floor &
our journey is done:
thank you
for coming ...

The arresting moments are almost lost in yardage: 'last day of the year: /I've been at this/25 days ...'

His 'Essay on Poetics' is a different matter. For the most part it is written in three-line stanzas with interludes in a lyrical style. Occasional slabs of quotation from technical books are introduced. Parts are engaging, thinking aloud:

poems are arresting in two ways: they attract attention with glistery astonishment and they hold it: stasis: they gather and stay: the progression is from sound and motion to silence and

rest: for example, I can sit in this room ...

But the poem lacks the inevitably of the shorter verses. It devolves into wilful exercises: 'three quatrains rhyming alternate lines: let me see if I can/write a poem to help heave the point ...' 'Hibernaculum', another poem in this style, includes the lines, 'the point is just to get this page full so I can/take it out of the typewriter and write a letter ...' The humour is weak. Randall Jarrell's quip about the poem written on a typewriter by a typewriter comes to mind.

In the short poems, however, Ammons is a formidable writer. The art is more exacting, and he is equal to its intensities. Each group has its particular momentum. The variety is surprising. The narrow field of subject matter makes his diversity of effect the more compelling:

My subject's
still the wind still
difficult to
present
being invisible ...

He manages mysteriously to illuminate that 'invisible'.

W. S. Merwin born 1927

We shall find
Dictions for rising, words for departure ...

– 'Dictum: For a Masque of Deluge'

W. S. Merwin's style changed radically in the midst of
his career, in reaction to external circumstances. The
change is so complete that Merwin seems to be two
poets, one of him now safely dead, the other still evolving.

William Stanley Merwin was born in New York City
in 1927, the son of a Presbyterian minister. After studying
at Princeton, he went to France and Spain and finally
to England, where his reputation as a poet was first
established. He now spends part of his time in France,
part in the United States, and part in Mexico.

His first book, *A Mask for Janus* (1952), won the Yale
Series of Younger Poets contest. He was awarded the
Pulitzer Prize for his seventh collection of poems, *The
Carrier of Ladders* (1970). In 1968 he won the PEN
Translations Prize for his *Selected Translations 1948–
1968*. His work as a translator has been extensive, and
his translations are seldom less than distinguished. They
have included *The Cid* (1959), and poetry and plays
from various languages, notably Spanish. A recent volume, *Asian Figures* (1973), includes reworkings of sayings
and poems from the East.

In his translation work, Merwin is drawn to primitive poetry and to modern work, much of the latter surrealist in manner. There can be little doubt that his translations helped to bring about the change of style in his own poetry, for that change implied a revision not only of his attitude to form and image, but to language itself.

In an introduction to Merwin's first collection, W. H. Auden wrote of the historical experience latent in the poems: 'By translating these feelings into mythical terms, the poet is able to avoid what a direct treatment could scarcely have avoided, the use of names and events which will probably turn out not to have been the really significant ones.' In other words, Merwin chose the archetypal mode and archetypal figures in preference to modern, patently historical, or even legendary material. The book includes no reference to the United States of the 1950s. It develops stylized landscapes and seascapes, and Greek myth (Odysseus in particular) is used. There are ballad-like poems on medieval themes and references to ancient China and Christian Palestine. The poems do not suggest an historical context: Janus, the two-faced god who looks forward and backward but belongs to the present, presides.

Merwin's early style is trimmed to his myths, presenting the perennial themes of birth, death and renewal, sometimes developed in the extended metaphor of the voyage. Self-conscious, archaic, including awkward inversions and stiffly traditional metres, the style is resolutely *not* 'contemporary'. But Merwin's technical assurance for the most part elevates his parables to myth. The tenses themselves waver:

Fixed to bone only, foreign as we came,
We float leeward till the mind and body lose
The uncertain continent of a name.

In 'Dictum: a Masque of Deluge' he tells of an apocalyptic flood:

          We shall find
Dictions for rising, words for departure;
And time will be sufficient before that revel
To teach and order and rehearse the days
Till the days are accomplished: so now the dove
Makes assignations with the olive tree,
Slurs with her voice the gesture of time:
The day founders, the dropping sun
Heavy, the wind a low portent of rain.

Merwin's second book, *The Dancing Bears* (1954), develops archetypal themes in an increasingly romantic manner. The prosody is freer than in his first book, often with longer lines and a wider range of technical possibilities. However elaborate the technique, the poet remains tightly in control:

And there where the spume flies and the mews echoed and
    beckoned
The bowing drowned, because in her hands love and the one
    song
Leap and the long faith is born gladly, there through the
    waters
Of the dead ...

Green With Beasts (1956), Merwin's third collection, shows his complete mastery of the early style. The image of the sea attracts him, powerfully in 'Low Fields of Light' where the sea gradually takes over the land:

My father never plowed there, nor my mother
Waited, and never knowingly I stood there
Hearing the seepage slow as growth, nor knew
When the taste of salt took over the ground.

He evokes the image through negatives: we see what he did not see. This nice mastery is carried further in other poems. And his third book includes 'Chapters for a Bestiary', describing the allegorical character of various animals.

With *The Drunk in the Furnace* (1960) the dramatic change of style is adumbrated. Though Odysseus hovers in the background, the sea is experienced more immediately, as a fact rather than a figure. The allegory, still in evidence, is more open, and there are fewer archaisms and inversions. 'The Bones' is an example of the clearer syntax and diction:

Shells were to shut out the sea,
The bones of birds were built for floating
On air and water, and those of fish devised
For their feeding depths, while a man's bones were framed
For what? For knowing the sands are here,
And coming to hear them a long time; for giving
Shapes to the sprawled sea, weight to its winds,
And wrecks to plead for its sands ...

The wilfully complex imagery is giving way, and in 'The Gleaners', for example, there is a positive extension of subject matter.

The dramatic change in Merwin's style reflects a wider tendency in American poetry towards the open forms suggested by the Projectivists. Merwin's themes remain the same, but he chooses to present them in a more immediate form. His idiom in *The Moving Target* (1963), avoiding closed structures of imagery, shunning syntactical clarity and rhythmic regularity, moves counter to his early style. He has learned from the surrealists as well. His language is now as colloquial as the earlier language was archaic. What is common to both styles is a curious aestheticism, a sense that he is engaging issues of language rather than human issues:

The inspector of stairs is on the stairs
Oh my God and I thought it was Sunday,
His advance like a broom and those stairs going
Down to meet him, alright
What that's mine will he show me
To be ashamed of this time

The spiders in my face, the whistles
In the cupboards,
The darkness in my shoes ...

In a longer poem, 'For Now', there is no punctuation:

Goodbye cement street address of cement tears
Grief of the wallpaper the witness
Cold banisters worn thin with fright
Photo of me wondering what it would be like
The girls at last the hips full of dice ...

Melancholy, voyages, farewells dominate the book. The
collection is disturbing in its implications, after the formalism of the earlier work – and yet the later poems are
better work. Does this imply that form, clear syntax,
strong rhythms and metre, inhibit the modern poet? In
Merwin's case, this was true. Only by breaking with his
finally arid early style could he draw nearer to experience
without surrendering his 'timeless' approach. His later
poems rely on more than structure to keep them going.
They take less for granted. They answer to the logic of
dreams.

In *Lice* (1967) the new style is consolidated. The surrealism, derived from the Spanish poets he has translated,
is developed. In 'For a Coming Extinction' the surrealism
and the archetypal approach are effectively fused:

When you will not see again
The whale calves trying the light
Consider what you will find in the black garden
And its court
The sea cows the Great Auks the gorillas
The irreplaceable hosts ranged countless
And fore-ordaining as stars
Our sacrifices ...

Is Merwin merely reflecting trends in modern poetry or
reacting to them in a positive way? William Dickey,

reviewing *Lice*, said, 'if accident is fashionable, I should expect to find Merwin embracing accident, and I did ...' Merwin's seventh book, *The Carrier of Ladders* (1970), expresses a quieter sense of loss, of exhaustion. But it is unrepentantly in the newer style. *The Miner's Pale Children* (1970) takes the style a step further into prose poems, small parables with large themes, recalling Samuel Beckett. Is this further evidence of Merwin's fashionableness?

In *Writings to an Unfinished Accompaniment* (1973) the emotions are more intense and so is the expression. It does not *seem* to be an imitated rhetoric. Merwin is a poet aware of new developments around him. Eclectic, responsive, he is marked by what he reads and responds to, but he makes his own poetry out of his won experience:

Even in the middle of the night
they go on handing me around
but it's dark and they drop more of me
and for longer

then they hang on to my memory
thinking it's theirs

even when I'm asleep they take
one or two of my eyes for their sockets ...

The poetry verges on hysteria, but significantly remains *on* the verge. Confessionalism is not for him. He attempts the common language of the dream. Perhaps the language in his recent work is less dense, his poise less artificial: but if translation has got Merwin into the habit of an English no longer conscious of its etymologies nor bounded by prescriptive forms – of syntax, metre and association – it is also an English more directly able, with surprising clarity, to articulate the intensities of dreams.

John Ashbery born 1927

And, as my way is, I begin to dream, resting my elbows
    on the desk and leaning out of the window a little ...

– 'The Instruction Manual'

John Ashbery has developed, regressed, experimented and
discovered in various styles and forms, wisely uncommit-
ted, unprescriptive, unpolemical. The constant is 'the
dream', explored in various ways. He has written, 'I often
change my mind about my poetry: I do not, for instance,
think it has much relation to painting, though I have
said it did in previous statements of this kind. I would
prefer not to think I have any special aims in mind, as
I might then be forced into a program for myself ...' He
is as indefinite as much of his best poetry, 'Spring Day',
for example:

And whether it is Thursday, or the day is stormy,
With thunder and rain, or the birds attack each other,
We have rolled into another dream.

John Ashbery was born in Rochester, New York, and
grew up on his father's farm in Sodus, New York. He
graduated from Harvard in 1949 and took his MA in
English at Columbia University in 1951. He worked for
four years in publishing before travelling on a Fulbright
Scholarship to France in 1955. He lived mostly in France
until 1965, when he returned to New York. While in

France he was art critic for the Paris *Herald Tribune,* edited the quarterly *Art and Literature* (1964–7) and is now an editor of *Art News.* He was on the editorial panel for the five issues of *Locus Solus* (1961–2), and thus became associated with a group of New York artists and writers which included Kenneth Koch, James Schuyler and Frank O'Hara. He was influenced not only by the New York action painters but also by the French surrealists *and* Wallace Stevens – a complex heritage. A few of his poems he wrote first in French, 'and translated them myself in English, with the idea of avoiding customary word-patterns and associations.'

His first collection of poems appeared in 1953, *Turandot and Other Poems,* and his second book, *Some Trees* (1956), won a prize in the Yale Series of Younger Poets. Other collections have included *The Poems* (1960), *The Tennis Court Oath* (1962), *Rivers and Mountains* (1965), *Double Dream of Spring* (1970), and *Three Poems* (1972). A *Selected Poems* (1967) was published in Britain, and a smaller section was included in *Penguin Modern Poets 19* (1971). *Self-Portrait in a Convex Mirror* was also published in Britain (1977). His most recent book of poems is *Houseboat Days* (1978). He has written plays – *The Compromise* (performed in 1955, published in 1960), and *The Heroes* (1950). He collaborated with James Schuyler in the novel *The Nest of Ninnies* (1969).

The difficulty of Ashbery's work is its apparent lack of consistency. It is difficult to reconcile the author of 'Europe' (in *The Tennis Court Oath*) with the author of 'Soonest Mended' in *The Double Dream of Spring.* In 'Europe' he writes,

17. I moved up
            glove
        the field
18. I must say I
    suddenly

she left the room, oval tear tonelessly fell.
19. Life pursued down these cliffs.
   the omened birds
   intrusion;

In 'Soonest Mended', a different poet seems to be at work:

... For time is an emulsion, and probably thinking not to grow
   up
Is the brightest kind of maturity for us, right now at any rate.
And you see, both of us were right, though nothing
Has somehow come to nothing; the avatars
Of our conforming to the rules and living
Around the home have made – well, in a sense, 'good citizens'
   of us,
Brushing the teeth and all that, and learning to accept
The charity of the hard moments as they are doled out ...

A long, quietly spoken cadence is developed in the second passage, without interruptions, following the line of thought. 'Europe' is entirely different, elliptical, without the *sense* of sense, apparently wary of coherence. It is a collage; the poet relies on the happy chance of juxtaposition of words, phrases, images and ideas. But the chance is not frequently happy. It is a poetry of serendipity, the element of accident as in Action painting is crucial. At times the poem darts into meaning:

36. he ran the machine swiftly across the frosty grass.
   Soon he rose, and skimming the trees, soon
   soared away into the darkness.

But then it is gone again, evasive, progressing in hope of a deeper coherence. Another poem, 'Idaho', progresses in a similar way, then suddenly asks, 'What does it mean??????????????' The fourteen question marks express the reader's confusion, too. But meaning, the poems suggest, may exist beneath the fragments. 'Europe' does not succeed. The fragments are too jagged, the ellipses and discontinuity too rigorously contrived.

Gertrude Stein has influenced Ashbery's work here. She attempted to develop a 'cubist literature' in which meaning was to be abandoned in order to generate a new art, multi-dimensional. She began by a simplification of syntax and concentration on 'automatic writing': 'Custard is this. It has aches, aches when. Not to be. Not to be narrowly. This makes a whole little hill.' Nonsense perhaps, but with compelling rhythms. And she, like Ashbery, attempted to clear the ground in order to restore a cliché. But Ashbery is not so theoretical as Stein, he is always 'leaning out of the window a little'. The dream engages him, and once engaged, the medium of language has to accommodate the dream. But his poetry is evasive, whether he uses expansive, Whitmanesque lines or elliptical modernist forms. He is evasive even in the fluent seeming logicality of 'Soonest Mended'.

Ashbery's earlier books waver between the elliptical and the expansive. 'A Boy' (1952) begins:

I'll do what the raids suggest,
Dad, and that other livid window,
But the tide pushes an awful lot of monsters
And I think it's my true fate.

It had been raining but
it had not been raining.

The poem is missing the bridge over to meaning. It puzzles itself with its riddles. As if to compensate for the incomplete style, 'The Instruction Manual' includes every detail. The poet looks out on the square in Guadalajara:

The couples are parading; everyone is in a holiday mood.
First leading the parade, is a dapper fellow
Clothed in deep blue. On his head sits a white hat
And he wears a mustache, which has been trimmed for
     the occasion.
His dear one, his wife, is young and pretty; her shawl is
     rose, pink and white.
Her slippers are patent leather, in the American fashion ...

Finally, this too is evasive. Meaning comes from selection, Ashbery chooses to be inclusive. The contrast between the styles is so extreme, their effects so similar, that we suspect a merely literary motive, the poet wishes to show that the opposite style confirms rather than refutes the elliptical manner. Many of the poems, particularly in *The Tennis Court Oath*, read like exercises. Even the 'happy chance' poems are marked by a wilful, contrived experimentalism.

Ashbery struck a successful balance in his finest poems where he is at once less aridly experimental, and truer to himself and his medium. The poems remain elliptical – but the ellipsis is thematic rather than formal. The poems work as lyrical explorations of uncertainty. *The Double Dream of Spring* includes many of the best of them.

There is that sound like the wind
Forgetting in the branches that means something
Nobody can translate. And there is the sobering 'later on,'
When you consider what a thing meant, and put it down.

The poem is unresolved. He writes how 'The sagas purposely ignore how better off it was next day,/The feeling in between the chapters, like fins.' His own poems attempt to illuminate the 'in between'. Time changes the immediate meaning of experiences and therefore confirms uncertainty. We have to learn to accept:

The charity of the hard moments as they are doled out,
For this is action, this not being sure, this careless
Preparing, sowing the seeds crooked in the furrow,
Making ready to forget, and always coming back
To the mooring of starting out, that day so long ago.

Ashbery once suggested that dreams might have a power to persuade that an event has a meaning not logically connected with it, that there is a 'hidden relation among disparate objects'. In his outstanding poems he communicates that power by allowing them to produce an inner narrative of disparate objects. His experiments with words, phrases and images were too halting to compel like dreams. The later work, particularly a poem such as 'Fragment', can of itself create a dreamlike world in which association thrives, in which the apparently disparate is given a context in rhythm if not in logic. 'Fragment' is addressed to an unnamed woman and takes the form of rapt meditation on a relationship: 'Out of this cold collapse/A warm and near unpolished entity could begin ...' He writes of 'the way love in short periods/ Puts everything out of focus, coming and going.' His poems, out of literal focus, have the compelling elusiveness of dream-focus: 'the plaits of argument,/Loosened...':

> On flat evenings
> In the months ahead, she would remember that that
> Anomaly had spoken to her, words like disjointed beaches
> Brown under the advancing signs of the air.

Three Poems is for the most part in prose. The first of the three hovers between verse and prose. Together the poems pursue meaning where no logical answer is possible: 'how beautiful a thing must have been to have been so much prized, and its noble aspect which must have been irksome before has now become interesting, you are fascinated and keep on studying it ...' He ruminates with himself as poet, seeking renewal in time: 'It is time we have now, and all our wasted time sinks into the sea and is swallowed up without a trace. The past is dust and ashes, and this incommensurably wide way leads to the pragmatic and kinetic future.' The power of Ashbery's work is that each book is a renewal and, to the reader, a surprise. It is as though he cannot repeat himself.

Adrienne Rich born 1929

A too-compassionate art is only half an art.
Only such proud restraining purity
Restores the else-betrayed, too-human heart.

– 'At a Bach Concert'

Adrienne Rich is a prolific poet whose work has developed and changed radically. There is an implicit logic in that development, but no sense of a programme – more an evolution of style and theme towards a greater directness and lucidity. Though her recent work includes self-indulgent poems, and her committed involvement in feminism and politics generates at times a naïve rhetoric, she is aware of the dangers and normally avoids them.

Adrienne Cecile Rich was born in Baltimore, Maryland, and educated at Radcliffe College in Cambridge, Massachusetts. She graduated in 1951. Her first book, *A Change of World*, appeared in the same year, chosen by W. H. Auden for the Yale Series of Younger Poets. A pamphlet of selected poems was published in the Fantasy Poets series in England when she came to Europe on a Guggenheim award. Other collections include *The Diamond Cutters* (1955), *Snapshots of a Daughter-in-Law* (1962), *Necessities of Life* (1966), *Leaflets* (1969), *The Will to Change* (1971), and *Diving into the Wreck* (1973). Some of the volumes include translations from the Dutch and Russian. Adrienne Rich now lives in New York City.

In her first book, she wrote the lines,

I draw the curtain as the sky goes black
And set a match to candles sheathed in glass
Against the keyhole draught, the insistent whine
Of weather through the unsealed aperture.

From this detached formalism, this scrupulous decorum, she has moved to the intense, questioning open poetry of *Diving into the Wreck*:

why do the administrators

lack solicitude, the government
refuse protection,

why should the wild child
weep for the scientists

why

The same poet chose the word 'aperture' and 'solicitude', but the later voice is not hedged behind form nor metrical regularity. Her recent poems belie that earlier cultivation of 'the detachment from the self and its emotions' that Auden praised in her first collection. He described her poems then as 'neatly and modestly dressed', they 'speak quietly but do not mumble, respect their elders.' Those elders include Yeats, Frost, Stevens, Robinson, Dickinson, and Auden himself. But the poems, Auden adds, are 'not cowed' by their elders, and they 'do not tell fibs'. Her early work, written just after World War II, is *contained* by its forms, sustained by a variety of metres and rhymes. Technique provides a protective solace for both poet and reader. All is understated but observed accurately. The sense of mutability is neutralized emotionally, if not intellectually, by her detachment:

This is our sole defense against the season;
These are the things that we have learned to do
Who live in troubled regions.

The first two books exemplify a poetry that, by reason of its clarity, is intellectually immediate and, because of the poet's controlled technique, can generalize. She writes *about* Thoreau on Concord River, but her real concern is with 'absolutes':

Lover and Child and fisherman, alike
Have in their time been native to this shore
As he would have it peopled: all entranced
By such concerns in their perfected hour
That in their lives the river and the tree
Are absolutes, no longer scenery.

She reveals an acute historical consciousness, particularly in *The Diamond Cutters* which she wrote, for the most part, while touring Europe after the war:

We come like dreamers searching for an answer,
Passionately in need to reconstruct
The columned roofs under the blazing sky,
The courts so open, so forever locked.

And some of us, as dreamers, excavate
Under the blanching light of sleep's high noon,
The artifacts of thought, the site of love,
Whose Hadrian has given the slip, and gone.

She feels she is obscurely the custodian of the past and its culture: 'We stand between the dead glass-blowers/ And murmurings of missile-throwers.' Nonetheless, the inadequacy of her approach, 'A too-compassionate art is only half an art', worries her. Finally, neither restoration nor nostalgia were sufficient. In 'Diving into the Wreck' she writes,

I came to explore the wreck
The words are purposes.
The words are maps.
I came to see the damage that was done
and the treasures that prevail ...

But now she senses, 'we are the half-destroyed instruments/that once held to a course ...'

Compassionate art is replaced by a more open, passionate and committed art, a greater immediate intensity, a less resolute clarity of perspective. The change is gradual. It first becomes clear in the title poem of *Snapshots of a Daughter-in-Law*. The book begins with her earlier assured formal control, but her restlessness increases. She has stood back long enough. She speaks the title poem with a new voice, herself implicated in the themes. The ten snapshots show women – Mary Shelley, Fanny Burney and Emily Dickinson among them – as figures of strength in action or achievement:

Reading while waiting
for the iron to heat,
writing, *My Life had stood – a Loaded Gun –*
in that Amherst pantry while the jellies boil and scum,
or, more often,
iron-eyed and beaked and purposed as a bird,
dusting everything on the whatnot every day of life.

Emily Dickinson, referred to here, is evoked in protest and celebration. The stylistic decorum is dissipated by anger:

Dulce ridens, dulce loquens,
she shaves her legs until they gleam
like petrified mammoth-tusk.

It is a crucial development of directness that opened up a field of new possibilities for the poetry. She moved from style to voice.

In 1964 she said, 'I find that I can no longer go to write a poem with a neat handful of materials and express those materials according to a prior plan: the poem itself engenders new sensations, new awareness in me as it progresses. Without for one moment turning my back on conscious choice and selection, I have been increasingly willing to let the unconscious offer its materials, to listen to more than the one voice of a single idea. Perhaps a simpler way of putting it would be to say that instead of poems *about* experience I am getting poems that *are* experiences, that contribute to my knowledge and my emotional life even while they reflect and assimilate it.'

While this approach can lead to solipsistic verse, poems in which the poet is writing for herself alone, Rich has the skill to avoid this pitfall. Firmer control is needed in her new manner if the poem is to escape sentimentality or mere rhetoric. Adrienne Rich takes the risks, and her recent successes are certainly more powerful than the even-paced achievement of her earlier poems. In *The Will to Change* she wrote:

What happens between us
has happened for centuries
we know it from literature

still it happens

sexual jealousies
outflung hand
beating bed

dryness of mouth
after panting

there are books that describe all this
and they are useless

Unpunctuated, each line becomes a rhythmic unit, matter

of fact and final. In *Diving into the Wreck* she wrote:

... the mirror of the fire
of my mind, burning as if it could go on
burning itself, burning down

feeding on everything
till there is nothing in life
that has not fed that fire

The recent verse gets perilously near 'statement', consciously limiting its wider implications. Sometimes latterly her involvement in the themes she develops has contributed to an intellectual slackness, where rhetoric supplies the ready solution. But the successes are more resonant, because gained with more difficulty.

Gary Snyder born 1930

Wrap up in a blanket in cold weather and just read
Practise writing Chinese characters with a brush
Paint pictures of the mountains ...

– 'Things to Do around a Lookout'

The relaxed tone of Snyder's poetry pervades even the
poems of anger. The anger dissolves into lucid incomprehension, as effective as lampoon:

        all
Pains or pleasures hells or
What in sense or flesh
Logic, eye, music, or
Concoction of all faculties
& thought tend – tend – to this:
      This gaudy apartment of the rich.
The comfort of the U.S. For its own.

In Snyder's philosophy, social action is inadequate, for:
'freedom is a void,/Peace war religion revolution/Will
not help.' Snyder's is a radicalism of consciousness, not
conscience, engaged with causes before effects. The 'Intricate layers of emptiness' where 'Human tenderness
scuttles/Down dry endless cycles' Snyder attempts to fill
with positive quiet, resembling that which Thoreau tried
to find in nature. Snyder's positive quiet is the Buddhist

Nirvana, where the cycle of rebirth is stilled in the peace of enlightenment. There are moments when self-transcendence is possible. Snyder uses an anecdote about John Muir who, climbing Mt Ritter, is stuck on a ledge unable to move:

My mind seemed to fill with a
Stifling smoke. This terrible eclipse
Lasted only a moment, when life blazed
Forth again with preternatural clearness.
I seemed suddenly to become possessed
Of a new sense.

Elimination of the self is a recurrent ambition.

The poetry is not built on the normal tensions of languages: syntax, varied vocabulary, imagery. For when one is,

Working with an old
Singlejack miner, who can sense
The vein and cleavage
In the very guts of rock ...
What use, Milton, a silly story
Of our lost general parents,
          eaters of fruit?

Such a sweeping dismissal of possibilities in his own verse, to make it comprehensible to his workmate, begs the question: will his workmate wish to read it? But direct simplicity and lucidity, a limited range of imagery and open forms, characterize most of Snyder's work.

Gary Snyder was born in San Francisco and grew up in a farm just north of Seattle, Washington. He took his degree in anthropology at Reed College, Oregon, and later became a friend of Kerouac and Ginsberg. His time in the early 1950s was divided between working as a logger and forester and studying Japanese and Chinese at the University of California at Berkeley. In 1956–7 he underwent formal Zen Buddhist training in Japan, and

after working on a tanker for a short period he returned
to live in Japan until 1968. He went to California where
he now lives with his Japanese wife Masa and two sons in
the foothills of the Sierras. His books have included
Riprap (1959), reprinted in *Riprap and Cold Mountain
Poems* (1965), *Myths and Texts* (1960), *Six Sections from
Mountains and Rivers Without End* (1965), *A Range of
Poems* (1966), *The Back Country* (1967), *Regarding
Wave* (1970), and a collection of essays and journal
excerpts, *Earth House Hold* (1969).

Although the poetry is still, with few linguistic tensions,
it has narrative and what can only be called dramatic
tensions. Often experiences and incidents are presented
fragmentarily, but the fragments contribute to a common
end. Snyder kept a journal which is reproduced in *Earth
House Hold*, and like those of Thoreau and Emerson it
is not a mere diary but part of a discipline, both descriptive and didactic. The journal, particularly the first
part called 'Lookout's Journal', recording the summer of
1952 when Snyder was a forest lookout on Crater Mountain, reveals the steps by which he moved towards his
particular vision. An entry for July 9th reads:

the boulder in the creek never moves
　　　　the water is always falling
　　together!

The *Riprap* poems clearly have their source there:

Down valley a smoke haze
Three days heat, after five days rain
Pitch glows on the fir-cones
Across rocks and meadows
Swarms of new flies.

Zen encourages the enjoyment of nature and the out-
doors. Its art is full of landscapes represented by a few
deft brush-strokes. It is characterized by understatement,
requiring vision. The artifice must be second-nature, so
that experience can be given with immediacy, intuitive

spontaneity, and impersonality. It is this directness that Snyder pursues when he discards simile, metaphor and 'reasoning'. Illumination comes rather from the experience of objects and living things, from living among objects, than from books. The poems often present solitary experience, suppressing the first person 'I':

sat on a rock in the sun,
watched the old pine
wave
over blinding fine white
          river sand.

But the poet isn't always meditating. He tells us, 'the rhythms of my poems follow the rhythm of the physical work I'm doing and the life I'm leading at any given time – which makes the music in my head which creates the line.' From the rhythms we can surmise that Snyder is generally relaxed, if this is the case. Of the quieter poems in *Myths and Texts* – probably his most important book – he writes, they 'grew between 1952 and 1956. Its several rhythms are based on long days of quiet in lookout cabins; setting chokers for the Warm Springs Lumber Co (looping cables on logs and hooking them to D8 Caterpillars – dragging and rumbling through the brush); and the songs and dances of Great Basin Indian Tribes I used to hang around.' *Myths and Texts* includes forty-eight untitled poems and is divided into three sections, 'Logging', 'Hunting', and 'Burning'. Together they develop the themes of destruction, creation and rebirth. Pound's influence is evident in their forms and structure. In 'Logging' Snyder laments the destruction of forests for human use:

Men who hire men to cut groves
Kill snakes, build cities, pave fields,
Believe in God, but can't
Believe their own senses.
Let alone Gautama. Let them lie.

Gautama is another name for the Buddha.

'Hunting' evokes the necessary ritual of the hunt and hardly distinguishes between man and beast. American Indian folklore plays a part. In one poem, he says '–not that we're cruel –/But a man's got to eat.' Nonetheless, his compassion is comprehensive:

All beaded with dew
          dawn grass runway
Open-eyed rabbits hang
          dangle, loose feet in tall grass
From alder snares.
The spider is building a morning-web
From the snared rabbit's ear to the snare ...

The section concludes with the birth of a child,

Meaning: compassion.
Agents: man and beast, beasts
Got the buddha-nature
All but
Coyote.

'Burning', the final section, suggests the Buddha's Fire Sermon. It concentrates on purification of the inner self and the possibility of renewal in the confused world: 'This whole spinning show .../It's all falling or burning...'

Smoke like clouds. Blotting the sun
Stinging the eyes.
The hot seeds steam underground
          still alive.

Mountains and Rivers Without End takes its title from a Chinese scroll painting. Snyder tries to revive the sense 'that modern people have lost' of journeying through space. The book does provide a sense of travel, history, movement. Though it is as yet incomplete, it seems to lack the necessity of the earlier book. The poems read more as extended snippets from a journal than an intensification of the tranquil experiences of that journal:

slipped on the ice turning
       in to a driveway
   and broke all nine milkbottles

or,

I came to buy
  a few bananas by the ganges
    while waiting for my wife.

This isn't particularly interesting. There is no sense of transformation, the effect William Carlos Williams achieves in poems of similar simplicity but greater depth and variety.

Regarding Wave develops his recurrent theme of the *wholeness* of creation in a relaxed – sometimes lazy – loose style. This is a basic flaw. Many of the poems are flat and uninteresting on the page. They demand the reader's voice. The apparent facility of writing, the lack of inner tensions of rhythm and language, make for slackness. In artistic terms, the flaw is deep. Yet the poetry is engaging. For one thing, Snyder's Buddhism does not partake of the fashionable commitment of the more superficial followers of Zen. He has accepted it as a discipline, not a pose. The relaxed tone of the poems is an aspect of his voice. And yet, in the recent poems we hanker after the greater sharpness and linguistic interest of the fine title poem of *Riprap*:

Lay down these words
Before your mind like rocks.
      placed solid, by hands
In choice of place, set
Before the body of the mind
     in space and time:

Solidity of bark, leaf or wall
     riprap of things:
Cobble of milky way ...

Whatever the changes of style, Snyder has remained constant to his themes. He has described them: 'I try to hold both history and the wilderness in mind, that my poems may approach the true measure of things and stand against the unbalance and ignorance of our times. The soil and human sensibility may erode away forever, even without a great war.'

Sylvia Plath 1932–1963

The fountains are dry and the roses over.
Incense of death. Your day approaches.

– 'The Manor Garden'

Sylvia Plath said of her work, 'I think my poems come
immediately out of the sensuous and emotional experiences I have, but I must say I cannot sympathize with
these cries from the heart that are informed by nothing
except a needle or a knife or whatever it is. I believe that
one should be able to control and manipulate experiences,
even the most terrifying – like madness, being tortured,
this kind of experience – and one should be able to
manipulate these experiences with an informed and intelligent mind. I think that personal experience shouldn't
be a kind of shut box and mirror-looking narcissistic
experience. I believe it should be generally relevant, to
such things as Hiroshima and Dachau, and so on.' James
Dickey finds such poets – and Plath in particular –
'slickly confessional; they are glib ... and if there is one
thing I find intolerable in either literature or in the world,
it is slick, knowing patter about suffering and guilt,
particularly about one's own.' Al Alvarez sees Plath as far
from glib. He writes of the poems, 'It needed not only
great intelligence and insight to handle the material of
them, it also took a kind of bravery. Poetry of this order

is a murderous art.' If either of these critics is right, then Plath's poems fail, for slickness is no part of the poetic art; and if, as Alvarez adds, 'The achievement of her final style is to make poetry and death inseparable,' this implies the finality of rhetoric rather than the balanced truth of poetry.

Most critical attention has been lavished on her later work, taking her suicide as a sort of validation of the poems' thematic power. Yet there are the outstanding early poems to accommodate in any assessment of her work, and in attending to her life the fact must be borne in mind that she was a busy housewife and mother as well as a poet: the poetry and the life with their different but complementary intensities were for the most part separate. She wrote in a radio script, 'These new poems of mine have one thing in common. They were all written at about four in the morning – that still, blue, almost eternal hour before cockcrow, before the baby's cry, before the glassy music of the milkman, settling his bottles.'

She portrays, not altogether accurately, her early life in the autobiographical novel *The Bell Jar* (1963) as bristling with neuroses. She was born in Boston, Massachusetts, in 1932. Her father, of German extraction, was a biologist. He died when she was eight. She used his death many years later as the starting point of her poem 'Daddy':

Daddy, you can lie back now.

There's a stake in your fat black heart
And the villagers never liked you.
They are dancing and stamping on you.
They always *knew* it was you.
Daddy, daddy, you bastard, I'm through.

The figure of Daddy, dressed out as a Gestapo man, as Count Dracula, as a cold, inhumanly passionate creature, is more a complex image of Plath's attitudes than the unfortunate Mr Plath. The poem is 'confessional' only in what it reveals about Sylvia Plath, and – as all her confessional poems attempt to do – she relates her experience to a wide context through the deft control of imagery and the strong rhetoric of her style. Sylvia Plath *changes* facts for the very good reason that the experience interests her as poetic experience, not as autobiography. Almost in spite of the autobiographical details, the poem is not limited by her biography. She said, 'Here is a poem spoken by a girl with an Electra complex. Her father died while she thought he was God. Her case is complicated by the fact that her father was also a Nazi and her mother very possibly part Jewish. In the daughter the two strains marry and paralyse each other – she has to act out the awful little allegory once more before she is free of it.'

Sylvia Plath was educated at Smith College and graduated in 1955. She had attempted suicide in 1953 after fierce depression, and her poem 'Lady Lazarus', written much later, celebrates the act and the 'resurrection':

The second time I meant
To last it out and not come back at all.
I rocked shut

As a seashell.
They had to call and call
And pick the worms off me like sticky pearls.

Dying
Is an art, like everything else.
I do it exceptionally well.

She attended Robert Lowell's poetry course at Boston University. He was moving towards the 'confessional' poetry eventually collected in *Life Studies* (1959) and his example affected her.

On a Fulbright Award she came to England to study at Newnham, Cambridge, where she met the English poet Ted Hughes. They were married in 1956. They spent their time in England and America until 1960, at the birth of the first of their two children, when they decided to settle in England. Plath's first collection, *The Colossus*, was published in 1960.

Some critics have complained that it is a collection of 'compositions' rather than poems. To judge the early work in the light of her later poems is misleading. In the first book her preoccupation with death is explored in the controlled – possibly over-controlled – early style, responsible but quietly emphatic. It takes fewer risks than her later poetry, but it reveals substantial achievement. The risks came in *Ariel* (1965) published after her suicide in 1963. In this latter book we witness an almost total reconception of form, the replacement of the authority of form with the authority of voice, as though the poems were composed for recitation. *The Colossus* is no less genuine for trusting its forms. There is excitement in the literary wit with which Plath chooses the right but unexpected word. The terror has a pattern, but there is a world besides the terror. Even in a grim poem like 'Suicide Off Egg Rock' we respond both to the 'hotdogs split and drizzled/On the public grills', with its arresting and amusing sound organization, and to the experience central to the poem: 'He heard when he walked into the water/The forgetful surf creaming on those ledges.'

The early poems suggest the later style. In 'Lorelei', 'It is no night to drown in' but there is temptation:

> Sisters, your song
> Bears a burden too weighty
> For the whorled ear's listening
>
> Here, in a well-steered country,
> Under a balanced ruler.
> Deranging by harmony
>
> Beyond the mundane order
> Your voices lay siege ...

Those voices speak *Ariel*. If *The Colossus* presents death at a formal remove, *Ariel* brings death up close – along with the killer and his victims. We accept the extreme vision because her voice handles the shifts of tone and imagery and the rhythms so skilfully. The poems, *because* they affect us, are dangerous to read. There is no pattern beyond the terror. The early poems attempt to transcend the terror, the later poems to plumb it.

Often the poems in *Ariel* are less lucid than those in *The Colossus*: the speaker is implicated in them, and the occasionally surreal effects answer subconscious fears. In 'Tulips' the flowers draw her from hospital sleep: 'The tulips are too excitable, it is winter here.' She does not want to return to life:

I am nobody; I have nothing to do with explosions ...

I didn't want any flowers, I only wanted
To lie with my hands turned up and be utterly empty.

Fear informs 'A Birthday Present': 'What is this, behind this veil, is it ugly, is it beautiful?/It is shimmering, has it breasts, has it edges?' The most effective expression of fear is in the 'bee' poems, especially in 'The Bee Meeting', where the fear is transferred to the allegorical plot:

Who are these people at the bridge to meet me? They are the
    villagers –
The rector, the midwife, the sexton, the agent for bees.
In my sleeveless summery dress I have no protection,
And they are all gloves and covered, why did nobody tell me?
They are smiling and taking out veils tacked to ancient hats.

I am nude as a chicken neck, does nobody love me?

She steps into the pattern of terror which implicates members of the village's crucial professions. Without understanding what is being done to her, she asks – but her questions remain unanswered: 'Which is the rector now, is it that man in black?/Which is the midwife, is that her blue coat?' The final transformation of the imagery into a final allegory, prepared for throughout the poem, none the less confirms the terror:

I am exhausted, I am exhausted –
Pillar of white in a blackout of knives.
I am the magician's girl who does not flinch.
The villagers are untying their disguises, they are shaking
    hands.
Whose is that long white box in the grove, what have they
    accomplished,
        why am I cold?

In 'Edge' death is an achievement:

The woman is perfected.
Her dead

Body wears the smile of accomplishment ...

Even mother's love becomes a nightmare. In 'Nick and the Candlestick' she moves towards her child, having to will the action:

I am a miner. The light burns blue.
Waxy stalactites
Drip and thicken ...

The child sleeps. The mother is swarmed by images of destruction:

A vice of knives
A piranha
Religion, drinking

Its first communion out of my live toes ...

She is the victim, devoured, the sacrificial victim nourishing others, herself suffering. The candle flickers, and she sees the child as Christ, 'Remembering, even in sleep,/

Your crossed position.' It too is implicated in the terror. 'You are the baby in the barn.' Compassion makes a poem such as this more than confessional – prophetic, profoundly responsible. The cruelty of the poems resides in part in their black humour – in 'Daddy' and 'Lady Lazarus' particularly, where the voice speaks its hyperboles and vaunts with ironic self-awareness.

Two further collections have been published since her death: *Crossing the Water* (1971) and *Winter Trees* (1971). The first of these includes poems written in the period of transition between *The Colossus* and *Ariel*. The later technique is evolving grimly in them:

This red wall winces continually:
A red fist, opening and closing,
Two grey, papery bags –
This is what I am made of, this and a terror
Of being wheeled off under crosses and a rain of pietas.

The abundance of similes in this collection – lacking in the later work – helps distance the terror. What is unachieved is the rhythm, neither spoken nor metrical. In *Winter Trees*, too, familiar images occur:

Spiderlike, I spin mirrors,
Loyal to my image,

Uttering nothing but blood –

This book includes the radio play *Three Women – A Poem for Three Voices*, which takes place in 'a Maternity Ward and round about'. One voice says,

I last. I last it out. I accomplish a work.
Dark tunnel, through which hurtle the visitations,
The visitations, the manifestations, the startled faces.
I am the centre of an atrocity.
What pains, what sorrows must I be mothering?

Sylvia Plath has attracted many imitators. But her

anguished and humane vision cannot be trumped up, cannot be imitated. Like Lowell's, her 'confessionalism' exists within a context, her experience is *inclusive*, her response is not whimsical, not solipsistic but – for all its extremity – an attempt to come to the world which includes Hiroshima and Dachau on that world's terms, to record it on her body. In the poetry this is reflected in the painful dislocation of imagery, the intense awareness of fear.

Select Bibliography

ANTHOLOGIES

Donald M. Allen (ed) *The New American Poetry*, London, 1960
(NAP)
Richard Ellman (ed) *New Oxford Book of American Verse*,
New York, 1976 (NOB)
Donald Hall (ed) *American Poetry – an Introductory Anthology*,
London, 1969 (AP)
Geoffrey Moore (ed) *American Literature: A Representative
Anthology of American Writing from Colonial Times to the
Present*, London, 1964 (AL)
Geoffrey Moore (ed) *Penguin Book of American Verse*,
Harmondsworth, 1977 (PBA)

GENERAL CRITICAL AND
HISTORICAL WORKS

Marcus Cunliffe *The Literature of the United States*
(including a generous bibliography), Harmondsworth, 1970
(revised edition)
Irvin Ehrenpreis (ed) *American Poetry* (Stratford-upon-Avon
Studies 7), London, 1965 (SOA7)
James D. Hart *Oxford Companion to American Literature*,
New York, 1975
Max J. Herzberg *Reader's Encyclopedia of American Literature*,
London, 1963
James Scully (ed) *Modern Poets on Modern Poetry*, London, 1970
(SCULLY)
Robert B. Shaw (ed) *American Poetry Since 1960: Some Critical
Perspectives*, Manchester, 1973 (SHAW)

Robert E. Spiller; William Thorpe; Thomas H. Johnson;
Henry Seidel Canby; Richard M. Ludwig (eds) *Literary History
of the United States* (4th edn, revised), London, 1975
Stephen Stepanchev *American Poetry Since 1945: A Critical Survey*,
New York, 1965
Leonard Unger (ed) *Seven Modern American Poets – an
Introduction* (Pound; Ransom; Stevens; Eliot; Frost; Tate;
Carlos Williams), London, 1967 (UNGER)
Walter Wager *American Literature – A World View*, London, 1970

Many of the statements by recent poets about their own work are
taken from *Contemporary American Poetry* (undated), edited by
Howard Nemerov, published by the United States Information
Agency, and containing a series of Forum Lectures broadcast by
the Voice of America. Other statements are taken from SCULLY
(above).

The Poets

Anne Bradstreet

Works, ed Jeannine Hensley, Harvard, 1967
Poems, ed Robert Hutchinson, New York, 1970
Also in NOB, PBA, AL, AP
Elizabeth Wade White *The Tenth Muse*, Oxford/New York, 1972

Edward Taylor

Poems, ed Donald Stanford, Yale, 1960
Poetical Works, ed T. H. Johnson, Princeton, 1967
Also in NOB, PBA, AL, AP
Donald Stanford *Edward Taylor* (Pamphlets on American Writers),
Minnesota, 1966

William Cullen Bryant

In NOB, PBA, AL, AP
H. H. Peckham *Gotham Yankee: A Biography of William Cullen
Bryant*, New York, 1950

Ralph Waldo Emerson

Essays, London 1972
Selected Prose and Poetry, New York, 1950

Journals and Miscellaneous Notebooks (in 10 vols), Harvard, 1960/74
Also in NOB, PBA, AL, AP

Josephine Miles *Ralph Waldo Emerson* (Pamphlets on American Writers), Minnesota, 1965
Hyatt H. Waggoner *Emerson as Poet*, Princeton, 1974

Henry Wadsworth Longfellow

Poems, London, 1970
Also in NOB, PBA, AL, AP

Newton Arvin *Longfellow: His Life and Work*, Greenwood/USA, 1977
Edward C. Wagenknecht *Henry Wadsworth Longfellow: Portrait of an American Humanist*, New York, 1966

Edgar Allan Poe

Collected Works; Vol 1: Poems, ed Mabbott, Harvard, 1970
Poems and Essays, London, 1969
Selected Writings, Harmondsworth, 1970
Also in NOB, PBA, AL, AP

Edward Hutchins Davidson *Poe: A Critical Study*, Harvard, 1957
Geoffrey Rans *Edgar Allan Poe*, Edinburgh, 1965

Henry David Thoreau

Collected Poems, ed Bode, New York, 1966
Walden, London, 1973
Also in NOB, PBA, AL, AP

Leon Edel *Henry David Thoreau* (Pamphlets on American Writers), Minnesota, 1970
Walter Harding *Thoreau Handbook*, New York, 1959

Herman Melville

Selected Tales and Poems, ed Chase, New York, 1950
Portable Melville, ed Leyda, London, 1968
Moby Dick, Harmondsworth, 1972
Also in NOB, PBA, AL, AP

D. E. S. Maxwell *Herman Melville*, London, 1968
Charles Olson *Call me Ishmael*, London, 1967
Reader's Guide to Herman Melville, London, 1962

Walt Whitman

Choice of Verse, ed Donald A. Hall, London, 1968
Complete Poetry, Selected Prose and Letters, ed Emory Holloway, London, 1938
Leaves of Grass, ed Blodgett and Bradley, London, 1965
Portable Walt Whitman, ed Van Doren, London, 1971
Selected Poems and Prose ed Jeffares, London, 1966
Selected Poetry, ed Robert Creeley, Harmondsworth, 1973
Selected Poetry, ed Reeves and Seymour-Smith, London, 1976
Also in NOB, PBA, AL, AP

Francis Murphy (ed) *Walt Whitman; A Critical Anthology*, Harmondsworth, 1969
Geoffrey Dutton *Walt Whitman*, Edinburgh, 1961
Milton Hindus (ed) *Walt Whitman* (Critical Heritage Series), London, 1971
See also: J. Albert Robbins 'America and the Poet', in SOA7

Emily Dickinson

Complete Poems, ed T. H. Johnson, London, 1970
Selected Poems, ed James Reeves, London, 1959
Choice of Verse, ed Ted Hughes, London, 1968
Also in NOB, PBA, AL, AP

Denis Donoghue *Emily Dickinson* (Pamphlets on American Writers), Minnesota, 1970
John B. Pickard *Emily Dickinson* (American Authors and Critics), New York
Richard B. Sewall (ed) *Emily Dickinson: A Collection of Critical Essays*, Englewood Cliffs, 1965
Charles R Anderson: *Emily Dickinson's Poetry: Stairway of Surprise*, London, 1963
See also: Elizabeth Jennings: 'Idea and Expression In Emily Dickinson, Marianne Moore and Ezra Pound', in SOA7

Edwin Arlington Robinson

In NOB, PBA, AL, AP

Francis Murphy (ed) *Edwin Arlington Robinson: A Collection of Critical Essays*, Englewood Cliffs, 1970

Edgar Lee Masters

Poems, ed Denys Thompson, London, 1972
Spoon River Anthology, London, 1962
Also in NOB, PBA, AP

Stephen Crane
Complete Poems, ed Joseph Katz, New York, 1972
Poems, ed Denys Thompson, London 1972
Red Badge of Courage, London, 1971
Also in NOB, PBA, AL

Richard M. Weatherford (ed) *Stephen Crane* (Critical Heritage Series), London, 1973

Robert Frost

Poetry, ed Edward Connery Latham, London, 1971
Selected Poems, ed Ian Hamilton, Harmondsworth, 1973
Also in NOB, PBA, AL, AP

Edward Connery Latham (ed) *Interviews with Robert Frost*, London, 1967
Reuben A. Brower *Poetry of Robert Frost: Constellations of Intention*, New York, 1969
Richard Poirier *Robert Frost*, London, 1978
See also: Lawrance Thompson: 'Robert Frost', in UNGER

Carl Sandburg

Complete Poems, New York, 1970
Harvest Poems 1910–1960, New York, 1960
Also in NOB, PBA, AL

North Callahan *Carl Sandburg*, London, 1970
Gay Wilson Allen *Carl Sandburg* (Pamphlets on American Writers), Minnesota, 1973

Wallace Stevens

Collected Poems, London, 1955
Selected Poems, London, 1965
Also in NOB, PBA, AL, AP

Frank Kermode *Wallace Stevens*, Edinburgh, 1960
Helen Vendler *Wallace Steven's Longer Poems: 'On Extended Wings'*, Harvard, 1972

A. Walton Litz *Introspective Voyager: Poetical Development of Wallace Stevens*, Oxford/New York, 1972
See also: Andrew Waterman: 'Some notes on The Blue Guitar', in *PN Review 8*, Manchester, 1978
William York Tindall: 'Wallace Stevens', in UNGER
Wallace Stevens: 'The Noble Rider and the Sound of Words', in UNGER

William Carlos Williams

Collected Poems (2 vols) Norfolk, Conn., 1950–51
I wanted to Write a Poem, London, 1967
In The American Grain, Essays, London, 1967
Autobiography, New York, 1967
Collected Earlier Poems, New York, 1951
Collected Later Poems, New York, 1963
Pictures from Brueghel, New York, 1962
Paterson, Bks I–V, New York, 1963
Selected Poems, ed Charles Tomlinson, Harmondsworth, 1976
Also in NOB, PBA, AL, AP

Charles Tomlinson (ed) *William Carlos Williams* (A Collection of Critical Essays), Harmondsworth, 1972
See also: John Malcolm Brinnin: 'William Carlos Williams', in UNGER
William Carlos Williams: 'A New Measure', in SCULLY

Ezra Pound

Collected Shorter Poems, London, 1968
Cantos, London, 1976
Selected Cantos, London, 1967
Selected Poems, ed T. S. Eliot, London, 1948
Literary Essays, ed T. S. Eliot, London 1954
Letters (1907–1941), ed D. D. Paige, London, 1971
Also in NOB, PBA

Eric Homberger (ed) *Ezra Pound* (A Collection of Critical Essays), London 1972
J. P. Sullivan (ed) *Ezra Pound* (A Collection of Critical Essays), Harmondsworth, 1970
Noel Stock *A Life of Ezra Pound*, London, 1970
Donald Davie *Ezra Pound: Poet as Sculptor*, London, 1965
G. S. Fraser *Ezra Pound*, Edinburgh, 1960

See also: Ezra Pound, 'A Retrospect' in SCULLY
William Van O'Connor: 'Ezra Pound' in UNGER
Peter Jones: 'Introduction' to *Imagist Poetry*, Harmondsworth, 1972
Andrew Crozier: 'The Young Pound', in *PN Review 6*, Manchester,
1977

H.D. (Hilda Doolittle)

Hermetic Definition, Manchester, 1972
Tribute To Freud, Manchester, 1972
Trilogy, Manchester, 1973
and a selection of the earlier poems in *Imagist Poetry*, ed Peter Jones,
Harmondsworth, 1972
Also in NOB, PBA, AP

Peter Jones: 'Introduction' to *Imagist Poetry*, Harmondsworth, 1972
A. R. Jones: 'Imagism: a Unity of Gesture' in SOA7
Colin Falck: 'Cranking the Engine', in *Poetry Nation 1*,
Manchester, 1973
C. H. Sisson: 'H. D.' in *Poetry Nation IV*, Manchester, 1975

Robinson Jeffers

In NOB, PBA, AL, AP

Arthur B. Coffin *Robinson Jeffers: Poet of Inhumanism*,
Wisconsin, 1971

Marianne Moore

Complete Poems, London, 1968
Selected Poems, London, 1969
Also in NOB, PBA, AL, AP

Jean Garrigue *Marianne Moore* (Pamphlets on American Writers),
Minnesota, 1966
Charles Tomlinson (ed) *Marianne Moore: A Collection of Critical
Essays*, Englewood Cliffs, 1970
George W. Nitchie *Marianne Moore: An Introduction to the
Poetry*, New York, 1970
See also Elizabeth Jennings: 'Idea and Expression in Emily
Dickinson, Marianne Moore, and Ezra Pound', in SOA7
Marianne Moore: 'Idiosyncrasy and Technique', in SCULLY

John Crowe Ransom

Poems and Essays, New York, 1955
Also in NOB, PBA, AL, AP

John Lincoln Stewart *John Crowe Ransom* (Pamphlets on
American Writers), Minnesota (undated)
See also: Louis D. Rubin: 'Four Southerners' in SOA7
John L. Stewart: 'John Crowe Ransom', in UNGER
John Crowe Ransom: 'Poetry: A Note in Ontology', in SCULLY

T. S. Eliot

Complete Poems and Plays, London, 1969
Selected Poems, London, 1964
Selected Essays, London, 1973
The Waste Land: Facsmile and Transcript of the Original Draft,
ed Valerie Eliot, London, 1974
Also in NOB, PBA, AL

Helen Gardner *The Art of T. S. Eliot*, London, 1968
Helen Gardner *The Composition of 'Four Quartets'*, London, 1978
B. C. Southam *Students' Guide to the Selected Poems of T. S.
Eliot*, London, 1969
C. B. Cox and A. P. Hinchcliffe (ed) *T. S. Eliot's 'The Waste
Land'* (Casebook Series), London, 1968
Bernard Bergonzi (ed) *T. S. Eliot's 'Four Quartets'* (Casebook
Series), London, 1969
D. E. S. Maxwell *The Poetry of T. S. Eliot*, London, 1972

Conrad Aiken

Collected Poems, London, 1971
Selected Poems, Oxford/New York, 1970
Also in NOB, PBA

Rouel Denney *Conrad Aiken* (Pamphlets on American Writers),
Minnesota, 1965

Archibald MacLeish

In NOB, PBA, AL, AP

Grover Smith *Archibald MacLeish* (Pamphlets on American
Writers), Minnesota, 1972

e.e cummings

Complete Poems 1913–1945, London, 1968
Selected Poems 1923–1958, London, 1960
73 Poems, London, 1974
The Enormous Room, Harmondsworth, 1971
Also in NOB, PBA, AL, AP

Norman Friedman (ed) *e. e. cummings: A Collection of Critical Essays*, Englewood Cliffs, 1972
Eve Triem *e. e. cummings* (Pamphlets on American Writers), Minnesota, 1970
See also: 'e. e. cummings: An Introduction' in SCULLY

Hart Crane

Complete Poems and Selected Letters and Prose, ed Brom Weber, London, 1972
Also in NOB, PBA, AL, AP

John Unterecker *'Voyager': A Life of Hart Crane*, London, 1970
Herbert A. Leibowitz *Hart Crane: An Introduction to his Poetry*, Columbia, 1972
See also: A. Alvarez: 'The Lyric of Hart Crane', in *The Shaping Spirit*, London, 1967
Hart Crane: 'General Aims and Theories', in SCULLY

Allen Tate

Collected Poems 1919–1976, London, 1978
Swimmers and Other Selected Poems, London, 1970
Essays of Four Decades, London, 1970
Memories and Essays: Old and New, Manchester, 1976
Also in NOB, PBA, AL, AP

George Hemphill *Allen Tate* (Pamphlets on American Writers), Minnesota, 1965
See also: George Hemphill: 'Allen Tate' in UNGER
Louis D. Rubin: 'Four Southerners' in SOA7

Yvor Winters

The Collected Poems, Manchester, 1978
Function of Criticism, London, 1962
In Defence of Reason, London, 1947
Also in NOB

Laura (Riding) Jackson

Collected Poems, Manchester, 1980
Selected Poems: In Five Sets, London, 1970
The Telling, London, 1972

Langston Hughes

Rhythms, London, 1965
Also in NOB, PBA

Louis Zukofsky

'A' 1–12, London, 1966
'A' 13–21, London, 1969
'A' 22 & 23, London, 1977
All: The Collected Short Poems, London, 1966
Also in PBA

Robert Penn Warren

Selected Poems 1923–1975, London, 1977
Selected Essays, London, 1964
Also in NOB, PBA

Victor Strandberg *'Colder Fire' – the Poetry of Robert Penn Warren*, Westport, 1967
See also: Louis D. Rubin: 'Four Southerners', in SOA7

Theodore Roethke

Collected Poems, London, 1968
Selected Poems, ed Beatrice Roethke, London, 1969
Also in NOB, PBA, AP

Karl Malkoff *Theodore Roethke: An Introduction to the Poetry*, Columbia, 1971

Charles Olson

Maximus Poems, London, 1970
Call me Ishmael, London, 1967
Mayan Letters, London, 1968
Letters for Origin 1950–1965, ed Albert Glove, London, 1969
Also in NOB, PBA, NAP

Charles Olson: 'Projective Verse', in SCULLY

Elizabeth Bishop

Complete Poems, London, 1970
Selected Poems, London, 1967
Geography III, London, 1977
Also in NOB, PBA, AP

Delmore Schwartz

What is to be Given: Selected Poems, Manchester, 1976
Also in NOB, PBA

Richard McDougall *Delmore Schwartz*, New York, 1974
James Atlas *Delmore Schwartz: the Life of an American Poet*,
London, 1979

Randall Jarrell

Complete Poems, London, 1971
Poetry and the Age, London, 1973
The Third Book of Criticism, London, 1975
Also in NOB, PBA

M. L. Rosenthal *Randall Jarrell* (Pamphlets on American Writers)
Minnesota, 1973

John Berryman

Homage to Mistress Bradstreet, London, 1959
Seventy Seven Dream Songs, London, 1964
His Toy, His Dream, His Rest: 308 Dream Songs, London, 1969
Love and Fame, London, 1971
Delusions etc, London, 1972
Recovery, London, 1973
Henry's Fate and Other Poems, London, 1978
Selected Poems 1938–1968, London, 1972
Also in NOB, PBA, AP

Louis Martz *John Berryman* (Pamphlets on American Writers),
Minnesota, 1970
See also: Edward Mendelson: 'How to Read Berryman's *Dream
Songs*', in SHAW
John Haffenden: Introduction to *Henry's Fate* London, 1978

Robert Lowell

Poems 1938–1949, London, 1950
Selected Poems, London, 1965

For the Union Dead, London, 1965
Near the Ocean, London, 1967
Old Glory, London, 1966
Voyage, London, 1968
Life Studies, London, 1969
Notebook, London, 1970
Prometheus Bound, London, 1970
Phaedra, London, 1971
Imitations, London, 1971
The Dolphin, London, 1973
For Lizzie and Harriet, London, 1973
History, London, 1973
Day by Day, London, 1978
Also in NOB, PBA, AL, AP

Hugh B. Staples *Robert Lowell: The First Twenty Years*, London, 1962
Patrick Cosgrave *The Public Poetry of Robert Lowell*, London, 1970
See also: Irvin Ehrenpreis: 'The Age of Lowell', in SOA7
Frances Ferguson: 'Appointments with Time: Robert Lowell's Poetry through the *Notebooks*', in SHAW
'An Interview' in SCULLY

Robert Duncan

Derivations, London, 1969
First Decade, London, 1969
Opening The Field, London, 1969
Roots and Branches, London, 1971
Bending the Bow, London, 1971
Also in NOB, PBA

Richard Wilbur

Walking to Sleep, London, 1971
Selected Poems, London, 1977
Also in NOB, PBA

James Dickey

Poems 1957–1967, London, 1968
Deliverance, London, 1972
Also in NOB
Michael Mesic: 'A Note on James Dickey', in SHAW

Allen Ginsberg

Howl, San Francisco, 1967
Kaddish and Other Poems, San Francisco, 1967
Planet News 1961–1967, San Francisco, 1968
Ankor Wat, London, 1968
Wichita Vortex Sutra, London, 1969
Mind Breaths: Poems 1972–1977, San Francisco, 1978
Also in NOB, PBA, NAP

A. R. Ammons

Northfield Poems, Cornell, 1967
Selected Poems, Cornell, 1969
Collected Poems 1951–1971, New York, 1972
Also in NOB, PBA

W. S. Merwin

The Drunk in The Furnace, New York, 1960
The Moving Target, New York, 1963
Also in NOB, PBA
James Atlas: 'Diminishing Returns: the Writings of W. S. Merwin',
in SHAW

John Ashbery

Selected Poems, London, 1967
Self-Portrait in a Convex Mirror, Manchester, 1977
Houseboat Days, New York, 1978
Also in NOB, PBA, NAP

Harold Bloom: 'John Ashbery: The Charity of the Hard Moments',
in SHAW
Grevel Lindop: 'On Reading John Ashbery', in *PN Review 4*,
Manchester, 1977

Adrienne Rich

Selected Poems, London, 1967
Snapshots of a Daughter-in-law, London, 1970
Leaflets, London, 1972
Will to Change, London, 1973
Also in NOB

Albert Gelpi: 'Adrienne Rich: The poetics of Change', in SHAW

Gary Snyder

Back Country, London, 1967
Range of Poems: Collected Poems, London, 1967
Six Sections from Mountains and Rivers without End, London, 1967
Myths and Texts, New York, 1968
Earth House Hold: Technical Notes and Queries to Fellow Dharma Revolutionaries, London, 1970
Regarding Wave, London, 1971
Also in NOB, PBA

Bob Stending *Gary Snyder* (US Authors Series), Boston, 1977

Sylvia Plath

Ariel, London, 1965
The Bell Jar, London, 1967
Colossus, London, 1967
Crossing the Water, London, 1971
Winter Trees, London, 1971
Also in NOB, PBA

Charles Newman (ed) *The Art of Sylvia Plath*, London, 1970
Eileen Aird *Sylvia Plath*, Edinburgh, 1973
See also J. D. McClatchy: 'Staring from her Hood of Bone', in SHAW

Index

Note: for individual poems refer to poet